THE GREEN REVOLUTION IN THE GLOBAL SOUTH

NE**X**US

NEW HISTORIES ᴏꜰ SCIENCE, TECHNOLOGY, ᴛʜᴇ ENVIRONMENT, AGRICULTURE & MEDICINE

NE**X**US is a book series devoted to the publication of high-quality scholarship in the history of the sciences and allied fields. Its broad reach encompasses science, technology, the environment, agriculture, and medicine, but also includes intersections with other types of knowledge, such as music, urban planning, or educational policy. Its essential concern is with the interface of nature and culture, broadly conceived, and it embraces an emerging intellectual constellation of new syntheses, methods, and approaches in the study of people and nature through time.

The GREEN REVOLUTION
in the GLOBAL SOUTH

Science, Politics, and Unintended Consequences

R. DOUGLAS HURT

THE UNIVERSITY OF ALABAMA PRESS   TUSCALOOSA

The University of Alabama Press
Tuscaloosa, Alabama 35487-0380
uapress.ua.edu

Typeface: Scala Pro and Scala Sans Pro

Cover image: Women engaged in maize field topdressing,
India, 2014; photograph by CIMMYT/Wasim Iftikar
Cover design: Michele Myatt Quinn

Cataloging-in-Publication data is available from the Library of
Congress.
ISBN: 978-0-8173-2051-5
E-ISBN: 978-0-8173-9282-6

For Evelyn Joy Hurt

Contents

Figures

Foreword

Doug Hurt takes one of the tropes of scientific-based modernity and explores how it played out outside of the United States and Europe. The Green Revolution, a grab bag of scientific techniques applied to agriculture to boost yields, promised to solve the Malthusian dilemma of populations expanding exponentially while food production was thought to increase only arithmetically. Its champions confidently predicted it would end or at least seriously diminish starvation, mitigate hunger and want, and redress income disparities in what used to be known as the developing world.

Claims that the Green Revolution would be a panacea proved a pipe dream. Everyone whose world vision was not confined to a laboratory readily and quickly understood that. Hurt carries the analysis significantly further. He traces in place after place the transformations that occurred and did not occur under the Green Revolution's onslaught. Even more arresting, Hurt posits what forces, policies, conditions, and activities contributed to the various outcomes. What emerges is a variegated story marked by some success but much failure.

Part of the genius of Hurt's work is that he humanizes the Green Revolution. No, he does not humanize uberscientist Norman Borlaug and his ilk. Rather he shows that applying any sort of technological or scientific solution to any significant problem begets any number of other problems that manifest themselves in the lives and activities of various populations. Some are physical, like death. But most are more diffuse and almost always place and culture specific. Structures—governmental and otherwise—are loath to relinquish whatever authority they have long exercised, even in the pursuit of noble goals.

Hurt's story, then, is a story that cuts across history's conventional disciplinary boundaries. It is a science story, a technology story, an agriculture story, and an environment story. It is even a medical story. Hence, it fits neatly within the Nexus series. Nexus was created to highlight those new life science–related questions historians are now regularly asking, questions of the past that place science explicitly at the core. The series reflects the self-conscious historical trend to push against old boundaries in a slew of new ways. Recognition of the centrality of science in an intriguing range of activities is translating into new syntheses, methods, and approaches within environmental, agricultural, technological, scientific, and medical history.

Nexus books explore the histories of the science of life and living in their myriad aspects rather than the identification of mechanical contrivances or the simple cataloguing of the accumulation of knowledge. Its authors are interested in books that have national and international significance, books that will leave a mark on the profession and make concrete contributions to scholarship. While the primary focus will be the United States and its regions, Nexus remains open to those international monographs that primarily engage America from outside its borders and intersect in a meaningful way with the histories of the science of life and living.

Alan I Marcus
For the Nexus editors

THE GREEN REVOLUTION
IN THE GLOBAL SOUTH

Introduction

The Green Revolution seemingly became the scientific solution to hunger, even famine, during the late twentieth century. The term conveys images of agricultural scientists at work in fields and greenhouses breeding new high-yielding crop varieties (HYVs) of wheat, maize, and rice to produce bountiful harvests on barren lands. The term also conveys a sense of speed, because revolutions happen quickly and bring dynamic, irreversible change. It conveys mental pictures of well-fed people who only a short time before suffered the daily agony of hunger with protruding ribs, bloated bellies, and vacant eyes as testimony to their plight. It also conveys a belief that science, unhindered by geography and politics, can solve all problems. Yet, politics and the environment determined the successes and failures of the Green Revolution in the food-deficit nations of Latin America, Asia, and sub-Saharan Africa. Governments appropriated the scientific benefits of the Green Revolution for their own nationalist and political agendas. Frequently, increased food production fostered by agricultural science did not reach the people who needed it. Politics perpetuated social and economic inequalities in the countryside and the distribution of and access to Green Revolution technologies and the food that resulted from it. Consequently, poverty and often hunger and malnutrition persisted for a majority of the rural population in developing nations.

I define the term "Green Revolution" to mean the substantially increased food production on traditional farmlands due to improved seed varieties that are nourished with heavy applications of fertilizer and water, the latter provided by irrigation. For example, early-maturing, semidwarf wheat and rice varieties that supported heavy grain heads produced bountiful harvests if irrigated and fertilized. Farmers not only could cultivate two crops where they raised only one before but they also could grow crops on lands that they had not previously planted given the right package of "inputs" (improved seeds, fertilizer, and irrigation). Farmers in less developed countries could now harvest more grain to feed hungry people.

Yet, as is true with many simple explanations of the past, the causes and consequences of the Green Revolution are more complex and problematic than the laudatory descriptions of its success based on genetics and agricultural productivity. Certainly, the Green Revolution founded on hybrid wheat, maize, and rice varieties as well as the expanded use of irrigation and chemical fertilizers, pesticides, and herbicides brought dramatic improvements in food production and income in developing regions, particularly in Mexico, India, Pakistan, and Southeast Asia, while land reform and science provided the basis for the Green Revolution in China. (Only sub-Saharan Africa seemed unable to capitalize on the new agricultural science.)

The Green Revolution, however, also has caused a major debate over its influence on the poor, with some critics claiming that it caused greater inequality between wealthy and poor farmers, forced people from the land, and spawned more poverty in the countryside as well as damaged the environment and upset traditional agricultural systems, perhaps for all time. Moreover, the extension of the Green Revolution to sub-Saharan Africa remained fraught with unresolved environmental and political problems, all influenced by continued rapid population growth, civil wars, and religious terrorism. By the twenty-first century, agricultural scientists sought a Gene Revolution, but social scientists, environmentalists, and the public often urged caution fearing the unknown.

I do not use the term Green Revolution in a pejorative fashion to suggest the failure of farmers to produce enough food to feed local, regional, and national populations from time immemorial due to race, culture, and class as well as ignorance. Readers should not consider my use of the terms "less developed" or "developing nations" as historical generalizations of economic modernization theory or a politically incorrect contention. Rather, these terms indicate that some people and regions did not have sufficient food to meet basic needs at a specific time for various reasons. Specifically, I use these terms to suggest that the nations under consideration in this study had less science-based agriculture than commercially oriented countries that produced crop surpluses and participated in the global market economy. I am not contending that starvation is a timeless condition. I do not accept the Malthusian theory that overpopulation alone creates hunger and famine. The historical evidence proves otherwise as in the case of the Sahel.

Agricultural scientists worldwide hailed this Green Revolution "package" as an opportunity to increase grain production, often by subsistence farmers to meet their food needs as well as provide sustenance for the urban poor. Green Revolution technologies also might enable them to generate some income with surplus production. The Green Revolution, however, did not depend on agricultural science alone but also on government support in the form of grain price supports, subsidies for fertilizers, and the development of irrigation systems, as well as research.

During the last half of the twentieth century, the term Green Revolution became the sobriquet for rapid and productive agricultural change in food-deficit nations. Research conducted at the International Maize and Wheat Improvement Center in Mexico and the International Rice Research Institute in the Philippines and disseminated to farmers in Mexico, India, Pakistan, and sub-Saharan Africa, among others, however, created unintended consequences. Although food production in the form of increased grain yields helped mitigate hunger, Green Revolution technologies created social, economic, and political problems that all food-deficit nations confronted and which limited the Green Revolution's effectiveness to feed hungry people.

This study analyzes the effects of science, technology, and politics on agricultural improvement and reform over a wide geographical area in selected nations in Latin America, the South Asian subcontinent, East and Southeast Asia, China, and sub-Saharan Africa. Historians generally refer to this area as the Global South. My purpose is to evaluate the different theories between agricultural scientists and social scientists of the benefits of the Green Revolution, including genetic engineering, a new and politically contentious aspect of the Green Revolution. The nations and regions selected are the most representative of Green Revolution agricultural success and failure. This work will show the geographical breadth of the Green Revolution and the complexities involved in crafting a history of agricultural change which it wrought. The book ends with a survey of the major issues regarding the Gene Revolution.

Throughout this study readers can trace opinions about the Green Revolution roughly by decade to see change, or the lack of it, over time. Readers also will see that the repetition of ideas over time reinforced the commitment to or opposition against the Green Revolution by agricultural and social scientists, journalists, and historians, among others. In many respects, this study reports and describes the assertions of those who often made imprecise or unverifiable claims about the Green Revolution for good or ill. This organizational approach will enable readers to gain a brief overview of the differences of opinion between the supporters of the Green Revolution and those who have been critical, if not opposed, to its social and economic implications. This study does not end with an overall, tight conclusion that many readers might prefer—to do so would be imprecise and misleading. The history and future of the Green Revolution has many stories and predictions. Absolute certainty about any position or argument would be invalid.

The literature on the Green and Gene Revolutions is immense and interdisciplinary. Those who have written about it are like theologians who write about God. They are concerned with origins, consequences, and salvation. They are argumentative, messianic, and contradictory with the truth contested and elusive. This survey of the Green Revolution is a highly selective effort to synthesize the literature and trace the acceptance or rejection of the Green Revolution over time. In many respects, this study traces the history of the Green Revolution. Someone else could write it again under the same title with an entirely different approach on the subject matter. Another scholar could write it a third time and others probably more without repeating anything. There could be chapters on the Cold War, the story of corporate capitalist imperialism, the tale of American trade encroachment under the guise of humanitarianism to feed hungry people, or subaltern theory. Historians, such as Jack Kloppenburg Jr., Nick Cullather, John Perkins, and Sigrid Schmalzer, have covered these issues.

Other historians, however, have given remarkably little attention to the Green Revolution. Economists, sociologists, geographers, anthropologists, environmentalists, journalists, regional planners, and political scientists have written the most about it, often prescriptive and negative. Some historians have called for a long look backward in order to give context to the Green Revolution, but most have neglected much of the agricultural and social science literature that would enable such perspective. Certainly, the agricultural antecedents of the Green Revolution date decades, if not centuries, before the official and public identification of that term post 1940s.

Several historians, however, have offered suggestions regarding how others might write the history of the Green Revolution. Some have encouraged historians to address agricultural modernization within the framework of a postcolonial critique of agricultural development. Others advocate the pursuit of subaltern and other non-elite relationships to understand how lower-caste politics changed as the Green Revolution altered traditional patron-client relationships. Still others urge historians to break with the Cold War explanation of the Green Revolution by those whose intellectual base is American foreign relations and area studies and pursue its business history to emphasize the intersection of multinational firms, scientists, and bureaucrats. Some scholars advocate more studies about plant breeding, racial theory, and gender as thematic ways to understand its history. Others urge historians to depart from placing agricultural science and scientists along with US philanthropists at the center of Green Revolution histories. Instead, they argue that historians should study the importance of institutional influences on the use of water, land, pesticides, and fertilizers to explain the intersection of the politics of agriculture with the industrial economy in national and international contexts. Other scholars stress the importance of social history over the economic and environmental metrics of the social scientists to help us better understand the history of the Green Revolution, particularly from the perspective of farmers and the rural poor. Some historians advocate greater attention to the Green Revolution's political history at the national, regional, and local levels to show the complexity of the Green Revolution, which, in fact, was not a singular event but a multiplicity of Green Revolutions. Few historians, however, have done much more than suggest these approaches for the study of the Green Revolution.

Moreover, synthesis is important, and it must include multiple areas in a single narrative, something that historians have not found easy to do. Put differently, historians often talk past each other and fail to agree about the core features of the Green Revolution. Consequently, we need more histories of the Green Revolution before anyone can write a major synthesis. Still, my effort to write a brief synthesis of the representational historical literature that discusses the success and failure of the Green Revolution across broad geographical areas provides a transnational snapshot of its history. It is a history in a moment of time and in the absence of the monographic studies suggested by various historians.

The possibilities for expanding our knowledge about the Green Revolution from non-Americanist or western perspectives are limitless. Historians can do much to enhance the work of social and agricultural scientists to help both scholars, students, and the public understand better what the Green Revolution was and is. Nevertheless, for the general reader, this brief overview of the Green Revolution will provide an understanding of its agricultural history as well as encourage the pursuit of the unrealized historical scholarship mentioned above.

This study, then, is an analysis of the intersection of agricultural science and politics regarding the Green and Gene Revolutions specifically regarding the production of wheat, maize, and rice, which agricultural scientists judged as the most important food grains. It shows that by the early twenty-first century the Green Revolution had become more important as an agent of economic change for elites rather than food-deficient people while agricultural science made important advances in crop breeding that improved grain production but often for the wrong farmers. No one argued that less food was better than more food for poor, hungry people. Rather, elites and governments often used agricultural science for their own purposes. While they benefited more from the Green Revolution, the poor benefited less. Promises for a better life often went unfulfilled.

This study is also a survey of the ways that agricultural and social scientists and the public have considered the Green Revolution over time and space (that is, geographically and historically). It is a beginning point that can lead to more in-depth study and research. I have written for nonspecialists, informed general readers, and anyone who wants a quick overview of the Green Revolution's history. To help facilitate that task this study asks several questions: What was and is the Green Revolution? What was its intent, results, and unintended consequences, particularly in relation to agricultural productivity, social equity, landholding, labor, migration, and government assistance? I have avoided using statistics as much as possible, but I could not always avoid numbers to make a point about production, benefits, and problems. I use the terms tonnes and tons interchangeably because the evidence often is presented by using one of these words. Tonnes is a slightly larger metric measurement, but it is impossible to determine whether reporters who used tons really meant tonnes. For the purpose of the survey and synthesis generalizations in this book, the interchangeability of these words does not make a great difference. Similarly, many of those who have written about a particular subject relating to the Green Revolution sometimes mix acres and hectares, the latter of which equals about two and a half acres. I have used the terms of the original writers for consistency, if not accuracy. More important, the Green Revolution is an area of historical inquiry where facts often are not clear evidence that supporters or opponents can easily marshal for explanations. In many respects, the Green Revolution is a matter of perception. Academics, scientists, and the public often have strong opinions about the successes and failures of the Green Revolution, but frequently they base their beliefs on ideology and their views about the positive and negative benefits of agricultural science on economic, social, and environmental circumstances. My intent is to provide an overview that will help readers understand the origins, developments, and consequences of the Green Revolution during the late twentieth and early twenty-first centuries.

This research and writing has taken more than a decade. The result is, I hope, a usable introduction to the agricultural history of the Green and Gene Revolutions. I also am grateful for the assistance many people provided over the years.

Juan Pan-Montoya at the Universidad Complutense de Madrid and Li Zhang at Beihang University in Beijing provided incisive critical insights about my work. They helped me think more broadly about the implications of the Green Revolution for subsistence farmers in food-deficit nations. Xiaoyu Peng at Peking University, Siming Wang at Nanjing Agricultural University, and Bo-Don Joo at Kyungpook National University gave me the opportunity to present my work to non-Western historians who saw the Green Revolution from a different perspective. Thanks also for the feedback upon the presentation of my work at National Taiwan University. Lorenzo Fernández Prieto at the Universidade de Santiago de Compostela in Spain provided essential assistance. Their comments immeasurably strengthened this book. Alan Marcus at Mississippi State University helped me see the proverbial other side of the coin in relation to many interpretive contexts.

At Purdue University, I received excellent assistance from Larry Mykytiuk, History Librarian, and Bert Chapman, Government Information, Political Science, History, and Sociology Librarian, both superbly skilled in locating essential sources. The staff of Interlibrary Loan provided their customary excellent assistance, and I do not take them for granted. My colleagues Will Gray and Margaret Tillman in the History Department at Purdue University also suggested important sources necessary for my work. Over the years, many graduate students helped locate essential sources: David Cambron, Erika Morin, Liberty Sproat, Yasir Yilmaz, and Ruisheng Zhang. I also am grateful for the photograph assistance I received from Valerie Collins, Digital Repositories and Records Archivist, and Jennifer Claybourne, Digital Projects Assistant, Archives and Special Collections, at the University of Minnesota; Brylle James I. Galang, Media Relations Officer at the International Rice Research Institute; and Clyde R. Beaver III, Creative Services Manager at the International Maize and Wheat Improvement Center. This study received financial support from the Office of the Executive Vice President for Research and Partnerships, the College of Liberal Arts, and the Department of History at Purdue University.

Thanks to all without whom I could not have completed this study.

1

Latin America

In 1968, William Gaud, director of the US Agency for International Development, remarked that "throughout the developing world . . . we are on the verge of an agricultural revolution. . . . I call it 'The Green Revolution.'" By the early 1940s, Latin America needed an agricultural revolution to increase productivity. Mexican farmers constituted 75 percent of the nation's population, but they could not meet the country's food needs. Mexico had already undergone a political revolution that changed landholding patterns but it had not helped farmers increase food, particularly grain, production. Traditional agricultural customs and methods that depended on human and animal power for planting and harvesting, insufficient irrigation, plant diseases, and insect infestations kept crop production low. Many farmers lived in poverty and endured insufficient diets, if not hunger. Moreover, the population increased rapidly and demographers predicted that it would double in the next twenty-five years. With the food supply in jeopardy, the government increased imports, which depleted its financial reserves and in part prevented a major investment to improve agricultural production.[1]

By 1940, Mexican farmers had experienced governmental land reform since the revolution in 1910. Under the presidency of Lázaro Cárdenas (1934–1940), the government appropriated many large estates and distributed those lands as small-scale, communally held tracts that farmers could inherit but not sell. During the Cárdenas administration, the government distributed approximately eighteen million hectares or 47 percent of the cultivable land to 811,000 farmers. These agriculturists comprised 86 percent of the farmers in Mexico. Marginal lands in remote areas constituted many of these tracts, and the government favored large-scale collective farms in areas with adequate rainfall and irrigation networks. Collectively small-scale farms contributed approximately 52 percent of Mexico's agricultural productivity. Most of the food for farm families, rural residents, and urbanites, however, came from a small number of commercial farms located in the fertile valleys and plains, particularly in northwestern and central Mexico. These relatively large-scale farmers feared expropriation of their land and distrusted advice for improvement from the Ministry of Agriculture. Mexico employed 65 percent of its labor force in agriculture. These workers contributed 23 percent of the gross domestic product.[2]

In 1940, President Franklin Delano Roosevelt sent Henry A. Wallace, vice president elect, to represent the United States at newly elected Manuel Ávila Camacho's inauguration. President Camacho (1940–1946) intended to abandon Cárdenas's efforts to improve subsistence agriculture through land reform. During his visit, Wallace conferred with US Ambassador Josephus Daniels who wanted to help Mexico improve its agricultural research and productivity to end rural poverty. Wallace expressed interest, but he knew that America's drift toward war would deplete government funds except for essential support at home for the United States Department of Agriculture. Consequently, Wallace asked or at least did not object to Ambassador Daniels pursuing Rockefeller Foundation assistance to develop programs in Mexico similar to its educational, health, and agricultural activities in the American South. Daniels wanted the Rockefeller Foundation to help improve Mexico's agricultural research and productivity to help feed a food-deficit nation of sixteen million people. The Rockefeller Foundation, which had conducted a cooperative public health program with Mexico since 1919, sent a Survey Commission of three agricultural experts to Mexico to investigate whether the Foundation could help improve its food production to aid the poor and make the improvement of the region a worthy cause.[3]

In 1941, Paul C. Mangelsdorf, a geneticist and maize breeder from Harvard University, Richard Bradfield, an agronomist from Cornell University, and Elvin C. Stakman, a plant pathologist who specialized in wheat from the University of Minnesota, constituted the Rockefeller Foundation's survey commission. They represented the land-grant tradition in the United States, historically dedicated to improving agriculture for commercial, not small-scale, subsistence farmers, based on new forms of agricultural science and technology. They unquestionably believed in the land-grant university tradition of research and extension as keys to eradicating hunger and improving the standard of living for Mexican farmers.[4]

The agricultural science developed at the land-grant institutions in partnership with the United States Department of Agriculture had made American farmers the most productive and prosperous in the world. The survey commission members saw no reason why they could not extend the American model for the development and application of agricultural science and technology everywhere. Naturally, the commission brought land-grant foundational assumptions regarding research and progress to their work in Mexico. The Rockefeller Commission and the US government also hoped that improved relations with Mexico would help prevent the establishment of a socialist or a fascist government on the border at a time when the United States drifted inexorably toward war with Germany and Japan.[5]

After touring Mexico during the summer, the survey commission recommended that the Rockefeller Foundation develop an agricultural research and extension program in Mexico. The Rockefeller Foundation approved the commission's report and offered to advise the Mexican Ministry of Agriculture about ways to improve farming and food production. Mexico agreed to accept American advisors, and work began in February 1943 to determine the research emphasis and the organizational structure between the Rockefeller Foundation advisors and the Camacho Administration, which led to the establishment of the Mexican Agricultural Program (MAP). George Harrar became the Rockefeller Foundation's director of this endeavor and Edwin J. Wellhausen served as a maize geneticist along with agronomist William E. Colwell. Other specialists joined later. The agreement of understanding between the Rockefeller Foundation and the Mexican government called for research to develop rust-resistant wheat and improved maize varieties.[6]

While the Mexican government understood the need to improve agricultural production and the standard of living for farmers, it did not have a strong tradition of scientific experimentation to improve agricultural productivity. Moreover, Mexican agricultural scientists were suspicious of American intentions and some resented the implication that American scientists were coming south to teach them their business. In many respects, they were correct even though the Rockefeller Foundation and the Ministry of Agriculture agreed to participate equally in an agricultural improvement program. Ultimately, in October the Mexican Ministry of Agriculture and Animal Husbandry established the Office of Special Studies (OSS) as a semiautonomous agency. Under American direction, it administered the research agenda for the Mexican Agricultural Program, which furthered the perception that Mexico's agriculture had failed. MAP scientists, however, conducted independent as well as collaborative research with other Mexican agricultural scientists. On December 31, 1960, the OSS terminated due to success, change of interests by the Rockefeller Foundation, and continued differences over the research agenda in the Mexican Agricultural Program. The National Institute of Agricultural Research replaced the OSS, but it had a brief existence before transforming on October 25, 1963, into the International Maize and Wheat Improvement Center, or the Centro Internacional de Mejoramiento de Maíz y Trigo (CIMMYT). In 1966, the center reorganized as a nonprofit international institution for agricultural science and education, no longer under the Ministry of Agriculture. It is from this organizational work that the Green Revolution emerged long before it had a name.[7]

$\sim$

If the Green Revolution ultimately succeeded in improving wheat production for the farmers who could afford the required technology, the efforts of agricultural scientists to increase maize production with Green Revolution technologies proved a failure, or at least a long-delayed success for reasons of science and politics. The Office of Special Studies and the Mexican government's Office of Experiment Stations, the latter renamed the Agricultural Research Institute, pursued separate research agendas and methods that targeted different groups of farmers. The Rockefeller Foundation's original survey team considered the maize improvement program of Mexico's Office of Experiment Stations promising but concluded that its research lacked accomplishment. Paul Mangelsdorf believed that the further development of improved open-pollenated varieties would be more beneficial than research to create new hybrid varieties that did not breed true and the seed of which farmers had to purchase anew each year. By using selected inbred open-pollinated varieties, yields would increase although not to the extent of hybrid production, but farmers could replant each year without a decrease in yield. Put differently, the improved open-pollinated varieties developed by the Mexican Office of Experiment Stations had the potential to meet the cropping and food needs of the majority of Mexican farmers who cultivated by traditional methods.[8]

In 1943, when the Rockefeller Foundation began supporting an agricultural improvement program for Mexico, scientists at the Ministry of Agriculture and the León Experiment Station had been breeding hybrid maize since 1941. Their efforts to use American varieties, however, failed because those varieties did not adapt to an environment substantially different from the Midwest. Political infighting among Mexican scientists also slowed the maize-breeding program, and traditional farming practices hindered the adoption of high-yielding varieties (HYVs). Moreover, the government did not provide a price support program to make the adoption of these varieties affordable. As a result, most farmers did not adopt the high-yielding, Green Revolution varieties. Subsistence farmers who cultivated about three hectares planted maize for subsistence purposes; they did not participate in a market economy. Moreover, the government did not provide an adequate extension service with agents to help farmers make the technical and financial adjustments from traditional to modern practices with the use of science and technology. Yet, these were the farmers who the advocates of the Green Revolution contended would benefit most from it.[9]

Despite these problems, in February 1944, Mangelsdorf and Wellhausen of the Rockefeller Foundation and Edmundo Taboada of the Mexican Office of Experiment Stations announced a cooperative plan to improve maize production. The experiment stations would provide inbred lines for further breeding by the MAP scientists. Eventually, the government would distribute the newly improved maize varieties to Mexican farmers. Wellhausen and Mangelsdorf organized the OSS research program to improve native varieties rather than develop hybrid varieties based on imported seeds. They planned a short-term goal to develop what became known as "synthetics," not hybrid maize as known in the United States. They did so by collecting open-pollenated maize from all areas in Mexico and planting them in isolated locations where they would cross naturally with windblown pollen. A random cross resulted that produced some superior lines regarding yields, growing periods, and disease resistance. The scientists then crossed these selected crossbred varieties, which had specific characteristics, with superior traditional open-pollinated varieties to produce a single hybrid cross. The result was a modified or "synthetic" hybrid, not a high-yielding, double-cross hybrid that produced 10–25 percent more maize than the traditional parent varieties. Synthetic varieties adapted to different microclimates produced greater yields than the traditional open-pollinated varieties, and farmers could save the seeds or kernels from the maize ears at harvest time for planting next year's crop without lowering the yield. They did not need to purchase expensive hybrid seed that they could only plant once, because the hybrid kernels produced a degenerated crop if planted. In 1948, MAP released some "synthetic" varieties, and the farmers who planted them achieved record yields.[10]

In addition, despite the MAP staff's optimism that they were on the verge of creating a Green Revolution for subsistence maize farmers as well as providing more food for urbanites, farmers generally rejected the higher yielding varieties. They preferred the more recognizable, traditional maize varieties rather than the synthetics. As a result, OSS scientists failed to increase maize yields quickly and cheaply. Moreover, Mexican maize breeders rejected the American desire to develop synthetic varieties in favor of producing hybrid double-cross varieties. As a result, a Green Revolution for traditional maize farmers in Mexico would not come for another decade. Put differently, the Mexican and American maize breeders sought the same goal of increased maize production for human food, but each pursued different research paths. The OSS scientists wanted quick results to meet both food needs and political pressure to distribute new high-yielding seeds. They prepared to sacrifice uniformity for some variability in the maize plants that would adapt to various regions and climates in Mexico. They would work to develop high-yielding hybrid varieties later.[11]

Mexican scientists under President Miguel Alemán Valdés (1946–1952) and his agricultural officials did not want to pursue this avenue of research. They preferred to take their time to develop hybrid varieties that would produce even higher yields on uniform maize plants. Yet, even had they accepted the OSS approach, Mexico did not have an extension service that could disseminate the improved open-pollenated and synthetic varieties to subsistence farmers. Even so, Mexican scientists continued their research to develop high-yielding varieties along the lines of hybrid maize development in the United States. During the 1950s a Green Revolution in maize production emerged in Mexico but it was at the hands of Mexican and not American scientists.[12]

Between 1945 and 1970, maize production increased 250 percent due to the introduction of synthetics and high-yielding, hybrid varieties and chemical fertilizer in the most favorable areas. By 1965, however, maize production had leveled off at about 9 million tons per year, but a decade later the demand reached 10.5 million tons annually for a shortage of 1.5 million tons or about 17 percent of Mexico's need. This deficit put Mexican consumers in the same positon they had experienced in 1945. Nevertheless, with maize production relegated to the subsistence farmers in rainfed areas who could not afford Green Revolution technologies, Mexico's maize production could not easily meet its food needs.[13]

Mexico's conservative governments favored the large-scale landowners rather than subsistence maize farmers. The commercial farmers would be privileged with government-funded irrigation systems, subsidized wheat prices, and generous credit terms. Moreover, the government could export grain surpluses to generate foreign exchange and feed an industrializing economy. The peasant communities or *ejidos* established during the Lázaro Cárdenas administration received little agricultural support from the Camacho government.

There would be no Green Revolution for them as Mexico increasingly turned to American-styled agricultural science that favored large-scale commercial farmers. In addition, the Mexican government wanted wheat not maize to provide an export surplus and urban demands for bread.[14]

The OSS scientists in the Mexican Agricultural Program soon learned that President Camacho wanted fewer subsistence farmers and more industrial workers. If agricultural science could improve the productive capacity of fewer farmers, more workers could develop Mexican manufacturing and industrial enterprises. President Camacho and his supporters also wanted to end land reforms that gave small tracts to peasant farmers within communal *ejidos*. To achieve this economic shift, agricultural science had to privilege commercial farmers who already operated on a scale far more efficient than Mexico's subsistence maize farmers.[15]

Wheat rust, however, plagued the large-scale farmers and kept production low. The Camacho Administration wanted to solve this problem and not divert resources to improving maize production for subsistence farmers. Mexico had accepted American technical and financial support for agricultural improvement, but on its own terms and for its own research agenda. The OSS scientists in MAP acquiesced. Instead, for both political and policy reasons, they began emphasizing the Mexican research agenda to end the wheat rust problem and thereby privilege commercial farmers rather than small-scale subsistent farmers. The American scientists in MAP had received their training at land-grant institutions where science and the concept of progress inextricably linked so this focus did not trouble them. Some, such as Norman Borlaug, embraced this emphasis. The result would be a Green Revolution that favored large-scale farmers and capitalists in urban areas. In addition, Mexican officials believed the best way to eliminate rural poverty was to reduce the need for subsistence farmers by encouraging them to stop raising more maize merely to feed themselves. If science permitted, commercial wheat farmers could produce enough food grain for home consumption and international trade. This was the premise of Mexico's agricultural policy and to which the Rockefeller Foundation scientists in the OSS willingly agreed.[16]

During the early 1940s, Mexican farmers produced an average of 11.5 bushels of wheat per acre compared to 15 bushels per acre in the United States. Mexico imported 10.1 million bushels or 275,000 metric tons of wheat for more than 55 percent of the nation's consumption at a cost of approximately 100 million pesos or $21 million for the greatest government expenditure for food. At that time, after considerable planning, the OSS determined that science could solve the stem rust problem and provide new varieties that would permit higher yields and the expansion of the wheat crop. Yet, no solution seemed obvious.[17]

To help resolve the problem, The Rockefeller Foundation hired Norman Borlaug, who held a PhD in plant pathology from the University of Minnesota. In 1944, Borlaug arrived in Mexico and soon realized that the improvement of wheat production required the breeding of superior drought- and disease-resistant varieties as well as improved cultivation methods. To achieve these goals, he organized an interdisciplinary team of geneticists, agronomists, plant pathologists, entomologists, and chemists. They did not achieve their goals easily or quickly. They would labor for more than a decade before developing a disease-resistant wheat variety that provided the foundation for the Green Revolution in Mexico and the world beyond.[18]

Borlaug believed that the only way to increase Mexican wheat production was to work with the large-scale farmers who had access to irrigation in the northwest and the highlands near Mexico City where small-scale but commercial wheat farms prevailed. These farmers could afford to purchase high-yielding varieties and the necessary fertilizers to produce a heavy grain crop. They also contended with wheat rust annually, and they welcomed research that would end their problems and put more money in their pockets from larger grain yields. The climatic differences between the dry northwest and the rainfed highlands enabled Borlaug to double crop by "shuttle breeding." With this procedure, Borlaug and his team could raise specific varieties during the northern growing season then crossbreed and develop new varieties in the south during the winter. This technique enabled him to produce two generations of wheat plants annually instead of one. It gained time because he crossed many varieties before the development of a rust-resistant wheat. Borlaug began this breeding program sometime between 1946 and 1948 in the highlands and the Pacific Northwest. The wheat varieties bred in the wet highlands of El Bajío and the dry Yaqui Valley of Sonora proved remarkably tolerant in both environments. By raising two generations of wheat plants each year, Borlaug reduced the customary rule from ten years to produce a new variety to five years or less. Borlaug knew that time to development meant success or failure to solve the food-deficit problem given Mexico's rapidly expanding population and its reluctance to support agricultural research to help subsistence maize farmers.[19]

Although Borlaug's team crossed more than seven hundred Mexican and imported wheat varieties and tested soils for fertility, they did not have a

rust-resistant variety for release to farmers on a trial basis until 1949. Borlaug remained optimistic, however, that science could solve the wheat rust
problem. By 1951, farmers planted rust-resistant varieties on 70 percent of
Mexico's wheat lands and in 1956 Mexico became self-sufficient in wheat.
Two years later Borlaug wrote that Mexico's wheat area had increased from
500,000 hectares (1.25 million acres) in 1946 to 840,000 hectares (2.1 million
acres) in 1957, with approximately 250,000 hectares planted to wheat in Sonora and Sinaloa. Landowners had developed much of this acreage with irrigation, lands that accounted for 60 percent of Mexico's wheat production.
Borlaug's applied agricultural science had made its mark, and proved, he believed, that breeding for widespread adaptability worked best. Wheat yields
now increased to approximately twenty bushels per acre. Put differently, wheat
production increased from 400,000 metric tons in 1945 to 1.25 million metric tons in 1956, which created a 200,000 metric ton surplus for food security.
Borlaug called the new high-yielding varieties an "insurance policy" against
crop losses if farmers also applied fertilizer and irrigation. By the late 1950s,
farmers planted HYV wheat on 90–95 percent of the wheat lands in Sonora
and Sinaloa. Mexico no longer needed wheat imports to meet public needs.
Borlaug acknowledged that the wheat farmers in the northwest proved recep-
tive to agricultural science and experts and willingly adopted MAP-suggested
techniques that brought a new technology to the land.[20]

   They also learned that the soils of the wheat regions lacked sufficient nitrogen to produce high wheat yields, except for the lands recently claimed from
the desert in Sonora and Sinaloa. Borlaug's team soon discovered that the introduction of improved varieties and chemical fertilizers increased production sufficiently to warrant the mechanization of the crop, which also meant
that large-scale farmers with sufficient hectares to merit investment in tractors, grain drills, and combine harvesters would be the beneficiaries of their
research. Heavy grain crops, however, also increased insect infestation as an
unintended consequence of the improvement of grain yields. Borlaug's team
also learned that the rust-resistant varieties, like those of other Mexican varieties, were not strong enough to hold heavy heads of grain when farmers fertilized their fields. To solve this problem, Borlaug turned to several Japanese
dwarf strains, probably Norin 10 along with a Norin-Brevoir cross, which he
then bred with varieties raised in the hot, dry fields of northern Mexico as
well as in the cool highlands near Mexico City. Two hard spring wheat varieties, Sonora 63 and Sonora 64, that fought rust, tolerated the climatic and
soil variations across Mexico, and resisted toppling resulted. These varieties

Figure 1. Norman Borlaug in a Sonora 64 test field in Mexico
Released for distribution in 1964, Sonora 64, a semidwarf, high-yielding, disease-resistant
spring wheat, became a leading variety that contributed to increased wheat yields in Mexico
and the Indian subcontinent. Borlaug, who believed that it would help farmers substantially
increase wheat production across a wide area, is shown here standing fourth from the right
in a test plot at the Campo Experiment Station near Ciudad Obregón, Sonora. Courtesy of the
University of Minnesota Archives, University of Minnesota–Twin Cities.

also produced large yields with the heavy application of nitrogen fertilizer and irrigation. Research and crop improvement, however, takes time. Although Mexico achieved self-sufficiency in wheat production by the mid-1950s, not until 1963, twenty years after he began working in Mexico, did Borlaug succeed in increasing the average wheat harvest to thirty bushels per acre.[21]

Agricultural implement and fertilizer dealers responded by opening businesses to serve the needs of wheat farmers using the new technology. Land values increased and rent rose dramatically with owners requiring cash rather than a share of the crop for a major unintended consequence of Green Revolution science and technology in the wheat lands. Borlaug cautioned, however, that farmers needed government price supports to encourage continued investments in Green Revolution technology because production costs would increase. When the 1950s ended, Borlaug's scientists worked to develop dwarf, rust-resistant wheat varieties that would increase yields from 30 percent to

Figure 2. An agronomist in a wheat test field in Mexico
Norman Borlaug's team of scientists bred wheat varieties
for quick distribution to farmers. They emphasized applied
rather than theoretical research to help farmers increase
food production as rapidly as possible. In this photograph, a
Mexican agronomist holds a semidwarf, high-yielding wheat
variety in a test field. Courtesy of the University of Minnesota Archives, University of Minnesota–Twin Cities.

40 percent above traditional non-hybrid varieties. By the mid-1970s, Mexican
farmers planted nearly all wheat lands with Borlaug's high-yielding varieties
that averaged three tons per hectare for a 400 percent production increase
since 1950.[22]

In Mexico, Borlaug's team emphasized "production-oriented" research and
restricted it to investigations that were "relevant to increasing wheat production." Borlaug sought the development of high-yielding, semidwarf wheat
varieties that had "unusual breadth of adaption." He believed that farmers
could plant improved varieties across wide areas. Varieties with the capability
of widespread adoption would meet the food needs of the largest number
of people. Borlaug never diverted from this belief, even when the evidence
proved otherwise, indicating that location-specific crop breeding produced

the best results. He recalled that "researches in pursuit of irrelevant academic butterflies were discouraged . . . because of the need to have data and materials available as soon as possible for use in the production program." As Borlaug's experimental plots produced increased yields, his staff distributed the improved seeds among farmers to help them improve their production. "We never waited for perfection in varieties or methods," he said, "but used the best available each year and modified them as further improvement came to hand."[23]

~

While the achievements of Norman Borlaug and his colleagues merit praise, their intent did not materialize as planned. Borlaug always believed that he worked to improve food production for hungry people by aiding commercial farmers. Improved grain varieties, such as wheat, would meet immediate household needs and provide food for city dwellers. At first, he did not see the unintended consequences of his research, although it troubled him in later years. In Mexico, the problems were fourfold. First, most people ate tortillas made from corn. They did not customarily eat wheat bread. Second, improved wheat varieties produced best in areas where large-scale landowners already operated and where they applied technology in the form of tractors and combines as well as fertilizer and irrigation to expand the crops planted and boost their production per hectare. Third, although Borlaug's work helped Mexico achieve self-sufficiency in wheat, the government used most of that grain for export to generate foreign exchange currency to pay for various imported goods. Fourth, Borlaug's Green Revolution succeeded because the large-scale commercial wheat farmers had access to the necessary capital or credit to purchase improved seeds and fertilizer and develop irrigation systems. Small-scale, particularly subsistence, farmers could not afford these "inputs" to adopt the Green Revolution "package." They also did not benefit equally with large-scale wheat farmers, particularly those in the Pacific Northwest and western central highlands where water for irrigation proved sufficiently available during the dry winter season.[24]

By 1950, MAP scientists contended that they were politically neutral. They only cared about helping Mexico end its food deficiency through agricultural science. By so doing, they avoided confrontational issues, such as land reform, democratization, birth control, and the redistribution of income, all matters for politicians not agricultural scientists, or so they contended. As a result, while arguing that their work also would improve subsistence farming and the rural standard of living, the Green Revolution scientists contrib-

Figure 3. Irrigation ditch along a maize field in Mexico
High-yielding wheat and maize varieties require irrigation for maximum production. This irrigation ditch along a Mexican maize field indicates the time and labor needed to construct irrigation systems. Many farmers could not afford the investment, which limited the Green Revolution to those who could command the capital or credit to develop irrigation canals and ditches and acquire pumping technology. Courtesy of the University of Minnesota Archives, University of Minnesota–Twin Cities.

uted to the further political and economic loss of influence, if not power, of subsistence farmers. Their humanitarian motives to help all farmers eventually proved admirable in theory, but they failed to reach fruition in reality. In many respects, MAP scientists could more easily aid commercially oriented wheat farmers than provide a path to modernity for all Mexican farmers. Their acceptance of the "tortilla" past for subsistence farmers proved professionally more acceptable. By so doing, the Americans in MAP abandoned their original intent to provide poor maize farmers with high-yielding varieties to prevent hunger and feed the rural and urban poor. Instead, almost from the beginning, based on government agricultural policy, they favored large-scale commercial farmers rather than research to save food-deficient people from hunger and want. Even so, Mexican and American agricultural scientists believed that they had created an agricultural revolution that would end fears of

Malthusian famine from overpopulation and inadequate agricultural production. Nevertheless, as long as agricultural production stayed ahead of population growth, an early unintended consequence of the Green Revolution was that it enabled the government to avoid dealing with the political issue of birth control in this Catholic nation.[25]

~

In 1958, Mexico became a wheat exporter. Commercial wheat farmers produced a surplus that fed the urban population and generated considerable foreign exchange. Although still an uncoined term, Mexican Agricultural Program scientists had created a Green Revolution that other nations would emulate with varying degrees of success. Subsistence farmers continued to raise maize but with little research assistance or support from MAP or the government. Many subsistence farmers, men and women, however, had fled to the cities where they remained part of the urban poor and their lives little improved from their days as subsistence farmers. The Green Revolution did not embrace them. Dismal days remained for the many subsistence farmers who remained on the land.[26]

By the mid-1960s, scientists at the International Maize and Wheat Improvement Center (which had replaced the Mexican Agricultural Program) believed that their work had benefited Mexico, but they did not assume that the future depended on small-scale subsistence farmers. Rather, Mexico's agriculture would best succeed by developing commercial, not by improving subsistence farming to enable poor agriculturists to feed their families. In 1967, with a remarkable misperception of reality, E. C. Stakman, Richard Bradfield, and Paul C. Mangelsdorf, authors of *Campaigns against Hunger*, the official history of the Mexican Agricultural Program and the early Green Revolution, stated that subsistence farmers did not have a place in modern Mexican agriculture. They reflected on the part that they and other MAP participants had played in the maize- and wheat-breeding programs with proverbial rose-colored glasses. They wrote, "In 1948, five years after the beginning of the program, Mexico, for the first time since the Revolution of 1910 had no need to import corn." They did not note that the new, improved seeds primarily went to increase the production of commercial maize farmers rather than to help subsistence farmers feed their families. They also noted that the Green Revolution had "release[d] many people no longer needed on farms for other needed services, as teachers, engineers, doctors, civil servants, and industrial workers." The Green Revolution had changed Mexican society by taking it "from backbreaking peasant farming to the intelligent business of farming."[27]

Figure 4. Workers filling grain sacks with Lerma Rojo 64
Lerma Rojo 64 became a major Green Revolution wheat variety
on the Indian subcontinent. This photograph from 1966 shows
Mexican workers filling grain sacks with the high-yielding wheat
variety. Note the destination of Bombay on the grain sack. Courtesy
of the University of Minnesota Archives, University of Minnesota–
Twin Cities.

Some critics countered that only politics could save Mexico's poor farmers
with more land reform, not agricultural science. Some agricultural scientists
charged that subsistence farmers were too uneducated to appreciate agricultural science and to use it properly to improve their economic and social conditions. One contemporary criticized subsistence farmers for their "impen-
etrable negligence, apathy, and inability to be sociable and cooperate." They
had neither the education, financial ability, nor character to participate in the
Green Revolution and, therefore, did not merit the attention of agricultural
scientists trying to improve seed varieties to increase production. Agricultural scientists considered their work to improve wheat production among

Figure 5. Grain sacks bound for India being loaded onto a
ship in Mexico
India became a major importer of high-yielding varieties
developed in Mexico. Farmers in Punjab planted these and
reaped high yields compared to traditional varieties. Courtesy of the University of Minnesota Archives, University of
Minnesota–Twin Cities.

the farmers in Sonora a success based on a "perfect union of technical experts and farmers." Others contended that hybrid seeds made rich farmers
richer and poor farmers poorer.[28]

By the late 1960s, then, the Green Revolution had mixed results. Farmers contended with price instability, inflation, decreasing government subsidies for seed and fertilizer, lower grain prices for wheat raised on irrigated
lands, and general neglect of the *ejidos* and small-scale agriculturists. Many
farmers fled the land to seek better paying opportunities in the cities. However, they did not get jobs as teachers, doctors, or even industrial workers as
Green Revolution supporters predicted. They simply joined the impoverished,
hungry, food-deficient, urban poor who lived in shantytowns surrounding

the cities. Moreover, the cost of HYVs and fertilizers were not entirely scale neutral. Although costs theoretically were divisible and affordable by small-scale farmers, in reality the Green Revolution favored the large-scale producers who had access to credit institutions and who had the education to apply Green Revolution technologies and negotiate the bureaucracy of lending institutions. Furthermore, Mexico's credit institutions that catered to small-scale subsistence farmers proved too undercapitalized to provide the necessary funds for Green Revolution investment.[29]

By the 1970s, some critics blamed "national high science" for harming the environment rather than helping to produce food for hungry people because farmers used heavy applications of fertilizers, herbicides, and pesticides to nourish and protect high-yielding crops. The Mexican government, however, rejected charges that the Green Revolution had failed to improve the lives of poor farmers while benefiting rich farmers, particularly wheat producers. Others called the long-floundering maize-breeding program a success, but without much hard evidence. Others argued that the hybrid-breeding program for wheat and maize had been a success but that the extension work to convince subsistence farmers to use this technology had failed for want of effort and interest and because the agricultural scientists preferred to work in their laboratories rather than deal with poor farmers in their fields. Mexican scientists responded to their critics saying that their work reached the poor and asked, "How can it be wrong to increase the amount of food . . . [and] the incomes of farmers?" They would not be a scapegoat for the social problems of Mexico.[30]

In 1970, Norman Borlaug joined the fight, if ever he had left it, by vociferously claiming that the Green Revolution could not "solve all the social problems that already existed." Green Revolution supporters admitted, however, that subsistence farmers did not adopt hybrid maize to any great extent because the government had bungled the seed distribution program, and these farmers did not trust officials to tell them the truth about anything, particularly how to improve their farming practices. Borlaug and others also believed that agricultural reform could be achieved by policies that removed subsistence farmers from the land. The large-scale, capital-intensive farmers could produce the most food and do so the most efficiently. Put differently, Mexico had too many farmers. Fewer farmers using Green Revolution technologies could best meet the food needs of the Mexican people.[31]

By the 1970s, however, Mexican farmers raised high-yielding maize varieties on less than 10 percent of their lands devoted to this crop. Mexico's Green

Figure 6. Ship workers loading seed wheat bound for India
In 1966, India imported eighteen thousand tons of high-yielding Mexican varieties. Mexico now exports seed wheat annually, primarily to Asian nations. Courtesy of the University of Minnesota Archives, University of Minnesota–Twin Cities.

Revolution rested on wheat production, and it remained concentrated in a few irrigated, not rainfed, areas. Although Green Revolution seed boosted production initially, wheat prices ultimately declined based on supply and as government price supports declined. Urban consumers benefited from low-cost flour and bread. The poor maize farmers, some optimists contended, also benefited because the government did not need to spend foreign exchange on wheat imports, thereby theoretically maintaining more resources for food assistance.[32]

The Green Revolution, then, had largely failed the subsistence farmers who raised traditional varieties of maize. Still, the Mexican Agricultural Program helped reduce food imports by producing the hybrid wheat varieties and technologies that increased production and by providing cheap subsidized food for urbanites, all of which helped keep the population well fed, peaceful, and unresponsive to community calls for major institutional and political reform. Equally important, Mexican scientists supported the government by emphasizing agricultural reform through science, not by politically inspired measures to break up large holdings or the *ejidos* for allocation to subsistence farmers. In turn, the government supported them with jobs and recognition of their professional credibility. Green Revolution agricultural science remained a top-down endeavor, the benefits of which remained at the top.[33]

By the mid-1970s, social, if not natural, scientists recognized that while the Green Revolution had provided food security for Mexican consumers in the form of wheat for bread, they had targeted the wrong farmers for assistance. This was not necessarily an unintended consequence of the Green Revolution but rather a miscalculation of approach (that is, strategy) from the beginning of the Mexican Agricultural Program. More than half of Mexico's cropland lay in the rainy central highlands where irregular precipitation fell from midsummer to late autumn. There, farmers primarily raised maize, but they also double cropped wheat during the winter if they had access to supplemental irrigation during the dry season. The central highlands constituted approximately 15 percent of Mexico's land area. Lowland tropical areas had potential for agricultural development, but they needed draining and infrastructure that could prevent periodic flooding.[34]

The agricultural scientists responsible for Mexico's Green Revolution did not target the lowlands or the central highlands for crop improvement. Instead, they focused on the dry northwestern coastal plain, particularly the states of Sonora and Sinaloa, where some farmers had developed irrigation and where year-round cropping of wheat, soybeans, cotton, and sorghum, among other crops, produced high yields. Smaller but similar agricultural areas existed in the states of Coahuila, Chihuahua, Baja California, and Tamaulipas. Green Revolution agricultural science had little to offer maize farmers who eked out a living on alluvial valley floors in the eastern and western mountains and southern highlands. In all, the National Bank of Mexico classified only 7.1 percent of the nation's 2.8 million farms as modern, progressive, or commercially oriented. These farmers had adopted the Green Revolution technological package to increase production. Approximately 40.5 percent of the semicommercial farmers applied some of the new technological improvements while 52.4 percent of the farms received a subsistence classification. In addition, about 50 percent of Mexico's farms were located in the central highlands with about six hectares each suitable for crops. In this area, overcrowding and subsistence agriculture prevailed given the small farm size, poor soils, and lack of sufficient rainfall.[35]

By the mid-1970s, 80 percent of Mexico's cropland remained under semicommercial or subsistence agriculture. Its farmers were the ones who most needed Green Revolution agricultural technology to improve subsistence food production and, if possible, a surplus for sale to improve their standard of living. In rainfed areas, however, farmers could not irrigate their fields for lack of surface and underground water. Green Revolution agricultural science did not improve dryland agriculture for them. Consequently, these subsistence farmers primarily raised rainfed maize and beans. At the same time, an annual 3.5 percent population increase pushed Mexico's population to 62 million. Approximately 23 million people lived in rural areas where 3.5 million remained unemployed. Some social scientists contended that agricultural science needed to make subsistence farming more productive so that this unemployed labor force could find work and refrain from migrating to the cities.[36]

Put differently, the dry central highlands contained about half of Mexico's cropland but it had only about 10 percent of the water for irrigation while the wet southeastern region had about 8 percent of the population, little cropland, and approximately 40 percent of the water resources. Either engineers had to move water to where needed or agricultural scientists had to determine ways to make these lands productive besides emphasizing wheat production. With the failure of farmers to meet the nation's food needs, Mexico imported 4 million tons of grain, mostly maize, but also some wheat and sorghum by the mid-1970s. The government increased its price support for these grains to encourage greater production, but subsistence farmers did not benefit from the price increases. Instead, chemical fertilizer, a Green Revolution "input," increased in price by 12 percent. Although fertilizer use increased significantly from 118,000 to 551,000 tons of nitrogen and to 183,000 tons of phosphorous fertilizer by 1974, with fertilizer imports increasing by 60 percent and pesticide imports by 15 percent between 1965 and 1975, most subsistence farmers still could not afford them.[37]

Mexico's National Institute of Agricultural Research did not respond to the need to increase subsistence production, and the International Maize and Wheat Improvement Center continued receiving strong government support in part to generate surplus grain production to earn income from international sales. Although the government made greater investments to expand irrigation networks and in 1970 created a separate agency for agricultural extension, it lacked trained personnel to improve Mexico's agriculture. With demand for grain estimated to increase at an annual rate of 5 percent for the next decade, social scientists urged the government to expand agriculture into the high rainfall areas where subsistence agriculture prevailed. Specifically, they urge greater maize production to enable Mexico to maintain self-sufficiency in this food. Green Revolution agricultural scientists needed to reorient their focus from wheat to maize and emphasize applied research to enhance production in drought-prone and high-rainfall areas. By so doing, they could increase grain production to feed hungry people, farmers, rural residents, and urbanites alike as well as increase farm income.[38]

The social and agricultural scientists both contended that agricultural research had to be "applied" rather than "pure" and that a well-organized and effective extension service skilled in communications had to take new knowledge to uneducated, traditional, and wary semicommercial and subsistence farmers. Social scientists also advocated improved credit and marketing assistance from the government to enable these farmers to participate in Green Revolution agriculture. Semicommercial and subsistence farmers had proven unwilling to incur debt without insurance against loss. Moreover, these farmers primarily raised maize, and they were unlikely to substitute other crops to improve their diets. They needed improved high-yielding, early-maturing, drought-resistant maize varieties that could produce large crops with small amounts of chemical fertilizer, and moisture conservation techniques. Green Revolution agricultural scientists once again ignored them.[39]

By the mid-1970s, the Mexican government distributed Green Revolution technologies at an increasing rate to the most commercially successful and promising farmers. Critics charged that the government also privileged the large-scale landowners with high price supports and low taxes. In irrigated areas, land values escalated and increased the wealth and borrowing power of the wheat farmers. The farmers, who could not compete, often overextended their obligations, went bankrupt, and sold out to large-scale commercial farmers who used the advantage of scale to expand their operations even further. They could best afford to invest in or own machinery businesses, fertilizer and insecticide outlets, tire dealerships, and other avenues of commerce in the agricultural service centers.[40]

Surplus production, however, presented another problem for the government. As wheat production increased beyond demand, domestic prices fell, and the government had to continue high price supports to maintain productivity and ensure grain for international sale to generate foreign exchange. Critics contended that too many people still suffered from malnutrition and hunger, because they could not afford adequate food. Put differently, many urban consumers could purchase food at higher prices because they had greater disposable income than rural dwellers. In this sense, government price supports that kept grain prices high for farmers and urban employment that en-

abled city residents to purchase adequate food had the unintended consequence of pricing poor rural dwellers out of an adequate food market. As a
result, they experienced the proverbial want in the midst of plenty.[41]

Moreover, large-scale grain farmers increasingly used tractors, combines,
and trucks to plant, harvest, and transport grain, so the need for farm workers gradually declined. Between 1965 and 1975, the importation of agricultural machinery increased from $42.6 million to $103 million. Although some
surplus labor went to the cities for employment, other rural workers had migrated north to the United States as legal workers in the bracero program
(1942–1964) or as illegal workers, thereby causing another unintended consequence or problem of the Mexico's Green Revolution.[42]

By the mid-1970s, critics charged the Green Revolution had not benefited
those who its early supporters had intended. Instead, they suffered continued
poverty and neglect while Mexico's agricultural investments in science and
technology went to the commercial farmers. By this time, the Green Revolution had become capital- rather than labor-intensive and market- rather
than subsistence-oriented, as well as linked to publically funded research institutions designed to make Mexican agriculture more productive, efficient,
and businesslike. Most Mexican farmers, however, remained subsistence oriented, labor intensive, and isolated from agricultural expertise as well as feared
failure upon expensive investments in Green Revolution technologies. They
also preferred open-pollinated maize varieties that enabled them to remain
independent of outside seed companies.[43]

Before the decade ended, some observers believed that the Green Revolution clearly had begun to wane. Although wheat production had substantially
increased over thirty years and while Mexico no longer had the dubious recognition as a food-deficit nation, the government still imported large amounts
of grain to ensure food security, approximately a quarter of the wheat, maize,
and soybeans required to meet food needs. While not starving, an estimated
27 percent of the population suffered severe nutritional deficiencies. Some
critics charged that Mexico needed a second Green Revolution with the introduction of new wheat varieties that would replace the dwindling productivity of older strains. Others believed that a second Green Revolution had
already occurred, but it rested on the production of sorghum. If wheat was
the "miracle crop" of the first Green Revolution, others now heralded grain
sorghum as the new high-yielding crop that provided a needed and profitable grain for the livestock industry. Sorghum is not a grain that Mexicans or
most people beyond sub-Saharan Africa eat, but it is a high-value cattle feed.[44]

Although wheat production increased to twelve million metric tons in 1980 because of Green Revolution technology, the hectares planted with wheat declined during the late 1960s and 1970s. Moreover, the maize area also had declined, due largely to falling prices and the inability of the government to provide price supports that provided farmers with sufficient incentive or profit to cultivate it. At the same time, sorghum provided a high-value alternative crop, which Mexican scientists had improved by developing high-yielding varieties. By 1980, Mexican farmers planted 1.5 million hectares with sorghum, more than double the area planted with wheat. They also used hybrid seeds for virtually all of the sorghum planted, and they fertilized more than 75 percent of this crop. The government did not support or encourage farmers to raise grain sorghum, but farmers increased production on their own because they could afford to forgo investing in irrigation technology since grain sorghum is a drought-resistant crop. The demand for sorghum came from livestock producers who responded to urban markets where workers with disposable income preferred to eat beef, and they willingly paid for it. As a result, poor, traditional, semisubsistent farmers in the rainfed areas produced most of the maize and beans, which remained their staple foods. These farmers fertilized little more than 50 percent of the maize lands, and they only planted 13 percent of these lands with high-yielding Green Revolution varieties. At the same time, wheat farmers irrigated 82 percent of their lands and applied fertilizer to 98 percent of their crop.[45]

By the mid-1970s, an increasing number of Mexican farmers who could afford fertilizer and pesticides also opted to raise high-valued winter vegetables. These crops brought good prices in the United States and provided greater income than maize and wheat. As a result, Mexico began to import more food grains. By the early 1980s, government efforts to promote food self-sufficiency and increase production by subsidizing grain prices, providing crop insurance, and committing more investment in agricultural research had failed with the collapse of oil prices which the government had depended upon to pay for a new commitment to agricultural development. More subsistence farmers left the land unable to compete with cheap grain imports or purchase expensive seeds, fertilizers, and pesticides. If anything, critics charged that the Green Revolution had eliminated many small-scale farmers from the countryside and replaced them with "efficient agribusinesses men" who produced for world markets.[46]

If anyone still believed that the Green Revolution emphasized improved production to aid poor, hungry people, they were naive to a fault. The Green

Revolution fed commercial agriculturists and agribusiness industries, not poor farmers. Had MAP and its descendent organizations emphasized research to help subsistence farmers, the Green Revolution might have achieved the original goal, because its supporters argued that hybrid crop varieties grew as well on small-scale as large-scale farms. Borlaug blamed any failures of the Green Revolution on politicians, not on the inability of agricultural scientists to reach poor farmers. He believed that "economists, sociologists, and politicians," not agricultural scientists, had the responsibility to improve food access and for making the Green Revolution a success in fighting hunger as well as enhancing the lives of poor farmers and others. Agricultural scientists did not have the responsibility to administer, control, or prevent social change.[47]

Yet, while Borlaug blamed politics for limiting the effects of Mexico's Green Revolution, the Social Division of CIMMYT confirmed that farmers did not share its benefits equally, and that the adoption of Green Revolution technologies depended on region and social class. Edwin Wellhausen observed that the Green Revolution reached the "larger, more commercial farmers, who were in a better position to afford fertilizer and other inputs." The key to improving the productivity of the subsistence farmers, the critics argued, was to develop seed varieties and nonchemical technologies that they could afford and use productively. Put differently, scientists should devote agricultural research to improve production and help farmers feed themselves and the rural and urban poor, an early goal of MAP scientists in the mid-1940s. Yet, not until 1991 did CIMMYT begin work to develop sustainable (meaning the seeds of each crop could be planted again the next year) wheat and maize varieties that had the potential to aid Mexico's subsistence farmers. CIMMYT scientists also experimented with genetic engineering to develop varieties with built-in tolerances to insects, disease, and environmental stress, thereby forgoing expensive chemicals that endangered humans and damaged the environment.[48]

Still, by the 1980s, some subsistence farmers used improved varieties, chemical fertilizers, and pesticides to the extent that they could afford the investment, thereby increasing their food supply and proving the basic neutrality of Green Revolution and that they would benefit proportionally to their investment in it. Yet, without improved maize varieties developed for varying regional soils and microclimates, subsistence farmers still preferred traditional varieties because they yielded a dependable harvest. Some critics charged, however, "the problems of Mexican agriculture are more than technical problems, they are social problems, and they should not be analyzed only in the cold context of science." Even some Mexican agricultural scientists said that they should study peasant farming practices and culture before they attempted to improve their lives with new high-yielding seed varieties and other technologies. At the same time, others thought the Green Revolution had been an unabashed success by favoring large-scale commercial producers, although Green Revolution technologies sometimes caused environmental degradation as they did at a colonization project in Yohaltún, Campeche, where experiments on rice lands made the soil incapable of absorbing water.[49]

By the 1980s, however, many farmers raised grain for livestock feed and not food for hungry, poor residents in the cities and countryside. When Green Revolution technologies in the form of fertilizers and pesticides damaged the land and water supplies and when lands became too infertile from overproduction and chemical applications proved too expensive to maintain profitability, farmers often abandoned those lands. As a result, agricultural employment declined and the rural poor increased. Greater soil erosion followed the abandonment of lands. Overall, the social and economic unintended consequences of Green Revolution agriculture proved increasingly detrimental to the intent of those who first advocated agricultural change.[50]

Although Green Revolution high-yielding wheat varieties had created a grain surplus, science could not yet do much about drought that kept the 1982 maize harvest 40 percent below the previous year. Mexico had no other solution than to import maize from the United States. With half of the arable land planted in maize and beans, and with maize primarily produced by the poorest farmers on the least productive lands under rainfed conditions, drought proved devastating to Mexico's chief food grain supply. At the same time, government price supports for maize and other basic crops favored large-scale farmers and the cooperative *ejidos*, both of which raised grain, especially wheat, for the urban and export markets. Yet, capital-intensive, market-oriented agriculture approached the limits of growth. Little land remained for new cultivation except in the mountainous rainfed areas. There, farmers could not afford hybrid seeds and instead planted indigenous, traditional, open-pollinated varieties that produced comparatively low yields. Inadequate transportation, unpaved roads, and insufficient credit further worsened the problem.[51]

By the 1980s, Green Revolution scientists at the International Maize and Wheat Improvement Center had thus far been unable to develop drought-resistant maize varieties, although they worked to breed high-yielding varieties for rainfed areas and to develop maize that reached maturity within three to four months rather than the six to nine months for traditional varieties.

At the same time, the poor subsistence farmers in the rainfed areas and the rural and urban poor most needed a Green Revolution in maize production. This area also had the highest rate of population growth and the largest migration to the cities.[52]

Although wheat and maize production increased 500 percent between 1940 and 1979, Mexico's population increased from 20.7 million to approximately 69 million and exceeded food production. By the mid-1980s, Green Revolution wheat and maize had not met the food needs of hungry people, particularly in poverty-stricken and low-productive, traditional farming areas. Mexico again became a wheat-importing nation. Moreover, the government had completed the irrigation projects designed to expand wheat production in the Pacific Northwest. Irrigated wheat lands had reached Mexico's natural limits based on the availability of water. Irrigation wheat farmers began shifting some fields to other more highly subsidized and price-supported crops. Farmers also increasingly focused on meeting the meat desires of urbanites because it paid more than raising wheat and maize.[53]

The Green Revolution had stalled, and it needed to be revitalized by the development of new plant-based crops, particularly wheat and maize, and government-subsidized prices to make production profitable for farmers who could feed people who could not afford expensive meat from sorghum-fed cattle, hogs, and chickens. By the mid-1980s, Mexico's Green Revolution still primarily benefited the wealthy and the middle class rather than food-deficient people in urban and rural areas. With estimates that 15 percent of the population consumed 50 percent of the food and that the bottom 30 percent of the population consumed only 10 percent of the food, the Green Revolution had failed to meet Mexico's food needs.[54]

Mexico's Green Revolution now emphasized food production for those who could pay for it, which was opposite the intent of the early American scientists who went to Mexico in the 1940s to produce high-yielding varieties of wheat and maize to feed hungry people. Many urban Mexicans with disposable income had abandoned their traditional dietary reliance on maize for tortillas and substituted with wheat bread. Wheat had become the crop of modern Mexico due to Green Revolution agricultural science and supportive government policy. In addition, maize production declined during the 1970s, which indicated a decrease in Mexico's subsistence farmers. A Green Revolution that produced luxury rather than subsistence foods resulted from many causes: industrialization, urbanization, inadequate agricultural support, and economic development not based on agriculture, among others. Mexico's rapid

economic and agricultural growth did not lead to equity for small-scale farmers and poor, food-deficient people in the cities and countryside. Social and
political constraints altered the direction and intent of the first Green Revolution. Many observers believed that Mexico needed another Green Revolution to sustain the gains of the first, meet the food needs of impoverished
urban and rural consumers, and elevate semisubsistent farm families from
poverty and want.[55]

∾

By the 1990s, a Green Revolution had not occurred for Mexican maize farmers. With more than half of the country arid and too steep for cultivation,
the poor subsistence farmers grew maize wherever possible without irrigation and depended only on rainfall for sustenance. These farm families constituted approximately 25 percent of all Mexicans. Subsistence farmers still
could not afford high-yielding varieties and fertilizer and their lands were not
sufficiently extensive to warrant mechanization, such as tractors. As a result,
they planted traditional varieties that often produced yields two-thirds less
than Green Revolution varieties. Although the government subsidized maize
production to ensure food security, albeit not from Green Revolution varieties, it purchased the entire surplus annually at nearly $200 per metric ton
for a $2 billion annual investment. Then it subsidized tortilla prices to keep
the cost of this basic food affordable. The government also imported maize
from the United States.[56]

Mexican agricultural scientists, however, still considered the needs of subsistence farmers an infringement, even an imposition, on their real work to
improve food crops for commercial farmers, particularly with biotechnology
that subsistence farmers could not afford. The new emphasis on producing genetically modified crops also kept scientists in the laboratories rather
than in experimental field plots, and extension agents cared little for disseminating new agricultural knowledge to Mexico's poor farmers. Many contemporaries believed that the Green Revolution had made life worse for these
neglected farmers.[57]

Mexico's government still wanted farmers to produce high-value crops for
export and the generation of foreign exchange. It would use the profits to purchase cheap grain on the international market. In 1992, Undersecretary of
Agricultural Planning Luis Téllez Kuenzler contended that while Mexico was
self-sufficient in cereal grains, success had come "at a very high cost." The
government now intended to shift support from Green Revolution grain production to "more value-added crops," such as fruits and vegetables, as well as

cattle, that agribusiness and consumers wanted to buy. Officials did not believe that they could transform subsistence farmers into commercial farmers by using Green Revolution technologies, and it was not worth the time, effort, and expense to change them. They would have the best chance for a better life in urban and industrial areas. The Mexican government intended to let the global market alleviate hunger and poverty, and not invest greatly in Green Revolution agricultural science for subsistence farmers. Political corruption made matters worse. At the same time, 10 percent of irrigated land, or 21 percent of all cropland, had become highly salinized, which some observers claimed reduced grain production by one million tons annually, or enough to feed four million people. An estimated 20 percent of the population suffered malnutrition. The twentieth century ended with the goals of the Green Revolution subverted and unaccomplished.[58]

Even so, the Green Resolution had sufficient success to keep food production ahead of population growth. Some critics believed that genetic engineering would make the plant-breeding methods of Green Revolution scientists obsolete and that better trained scientists from other countries would bring this new technology to Mexico. Or, worse yet, that scientists working for transnational companies would introduce costly new varieties in Mexico but not distribute them freely or cheaply because of patent restrictions designed to generate profits rather than help subsistence farmers feed their families and the poor. When the twentieth century ended, Mexican agricultural science remained biased against the small-scale subsistence maize farmers. If anything, Mexico's Green Revolution proved that agricultural science and technology could not solve social problems or contribute to greater economic equality. Whether the government intended to fund the development of biotechnology to aid subsistence farmers remained unclear. If biotechnological research could make agriculture sustainable rather than require annual renewals of the expensive new seed varieties, some contemporaries argued that Mexico could experience the benefits of a second Green Revolution. When the twentieth century ended, however, subsistence farmers did not trust the agricultural scientists and the scientists generally disregarded them.[59]

At the turn of the twenty-first century, the scientists at the International Maize and Wheat Improvement Center increased their efforts to develop high-yielding maize varieties to help subsistence farmers better feed themselves and other food-deficit nations, but the Center relied on private funding from seed companies to support much of its research. These seed companies demanded that the research they financed remain under their ownership and control. This forced the Center to patent its discoveries to prevent capture by the corporations. The Center also worked to improve the distribution of these new varieties to subsistence farmers. In contrast, the private seed companies wanted to control and sell their patented varieties.[60]

~

Despite the failure of the maize program and the unintended consequences of the wheat program by the late twentieth century, the collaborative work of the Mexican government and the Rockefeller Foundation in the Mexican Agricultural Program had laid the foundation for the extension of the Green Revolution to other Latin American countries. In 1950, Colombia began an agricultural research program to develop Green Revolution technologies for the improvement of maize production. During the mid-1960s, agricultural scientists at the International Center for Tropical Agriculture (CIAT) near Cali worked to develop high-yielding maize, wheat, and "miracle rice" varieties, similar to the efforts of Norman Borlaug and his researchers, to develop new HYV wheat varieties in Mexico. Although they succeeded in breeding new rice strains that produced abundantly and required little fertilizer on poor, acid soils, they would not resist "blast disease" (that is, rust). The Ministry of Agriculture made little progress and maize production lagged due to inadequate access to improved seeds. Uneducated farmers also preferred traditional methods, which prompted one observer to note that they farmed "much the same as at the time of the Spanish conquest." Moreover, climatic adjustments proved difficult to overcome, and the tide of achievement for the Green Revolution science ebbed and flowed.[61]

Colombian farmers planted high-yielding rice varieties on nearly all irrigated areas, and between 1966 and 1974 they increased production from 3 tons to 5.4 tons per hectare. Put differently, between 1967 and 1975, Colombia's rice production increased from 80,000 tons to 1.6 million tons from varieties acquired from the International Rice Research Institute, thereby making Colombia a rice exporter and no longer food deficient. By doing so, however, it, too, neglected the needs of the small-scale, poor farmers and privileged mill owners and consumers. In Colombia, as in other nations, consumers rejected the high-yielding, disease-prone variety known as IR-8, although farmers liked its high productivity. The government responded by providing a moderate price support to encourage production by offsetting the lower market price for IR-8 rice. The government also purchased and sold it at low prices through grain dealers and millers to encourage acceptance by the urban poor.[62]

New rice varieties soon replaced IR-8, and rice production improved. More rice meant lower food prices, which benefited the poor. This achievement caused one agricultural scientist to proclaim, "Agricultural research pays handsomely in developing countries." By the mid-1970s, however, the Green Revolution had not spread to Colombia although optimists believed in the inevitability of an agricultural revolution based on science. Late in the decade, oil prices quadrupled and increased the cost of petroleum-based fertilizers and pesticides which priced poor, small-scale farmers out of the market because they could not afford these chemicals.[63]

Moreover, CIAT scientists struggled to convince small-scale farmers to adopt their suggestions for agricultural improvement. These farmers could not afford to risk new Green Revolution techniques that might fail because they farmed only a few hectares. Traditional but low-productivity rice varieties ensured a crop. Crop failure often meant loss of the farm, but farmers could manage low prices and production from traditional crops. By the mid-1980s, high-yielding rice varieties met the basic food needs of Colombia's rapidly increasing population. CIAT scientists also experimented with upland rice (that is, rainfed or dryland varieties) rather than irrigated rice, to reduce costs. In many respects, the CIAT scientists had a more difficult task than those in Mexico during the 1960s because they also turned their attention to developing high-yielding rice varieties that also resisted disease, drought, and insects. They did not expect to develop any more miracle varieties, but they hoped that their work would increase productivity for reasons beyond genetic makeup for productivity alone.[64]

Colombia's CIAT scientists also pursued another avenue of Green Revolution research far beyond merely developing high-yielding grain varieties. They worked with scientists at a research center in Brasília, Brazil, to expand beef production for the benefit of the poor by developing grasses that could thrive on the poor soils in the savannah and jungle areas where raising grain crops proved problematic. They hoped to develop grasses and legumes to fatten cattle faster than on ordinary forage and pastures. By 1980, agricultural scientists had successfully demonstrated that the West African grass called *Andropogon gayanus* grew abundantly on poor soils, and it did not require heavy fertilizer applications. Cattle raisers became optimistic that they could fatten cattle quicker and cheaper and produce more beef to feed the population. Their definition of the population remained less clear, although poor people, farmers included, seldom could afford beef.[65]

Critics contended that the efforts to create a Green Revolution for Colombia had failed and merely replicated the Mexican experience where the large-scale, wealthy landowners benefited from agricultural science. Colombian agricultural scientists had achieved the most success by developing high-yielding rice varieties that required only two-thirds the amount of nitrogen fertilizer usually required. The large-scale farmers readily adopted it and soon added $150 million to the country's gross national product from increased production. Urban consumers and rural residents, not poor farmers, benefited the most from greater rice supplies at lower costs. The emphasis on this Green Revolution science, however, clearly focused on the commercial, not small-scale, poor farmers. Politics determined the research agenda. Latin American governments still did not care about bettering the conditions of the rural poor. They did not adequately support extension services that would take new agricultural science to farmers even though they still produced most of the food in Latin America. These governments also spent less on agricultural research as a percentage of agricultural production than any region in the world. Even though CIAT donors, such as the Rockefeller Foundation, wanted to help improve the lives of the rural poor, Latin American governments tended to treat agricultural research that would help subsistence farmers, such as developing highly productive varieties of beans and cassava, as merely institutionalizing poverty. Moreover, small-scale farmers in Latin America, who constituted 40 percent of the population, could not afford the improved seed varieties and fertilizer, which meant that increase food production had to come from the large-scale, more capital-intensive farmers.[66]

In addition, as late as 2016, Colombia's government encouraged cacao, not grain, production in rural areas where the army and rebels had fought for many years and from which farmers had fled the land. Government officials wanted to repopulate deserted rural areas with farmers who would raise cacao for international sale, not maize for subsistence agriculture or to feed hungry urban and rural people. Colombian officials sought to make the nation a major producer of cacao within fifteen years. They also wanted to develop the chocolate industry. An insufficient agricultural research system, however, continued to restrict Green Revolution achievements for any crop.[67]

Although the CIAT and the CIMMYT began focusing their research to improve the lives of small-scale farmers, John L. Nickel, director of the International Center for Tropical Agriculture, remarked, "Lots of social scientists have expected too much from the green revolution and international centers like ours." He contended, "Some people expect us to change social structures in farm areas and even influence changes in government policies. We have been blamed when small farmers did not have access to markets, machinery, credits, and water." Many social scientists, however, argued that the agricultural scientists should have been aware of these needs and potential problems and even worked with them simultaneously as they developed Green Revolution technologies that would have widespread social influences for both good and ill.[68]

The decisions of many Latin American governments to keep food prices low for urban consumers also kept agricultural prices low for farmers, thereby hindering their limited abilities to take advantage of Green Revolution science. Despite the pervasiveness of the rural poor, most of whom were farmers, Latin American governments lacked commitment to invest in irrigation, land reclamation, resettlement, extension services, fertilizer plants, and mechanization. Government officials also did not believe that they could extend the Green Revolution to small-scale, poor subsistence farmers. They contended that it was far better to generate foreign exchange from the sale of coffee and cotton and industrial goods and to purchase cheap grain on the international market than to feed their population with expensive food grains produced with Green Revolution technologies. Better to forgo political unrest, they judged, than to increase agricultural prices so that farmers could afford to adopt Green Revolution technologies.[69]

Guatemala provides another example of the negative unintended consequences of the Green Revolution. During the 1950s and 1960s, Mayan farmers in the highlands began using synthetic fertilizer. They welcomed increased maize yields that provided more food for their families and freed them from the necessity to migrate annually to find jobs on the cotton and coffee plantations after their food supply vanished. While Mayan farmers embraced the benefits of chemical or inorganic fertilizer, they also became dependent on it. When oil prices escalated during the 1970s, it became prohibitively expensive, and they necessarily returned to migratory labor during part of the year to earn enough money to pay for the costly fertilizer. Some Mayan farmers could no longer afford to cultivate with Green Revolution technologies and sold their land to large-scale operators who commanded the capital and credit to purchase it for their own use. By 1979, 2.5 percent of the farmers controlled 65 percent of the land.[70]

Guatemala's government, controlled by large-scale landowners and wealthy elites, welcomed opportunities to acquire cheap fertilizer from the United States. The Rockefeller Foundation and the US Agency for International Development (USAID) promoted Guatemala's acquisition of synthetic fertilizer to help increase food production and prevent hungry people from adopting

Communist ideology and overthrowing the government, all to the detriment, some believed, to Guatemalan and American security. Although the Mayan maize harvest had increased by the 1970s, many farmers not only had become dependent on expensive fertilizer to maintain large crop yields but they also began worrying about environmental degradation and danger to human health from the application of chemical fertilizers with high nitrogen and phosphorus contents. Chemical fertilizers, herbicides, and pesticides leached into water supplies, and the public soon attributed a host of illnesses and diseases, especially cancer, to these chemicals.[71]

Guatemala's government also did not provide adequate extension service to help educate and train farmers to use synthetic fertilizers, pesticides, and herbicides safely. At the same time, the United States sent its surplus maize to Guatemala, which the government sold at prices lower than production costs for Mayan farmers who produced it with Green Revolution technologies, particularly fertilizer. Many farmers gave up trying to produce surplus maize crops to feed their families and the urban and rural poor. By the 1970s, approximately 75 percent of Guatemala's children suffered from inadequate food and malnutrition. Overall, Green Revolution technology of synthetic fertilizer alone ultimately impaired agricultural production and contributed to poverty and social dislocation, while creating an agrochemical dependency.[72]

In retrospect, between 1940 and 1965, Mexico merited recognition as the birthplace of the Green Revolution. Maize production increased 400 percent and wheat 700 percent, and Mexico became self-sufficient in food during most years and no longer a food-deficit nation. By the late 1970s, however, grain production declined and imports increased. Salinization of land in some areas due to irrigation, deforestation, desertification, soil erosion, and pesticide contamination of land and water had become unintended consequences of the technological "package" required to significantly increase grain production, particularly wheat. Some observers contended that Mexico had a new food crisis. Between 1947 and 1960, the government facilitated the Green Revolution by building dams, electrical power plants, and roads. Irrigated land increased nearly 50 percent from approximately 28 million acres in 1930 to 41 million acres in 1960. Half of the water went to commercial farmers and half to the *ejidal* communities and their farms. The government supported grain prices to enable subsistence and commercial farmers to invest in Green Revolution technologies to the extent possible, thereby fostering the scale neutrality of the Green Revolution, meaning that all farmers could participate even with modest financial commitments.[73]

Yet, if the entry level for participating in the Green Revolution was scale neutral, the benefits were not equitably distributed or earned. Large-scale commercial farmers used their profits to buy out small-scale farmers. With better access to credit, they could acquire the financial resources for investment in Green Revolution technologies, particularly high-yielding seed varieties, irrigation, and fertilizers. The smaller-scale *ejido* farmers on marginal lands could not acquire technologies on a comparable scale, thus proving the fallacy of scale neutrality for participation in the Green Revolution for some critics. As late as 1960, 83 percent of Mexico's farmers practiced subsistence agriculture. At the same time, the market for luxury fruits and vegetables, such as strawberries, asparagus, and broccoli, expanded. With high prices north of the border, many commercial farmers planted less wheat and corn and more fruits and vegetables for export, all nourished with irrigation and fertilizers. Green Revolution food grain production could not keep pace with foreign and urban demands by consumers who could afford other foods. In addition, the population continued to increase, and Mexico began importing food grains with income from oil exports during the 1970s and 1980s. Low maize prices discouraged farmers from planting more acreage than necessary. Landowners increasingly used their hectares to raise cattle for fattening with cheap maize and grain sorghum or for sale in the United States. Low maize prices, set by government policy to keep urban food costs low, prevented subsistence farmers in poor, rainfed areas from participating in the Green Revolution because they could not afford it.[74]

In addition, subsistence farmers could participate in the Green Revolution only with government subsidies for seed and fertilizer and profitable crop price supports. When Latin American governments reduced or ended those supports, subsistence farmers could only return to traditional farming practices. As a result, the Green Revolution did not qualitatively improve their lives and farming practices. Put differently, the success of the Green Revolution in Latin America remained relative to whom the government supported the most with new agricultural technologies and policies.[75]

Government-sponsored irrigation development also caused a large drawdown of the underground water supply, particularly in Mexico's Ciudad Juárez area. Heavy applications of water for irrigation left salt residues in the soil, which reduced grain production, while fertilizers and pesticides polluted some water supplies, particularly near Mexicali. Government subsidization of the pesticide industry, some critics charged, favored profits for manufacturers who gave little concern to the environmental consequences of heavy applications. Most of Mexico's deforestation created grazing lands for cattle, not Green Revolution maize and wheat.[76]

Confronted with the impressive gains in wheat production, one must ask whether the Green Revolution technologies have been fairly shared by class and types of landholding. By using 1960 as a midpoint of this agricultural success story, the answer is no. Neither the increased income generated from Green Revolution production nor the technologies required to make it successful were equitably distributed. The farmers in Mexico's Pacific Northwest and North (known for its large-scale, privately owned farms) had the highest per capita income. These farmers irrigated their lands and used modern technology, which they could afford due to various government price supports and subsidies. Few farmers could be classified as poor in this region. The northern states also had the largest percentage of irrigated cropland varying from 32 percent to 72 percent. In contrast, the low-income states had only 1–6 percent of the land irrigated. Considering that irrigation covered only 15 percent of Mexican farmland, the benefits of Green Revolution technologies for the North are clearly apparent.[77]

Moreover, regional income declined among the poorest agricultural workers. Green Revolution efficiencies and increased production did not improve the ability of agricultural workers to make a living. During the 1960s, the percentage of income for the poorest class of workers nationwide declined by 14 percent, but it increased 61 percent and 11 percent among the middle- and upper-income wage earners in part because of Green Revolution production gains, which translated into more work and higher income. In the Pacific Northwest, the lower class of worker income declined by 60 percent while among the middle- and upper-income wage earners it increased by 66 percent and 42 percent respectively. Put differently, Green Revolution technologies benefited the states and regions where most workers were among the middle- and upper-income wage earners while those in the poorer regions—Central, Gulf, and Pacific South—failed to improve their incomes significantly.[78]

By 1970, the Green Revolution had improved the lives of farmers who not only had enough to eat but also marshalled the capital to invest in this new technology. The Green Revolution had not substantially aided the poorest class of farmers who raised maize and beans as insurance for their families, many of whom now left the land, although urban jobs never could absorb all of them. Mexico had gained self-sufficiency in food, and it primarily exported cotton, coffee, vegetables, fruits, and livestock. Mexico's government had invested heavily in irrigation, roads, storage facilities, long-term credit associations, and occasionally high price supports for wheat to achieve a Green Revolution. Those investments, however, did not guarantee equal access to the food produced from greater wheat harvests due to government policies and rapid population growth.[79]

Overall, the Green Revolution proved most successful in increasing wheat production because these farmers already were more capital-intensive, better educated, and credit worthy for the purchase of hybrid seeds, fertilizers, and irrigation. They were geographically unified in a relatively small area where they practiced commercial agriculture. The Mexican government could easily target its economic and logistical support to them, and their political ideology favored the government. In contrast, the widespread poor subsistence farmers raised maize. The government really did not expect them to succeed and provide grain surpluses for the nation's security and international trade. The culture of the Mexican wheat farmers had strong American commercial influence while the maize producers seemed nothing more than a poor class of ignorant farmers who could never improve themselves. In the end, the Rockefeller Foundation and the Mexican government considered their efforts to improve wheat production a success because it increased grain production and trained Mexican scientists to continue the work. Critics, however, always charged that this agricultural development program neglected subsistence farmers, farm families, and rural residents. Moreover, without agricultural education in the form of an adequate extension service, the trickle down of information for agricultural improvement could not have much effect. As a result, by the mid-1970s, Mexico's Green Revolution benefited a farm population that most resembled that in the American Midwest.[80]

The Green Revolution, then, failed significantly to improve the lives of the poor subsistence farmers and agricultural workers. It enabled, however, the improvement of agriculture by scientists who, with state support, developed a scientific professionalization. Some critics asked whether the Green Revolution fostered a socially responsible science. In the case of Mexico, many answered no, because the government ignored the needs of poor subsistence maize farmers to improve the productivity and standard of living of commercially oriented wheat farmers. Borlaug always bristled at that charge. In a 1975 interview, he said, "Our primary concern has to be to produce food. We're not a land-reform agency; we can't decide to split up land into small pieces." He argued that governments should provide seed, fertilizer, and water to farm-ers without cost to end charges that he and his fellow scientists favored the large-scale, wealthy landowners.[81]

The Mexican Agricultural Program scientists preferred to use science to modernize Mexican agriculture in the tradition of the United States, which had made the transition from an agrarian to an industrial society. They be-lieved that agricultural science could pave the way for modernization with commercial wheat farming and not by improving the lives of subsistence maize producers who would merely feed themselves and live traditional lives as poor farmers in isolated communities. Moreover, support for the subsis-tence farmers that would have required land and credit reforms were not po-litically possible through the 1950s and thereafter. In addition, agricultural scientists had little in common with the uneducated, lower-class, and cultur-ally different subsistence farmers. Instead, they catered to the politically in-fluential large-scale wheat farmers who controlled politics, research funding, and who reaped the greatest gains from the Green Revolution.[82]

Many agricultural observers considered plant breeders, such as Norman Borlaug, as "heroes" for developing high-yielding cereals that triggered an ag-ricultural revolution in food-deficit nations such as Mexico, India, Pakistan, the Philippines, and Kenya. They believed that the Green Revolution could eliminate most malnutrition and hunger worldwide. One contemporary cau-tioned, however, that "poorly managed[,] the new seeds and their associated technologies could displace millions in the countryside, forcing them into al-ready overcrowded cities." By the early 1990s, Mexican agricultural policy in many respects had failed the small-scale, poor subsistence farmers and guar-anteed that they would remain poor, socially and economically marginalized, and lacking adequate food. Although the Green Revolution benefited urban consumers with more and lower-priced food from wheat and maize, Mexican agricultural policy (that is, politics) had trumped Green Revolution agricul-tural science. The idealism of those agricultural scientists who in the begin-ning believed that Green Revolution technologies would provide food secu-rity to a food-deficit nation based on improved agricultural productivity by small-scale subsistence farmers lay in the distant past.[83]

2

South Asia

The Green Revolution came to the Asian subcontinent during the mid-1960s. The need for greater food production, particularly grain, remained dire. The Bengal famine (1942–1944) during British rule had cost the lives of at least 1.5 million people due to mismanagement of food supplies and rising population as well as government investments that privileged industry over agriculture. In 1947, India's war with Pakistan over Kashmir worsened the food supply and foreign nations declined to provide adequate food assistance until Mao Zedong gained control of the Chinese mainland. In 1949, Mao's victory, along with the testing of a nuclear bomb by the Soviet Union, transformed US grain exporting assistance from a humanitarian to a Cold War diplomatic policy. Yet, while US grain exports increased during the 1950s, Indian agricultural productivity lagged in part because low grain prices did not provide farmers an incentive to increase production. Prime Minister Jawaharlal Nehru did not support capital-intensive agricultural improvements or the provision of government price supports to encourage farmers to produce more grain. Instead, he used the American Public Law 480, which provided grain shipments to friendly nations who paid in their own currency, thereby keeping grain and food prices low and the public adequately fed, if they could gain access to those aid supplies through government distributions. Moreover, by the 1960s, low-yielding varieties along with severe drought, once again, stagnated agricultural production and brought India to the precipice of famine. After Nehru's death in January 1964, Minister for Food and Agriculture C. Subramanian changed Indian agricultural policy and began purchasing grain from its farmers at profitable prices while facilitating the adoption of new technology, such as improved seeds and chemical fertilizers, particularly in areas with an irrigation infrastructure.[1]

Although India and Pakistan suffered a grave food crisis that bordered on famine, both nations had closely watched the wheat-breeding program in Mexico. In 1963, they invited Norman Borlaug to observe the progress of the scientists and technicians who had trained under him along with other Rockefeller Foundation scientists in Mexico. They wanted him to evaluate their wheat-breeding program to determine whether his Mexican research could help increase yields for India. The work of the Indian and Pakistani agricultural scientists convinced Borlaug that his Mexican dwarf and semidwarf varieties could substantially increase wheat yields across West Pakistan and India. Mankombu Sambasivan Swaminathan, India's leading geneticist, also had urged Borlaug to come. Both would soon become known as the founders of the Green Revolution in India.[2]

At the end of his visit, Borlaug promised to send a selection of wheat varieties from Mexico that he thought might produce well on the Indian subcontinent and lend themselves to the ongoing crossbreeding efforts of Indian and Pakistani scientists. In the spring of 1964, these samples arrived from the International Maize and Wheat Improvement Center (CIMMYT) in Mexico. They were Sonora 63, Sonora 64, Lerma Rojo 64, and Mayo 64, and in West Pakistan Penjamo 62 and Lerma Rojo 64. The results from the test plantings created sufficient but guarded optimism for continued development at a time when India faced possible famine. As a result, in 1965, India purchased 250 metric tons of these wheat varieties to seed 700,000 acres, and in 1966, 18,000 metric tons of Mexican high-yielding varieties (HYVs). A year later, Pakistan acquired 42,000 tons of Mexican wheat varieties for seed production and distribution to farmers. This initial breeding and importation of high-yielding wheat varieties began the Green Revolution on the South Asian subcontinent. Subramanian supported fast-track agricultural development with the Mexican varieties but other government officials objected over the cost, which slowed these crop-breeding efforts.[3]

In 1966, food shortages, in part caused by a severe drought that had lasted two years, compelled the Indian government to establish a floor price—that is, a remunerative price for food grains, particularly wheat, which all grain dealers had to pay. The government also purchased grain at profitable prices from farmers through the Food Corporation of India and the State Marketing Federation. This agricultural policy, along with the recognition of farmers that the new wheat varieties were technically and economically superior to traditional local varieties, encouraged them to increase national production to 2.45 million metric tons, an increase from 1.9 million metric tons during the previous crop year. Swaminathan and other Indian agricultural scientists contributed to these gains by improving the Mexican varieties with Indian strains for widespread environmental adoption, all for the economic and social benefits of Indian society.[4]

Guaranteed, profitable prices, along with highly productive HYVs, soon succeeded in increasing food production. One observer noted that with price supports, Indian farmers would "turn sand into gold." Borlaug recommended that Indian and Pakistani scientists increase the application of water and fertilizer on their test plots. The results proved three to four times more productive than that of the Indian farmers who used traditional varieties and methods. This research attracted the attention of other farmers who then wanted the hybrid seeds for their own fields.[5]

India gambled that these new seed varieties would substantially increase wheat production and as government officials distributed the seed, these varieties impressed most farmers who accepted them. They knew that the varieties developed by Borlaug's team in Mexico had the potential to double or triple wheat yields. They were not impressed, however, by the taste. The Mexican wheats also had an unaccustomed reddish color. Indian women who made pancake-like chapattis preferred flour from white wheats. Soon crossbreeding of the Mexican varieties with Indian wheats changed the color and taste without reducing productivity to make them acceptable to consumers as a food.[6]

By 1970 the wheat areas in Pakistan's Punjab had increased to 6 million acres or 73 percent planted in HYV varieties. Approximately 95 percent of these farmers had used nitrogen fertilizer at least once while approximately 37 percent had used pesticides and 33 percent had used tractors. Fifty percent of these wheat farmers had used tube wells. Farmers who cultivated 50 acres or more produced enough wheat to market 86 percent of it while farmers who cultivated under 12.5 acres marketed only 43 percent of their wheat crop. Generally, Pakistani farmers sold their HYV wheat and rice and consumed local traditional varieties.[7]

Similarly, during the 1966–1967 crop year, India's Punjab farmers planted 1.6 million acres, or 3.6 percent, of the wheat area in high-yielding varieties. Yields increased ten times in some areas. By 1968, farmers planted 18 percent of India's wheat area with HYVs, which produced 36 percent of the total wheat crop. For the 1969–1970 crop year, they planted 65.6 percent of the wheat lands in HYVs. Indian and Pakistani farmers recognized the proven results of planting the Mexican high-yielding varieties. Between 1965 and 1970,

Figure 7. Clearing land with oxen in India
The high-yielding wheat varieties developed in Mexico and India required farmers to level
their fields for the most efficient distribution of water. Indian farmers who could not afford
tractors used traditional methods to prepare their fields for planting and irrigation. Courtesy
of the University of Minnesota Archives, University of Minnesota–Twin Cities.

Mexican HYVs increased wheat production in India by 50 percent and West
Pakistan by 60 percent. The largest increases in yield, however, occurred where
farmers used tube wells to irrigate their crop and where the environmental
conditions most closely approximated those at the CIMMYT in Mexico where
Borlaug's team had developed these varieties. Government price supports also
played a key role in India's and Pakistan's Green Revolution. Without profitable wheat prices, Punjab and other Indian and Pakistani farmers could not
have afforded fertilizers, herbicides, and pesticides as well as HYVs, equipment, and labor. This expansion of wheat acreage gave India and Pakistan
hope of becoming self-sufficient in this food grain. With this success, some
Green Revolution supporters contended that India and Pakistan were not over-
populated just under fertilized. In 1969, because of Borlaug's help, West Pakistan now became self-sufficient in wheat although political instability and
rapid population growth, landholding patterns, and inadequate credit continued to make that achievement tenuous.[8]

Figure 8. Norman Borlaug with fellow agricultural scientists in India
Borlaug and his followers believed that wheat bred for photoperiod insensitivity would enable widespread adaptation. They relied on genetic changes rather than environmental conditions, including sunlight, to improve crop yields. By the early twenty-first century, not all crop breeders agreed with that method. Courtesy of the University of Minnesota Archives, University of Minnesota–Twin Cities.

By the late 1960s, however, the Green Revolution had not spread across India. In the southern tip of the subcontinent in the state of Madras, the rice crop went unharvested because landless farm workers battled with landowners. Increased production with HYVs provided by the Ford Foundation had created considerable social tension. In the Tanjore District, the leading rice-producing area of Madras, agricultural wages increased unevenly, and the landless workers demanded a greater share of the profits from the rice harvests. They traditionally received twenty cents per day, usually in-kind. The landowners responded by forming the equivalent of a company union called the Rice Growers Association. They also employed outside workers to harvest the crops to keep wages low. Violence occurred between the two groups with the workers often members of communist unions. Tanjore fed most of the 40 million people in Madras, and officials feared that the benefits of the Green Revolution in terms of production and fair compensation lay in the distant future. Although Green Revolution science and technology had ended the threat of famine, hunger remained a daily part of life for many Indians. The large-scale landowners who raised HYV wheat, however, easily earned $200 per acre tax free due to government subsidy to encourage farming with Green Revolution technology, but new rice varieties had not improved production.[9]

The success of the Green Revolution had occurred in the northern wheat belt where production had substantially increased by the late 1960s. Tractor dealers in Punjab had difficulty filling orders from landowners. Small-scale farmers, however, could not qualify for low interest loans from the local credit cooperatives to purchase seed and fertilizer. Interest rates of 24 percent kept farmers with only a few acres in perpetual debt and poverty. Moreover, the new rice varieties imported from Taiwan proved highly susceptible to disease even though they tripled production compared to traditional varieties.[10]

By the late 1960s, 40 million of India's 60 million farm families could not invest in Green Revolution technology. Tenants and sharecroppers farmed about 20 percent of the land, and Green Revolution productivity often meant that landowners charged higher rents in grain. Landowners evaded government limits of thirty cultivated acres. Green Revolution agricultural science enabled greater production and profits but the large-scale landowners who had access to cheap credit profited not the landless farmers and agricultural workers. As landowners profited, they purchased tractors and other equipment and released workers who demanded land reform to gain access to Green Revolution farming opportunities. India needed greater industrial development to absorb surplus agricultural labor. Yet with Indians favoring large families for social security, Green Revolution agriculture could barely produce enough food for a rapidly expanding population.[11]

Ideally, Green Revolution farmers needed the "package" of high-yielding seeds, fertilizers, and irrigation as well as pesticides and labor, low interest credit, farm-to-market roads, storage facilities, truck and rail transportation, and floor prices. Few Indian districts had these optimal assets for Green Revolution success. India had achieved the agricultural production required to feed people on a subsistence level but not enough to eradicate hunger. The Department of Agriculture warned that the "uneven impact of technological change" threatened "disastrous" consequences because it favored the large-scale farmers who might push the subsistence farmers from the land, thereby creating "massive problems of welfare and equity." In 1969, Prime Minister Indira Gandhi's nationalization of the largest private banks did not improve credit for small-scale farmers, and land reform seemed distant at best. Gandhi addressed these problems saying that "the warning of the times is that unless the green revolution is accompanied by a revolution based on social justice, the green revolution may not remain green."[12]

India, however, had not evenly distributed the economic gains of the Green Revolution, particularly regarding wheat production. Moreover, rice cultivation still lagged because new HYV varieties did not adapt to the many environmental conditions of South Asia. The new varieties proved susceptible to pests and disease and adequate irrigation often did not exist, although the rice farmers who planted HYVs in Kerala, Tamil, Nadu, and parts of Andhra Pradesh and West Bengal had increased their productivity. Consumers did not like the taste or cooking quality of the new rice varieties. They preferred long-grained rice, which is non-glutinous. Short-grain HYV rice lumped together after cooking. Rice buyers also preferred indigenous varieties for which they paid higher prices than for HYVs. In addition, the new short-stemmed HYVs produced less straw, which farmers used for cattle feed. The "miracle" varieties from the Philippines and Taiwan also had not proven as productive as the new wheat HYVs. By the 1968–69 harvest, farmers had planted only 9 percent of India's lands with improved rice varieties due to inadequate access to water.[13]

Despite India and Pakistan's interest in using the Mexican high-yielding varieties, major production increases did not meet expectations. Efforts to expand wheat production slowed because war erupted in 1971 between India and Pakistan. Moreover, poor seed germination due to improper fumigation before shipment from Mexico limited the harvest. India's situation remained desperate with famine conditions prevailing. By 1970, with three-fourths of India's farmland without irrigation, the Green Revolution had proven "highly selective" and favored "small islands" of farmers even in Punjab. Environment and culture, the latter in the form of class discrimination, dampened unrestrained optimism about the Green Revolution. In Punjab and Bihar, where farmers increasingly practiced Green Revolution agriculture, landowners raised rents from a 50/50 share to a 70/30 split for sharecroppers. Many landowners continued to replace their tenant farmers and sharecroppers with hired labor. Some critics charged that surplus production eventually would decrease the need for farm labor as landowners reduced their wheat acreage based on market demands while also using more machinery to replace workers. Tenants and sharecroppers had become less secure due to the Green Revolution. Yet, most critics failed to realize that class and gender historically determined the social and economic problems of the subcontinent and not Green Revolution agricultural science. The Green Revolution emphasized production, not social change.[14]

Even so, by the early 1970s farmers in Rajasthan, Bihar, Orissa, and parts of Uttar Pradesh still lived in poverty and far from the benefits of the Green Revolution. In these areas communist leaders believed that a red revolution had to precede a Green Revolution. In 1974, India had another food crisis because of drought and the inability of the government to produce enough fertilizer and subsidize the cost to make it affordable. Critics charged Indira Gandhi's government with investing in heavy industry and manufacturing rather than agriculture. As a result, India suffered another food deficit. Government food procurement and distribution, particularly of wheat flour and rice for urban areas, failed to meet public needs. Inflation accelerated to 30 percent annually as consumers hoarded food. Prime Minister Gandhi urged farmers to produce more grain to solve the food-deficit problem. Critics charged that the Green Revolution had faltered because HYV seeds were prone to disease and fertilizer, insecticides, and irrigation had been inadequate to maintain high productivity and food security. They also complained that the government had lacked the vision to make a major commitment to agricultural development. Production fell from 108 million tons of grain in 1970–1971 to 103 million tons in 1973–1974 while the population increased by 36 million.[15]

With 75 percent of India's land without irrigation, most farmers depended on the monsoon season to water their crops no matter whether they planted HYVs or traditional varieties. Moreover, with 80 percent of India's 620 million people living in agricultural villages and half of that number marginal farmers, many could not afford Green Revolution technology despite Norman Borlaug's contention that it was scale neutral. The Green Revolution had not reached its potential to end hunger and want. By 1977, India had a grain reserve of 20 million tons, half from imports, to serve as a food safety net, but this too indicated a failure of Green Revolution agricultural science. In Pakistan, wheat rust and low government price supports reduced the incentive for farmers to adopt Green Revolution technologies even if they could afford it. For poor farmers, the hope of the Green Revolution meant little more than disappointment.[16]

By the 1970s, farmers who owned or cultivated fifteen to twenty acres in the major wheat-producing areas had the savings or access to credit that permitted them to invest in Green Revolution technologies. An estimated 20 percent of all farmers with less than ten acres, however, did not have that invest-

Figure 9. Farmers plowing their rice paddy
These farmers are "puddling" (that is, plowing their rice paddy) prior to setting out the plants. Small plots kept profits low, but Green Revolution rice varieties increased yields and income and produced more food. Photo: P. Lowe / CIMMYT, CC BY-NC-SA.

ment capacity. In the wheat areas of Bihar and Uttar Pradesh, more than 80 percent of all farmers cultivated less than eight acres, which essentially excluded them from the benefits of the Green Revolution, at least in terms of raising surplus grain for income and not just food for the table. The same results occurred in the rice areas where the majority of farmers cultivated only two to three acres. Approximately 75–80 percent of these farmers suffered a deteriorating living standard because landowners released them from employment. In addition, a disparity between the large- and small-scale farmers occurred in relation to credit. Many farmers had installed tube wells with the cost ranging from $1,000 to $2,500 each. Yet, a cost-effective commitment to groundwater irrigation required at least five acres for a profitable return on the investment, but the Indian government provided irrigation loans only to farmers who owned at least twenty acres. Although similar conditions existed in Pakistan, large- and medium-scale farmers readily adopted tube well irrigation and the application of more fertilizer because they already had been using a primitive form of irrigation and some organic fertilizer. They did not need to learn new techniques or assume great risk. For them, the Green Revolution meant enhanced farming, not introducing new agricultural methods.[17]

In the 1970s, some scholars believed that the economic achievements of the Green Revolution proved clear. One contended, "It appears to be a turning point in stagnating Indian agriculture." No one, however, could predict the long-term effects of the Green Revolution, and the social and political consequences remained problematic. Some observers estimated that the adoption of HYVs increased labor needs from 20–50 percent. However, when landowners mechanized, their labor needs declined from 42.5 days per acre of wheat to 18.5 days. Mechanization, particularly tractors, drove workers from the land. During the 1960s, farmers increased their tractor purchases from thirty thousand to ninety thousand implements. Critics argued that the Green Revolution created a surplus labor force that industry and manufacturing could not absorb, and the continued population explosion made a difficult situation worse. Increasingly, social scientists identified emerging social and economic problems and posed possible solutions ranging from expropriation of land and redistribution to poor farmers to improved credit for them if they would invest in Green Revolution technologies and cooperative programs. No one, however, had all-encompassing solutions.[18]

These concerns proved unwarranted because by the late 1970s, the Green Revolution had achieved increased food security for India and Pakistan, but its success was not due to biological transformations alone. In Punjab, for example, comparatively well-educated farmers, often landowners, who understood the correct application of fertilizer, used irrigation systems to water high-yielding wheat varieties, and a supportive environment enabled double or multiple cropping—that is, the planting of two crops in the same field consecutively during the growing season. Farmers could plant two wheat varieties, an early and a late-maturing crop, for example, to produce a total greater volume of the grain harvest. As a result, wheat production not only increased but agricultural workers had more employment opportunities, higher wage rates, and an improved standard of living. Punjab farmers also had the financial and credit resources to invest in mechanical technology, particularly tractors and threshing machines, that enabled them to process larger amounts of grain for market and plow their fields more efficiently than with bullocks (oxen).[19]

Intensive cropping provided more work for farm laborers, and cash wages also increased. With Green Revolution technologies best adapted to the wheat area of Punjab and Haryana where landholdings and irrigation helped produce abundant wheat crops, few small-scale farmers, tenants, or sharecroppers suffered displacement even though the large-scale farmers dominated the countryside. In the rice area, however, manufacturing and industry could not absorb the great displacement of farm workers for alternative employment. Some observers believed that agricultural reform, including government-mandated redistribution of land, would not occur as long as the major agricultural casts controlled local governments. Put differently, the Indian government emphasized production first and chose to consider land distribution later.[20]

By 1975, Indian farmers planted HYV wheat on 27 million hectares, which provided an estimated 62 percent of India's cereal production. Farmers increased wheat production from 200 percent to 300 percent in some locations. The other Indian states did not approach that success because only the farmers in Punjab had had access to the required technological package of the Green Revolution through cooperative organizations, which they also used to purchase needed supplies. Cast played a major role in the access of wealthy or large-scale landowners to Green Revolution technologies. By the 1970s, Indian agricultural officials and scientists hoped the Green Revolution would transform peasants into farmers who would conduct the business of agriculture (that is, farm for a profit) by moving them from subsistence to commercial agriculture. Consequently, the Green Revolution proved an economic success for some farmers but not a nutritional success for most Indians who still consumed food at least 25 percent below health requirements.[21]

In northern India, many economists designated landowners with more than 12 hectares as large-scale farmers, and they labeled farmers cultivating less than 4 hectares as small-scale agriculturalists. Advocates of the Green Revolution argued that farmers with 6 hectares could adopt most of the required "inputs" to improve production while farmers with 10 hectares could make major investments and provide plowing and harvesting services to other farmers to cover costs. They also argued that only farmers cultivating fewer than 2.5 hectares had difficulty affording HYVs and fertilizers. In addition, they welcomed the consolidation of farms to enable the more efficient use of mechanized implements, particularly tractors. Moreover, the multiplier effect of the Green Revolution supported tractor repair shops, seed, fertilizer, and herbicide suppliers, grain markets, and a variety of businesses that met the needs of rural consumers who now enjoyed more money to spend.[22]

Similarly, West Pakistan increased rice and wheat production, and by so doing, stimulated the agricultural service industries, such as well drillers and pump suppliers, which had a multiplier effect on the economy. Overall, by the late 1970s, Green Revolution supporters considered it an ongoing success. They believed that those who disagreed with them were "foolish," and they argued that the continuous development of new wheat and rice varieties to fight diseases and pests, new chemical herbicides, and family planning would ensure the benefits of the Green Revolution, despite some economic and environmental costs.[23]

In India and Pakistan, however, the critics concluded that the benefits of the Green Revolution went to the large-scale landowners, creditors, and investors, while small-scale farmers suffered further economic decline and hardship. They also charged that the Green Revolution caused greater inequality because wealthy property owners used technology to monopolize scarce land and water resources, and further impoverished the poorest farmers. Agricultural technology drove people from the land, they argued. High price supports made food grains expensive and further benefited the large-scale landowners, while the poorer, small-scale, often tenant, farmers suffered an income decline. For these critics, the benefits of the Green Revolution did not percolate down from the top level of society to the small-scale farmers and agricultural workers at the bottom. Critics also charged that Pakistan's agricultural extension service favored large-scale agriculturists, thereby hindering small-scale farmers from adopting the supposedly scale-neutral "inputs" of the Green Revolution. Moreover, by 1975 they also contended that Pakistani farmers still could not feed the population from 33 million irrigated acres in the Indus Basin.[24]

During the 1970s, the critics also argued that only select areas benefited because of limited irrigation as well as the suitability of environmental and agronomic conditions for the new HYVs. They charged that although the Green Revolution increased the demand for labor, and while wage rates increased in some areas, where irrigation did not exist few benefits developed from the new agriculture. Certainly, the Green Revolution eased some problems of hunger, unemployment, and poverty, but it also caused a decline in the production of crops other than wheat and rice. Although it had originally appeared to hold the solution to hunger and unemployment, the required technological adoptions had proven complex, expensive, and environmentally limited. For them, the success of the Green Revolution had been "highly exaggerated," despite the improvement of production which provided food security.[25]

Many rice farmers also held that view. Indian agricultural scientists did not successfully cross domestic high-yielding rice varieties with varieties from the International Rice Research Institute in the Philippines until the late 1970s. These new HYVs enabled the Green Revolution to spread to other rice-growing states. In 1966, Punjab farms raised only 290,000 metric tons of rice, but HYVs along with corresponding irrigation developments helped them produce 3.1 million metric tons in 1979, making Punjab the leading rice-producing state in India. By the late 1970s, Punjab contributed 63 percent of the wheat and 56 percent of the rice to government procurement.[26]

Some opponents went so far as to charge that "far from breaking the chains of rural poverty, [the Green Revolution] has left poor farmers worse off than before." The energy crisis of the early 1970s also raised the price of petro-based fertilizer, pesticides, and fuel and energy in the form of electricity to power pumps for irrigation beyond the means of poor, small-scale farmers on the Indian subcontinent. Critics argued that the benefits of the Green Revolution had been "oversold" and "overbought." Some now called the Green Revolution a "hoax." It was not even an experimental success because traditional varieties often outproduced HYVs.[27]

By the mid-1970s, most critics of the Green Revolution had focused on economic problems, but they also began attacking the technical process because the Green Revolution contributed a package of Western technology that transferred its problems to the Indian subcontinent. Genetic uniformity of the HYVs brought the most criticism because it created the possibility of crop failure from disease with few traditional varieties surviving to prevent famine. Optimists contended that the likelihood of such a catastrophe would require genetic links to another gene susceptible to some pathogen (that is, disease). Varietal diversity, they argued, prevented that occurrence and disaster. Critics also argued that the technical processes of close planting and multiple cropping encouraged insect infestation. Green Revolution advocates countered that the plant breeders had developed pest- and disease-resistant varieties that were "probably as resistant as the native varieties to many diseases," pending the constant development of new varieties to maintain varietal resistance to disease and pests. Moreover, critics charged that as farmers emphasized HYV wheat and rice, they planted fewer high protein pulses (that is, beans, peas, and lentils). Poor, small-scale farmers preferred dependable, small harvests to risks for big harvests that might prove costly failures from weather and disease, particularly due to monocrop conditions.[28]

Green Revolution advocates responded that HYVs produced more than traditional varieties even without fertilizer. While the highest yields occurred on the best lands, even poor lands planted with HYVs generally produced more than traditional varieties with a rule of thumb that the Green Revolution package of HYVs, fertilizer, and irrigation generally produced 50–100 percent greater returns for wheat and 10–25 percent greater harvests for rice than traditional varieties. Green Revolution opponents and supporters agreed, however, that further efforts to improve HYV breeding had to occur domestically on the national, regional, and local levels, and not from Western varietal introductions. The subcontinent could not abdicate to the catastrophic population explosion, droughts, and floods. Traditional agriculture provided no solution for this food-deficit and insecure region. Only agricultural science could save food-deficient people and nations. Those who considered the Green Revolution beneficial contended that it enabled the production of more food and that resulting social problems were better than the problems of food scarcity and insecurity (that is, hunger, want, and famine). "Progress with distribution," they contended, "is better than no progress at all." Still, agricultural scientists did not target dryland India with their crop-breeding research. They would not do so for nearly a half century.[29]

By the late 1970s, criticism that only larger-scale, more capital-intensive farmers could afford HYVs began to wane. Although farmers with more land to cultivate could make an investment in Green Revolution technology, eventually smaller-scale operators made some commitment to planting HYVs that increased their yield and hence food supply and perhaps contributed a surplus to sell. Evidence from the Punjab indicated that the new wheat technology had been "approximately" scale neutral in terms of capital and labor investment as well as production gains. Small-scale farmers, of course, did not have as much access to irrigation and credit compared to large-scale farmers but these constraints had not prevented them from committing to Green Revolution agriculture. Put differently, the average wheat yields per hectare of small-scale farmers equaled those of larger-scale farmers. They just had fewer hectares to plant and thus smaller total bushels of wheat harvested. Even so, landowners had relatively higher gains from their adoption of HYVs than tenants and sharecroppers. Tenant farmers, sharecroppers, and agricultural workers increased their incomes but landowners as a class gained more from Green Revolution agriculture.[30]

In other words, the Green Revolution created greater disparities in production and earnings for farmers and agricultural workers across regions than within the most favored regions, both environmentally and politically. At the same time, subsistence farmers, agricultural workers, and landless consumers gained because more grain production meant more food and lower prices than had farmers only planted traditional varieties. High-yielding wheat varieties helped keep food prices affordable. In addition, the government continued to subsidize grain prices and ensured a market, thereby encouraging the adoption of Green Revolution technologies.[31]

Essentially, by the late 1970s, where Green Revolution agricultural technologies had been introduced in India and Pakistan, where the infrastructure, including credit system, and governmental support were equitably distributed, farmers produced significantly more grain to feed their families and poor, landless, rural, and urban consumers. In less favorable areas determined by land quality, environmental conditions, and government support, Green Revolution agriculture proved less productive and created even greater inequality in the distribution of resources and the profits. Discrimination among classes in India and Pakistan, however, which hindered if not prevented economic, social, and political progress, was not the product of Green Revolution agricultural science.[32]

∽

By the early 1980s, much of the criticism against the Green Revolution had diminished because research proved that it had not upset social and cultural traditions while privileging the large landowners. This positive counterbalance came from social scientists who, as a group, had been opposed to the perceived social changes that the Green Revolution had caused during the 1970s. No one could truthfully contend that the Green Revolution had not increased grain (that is, food production). The increased grain supply kept food prices lower than would have been possible otherwise. Landowners had benefited more than agricultural workers, but the latter would have suffered greater economic problems, if not destitution, without the Green Revolution because it provided more labor and income. Widespread unemployment did not occur, and the Green Revolution had proved scale neutral because large- and small-scale farmers had been able to purchase its required technology, albeit in different quantities. Moreover, related and increasing off-farm employment opportunities absorbed agricultural workers and tenants who left the land. The Indian Agricultural Research Institute and India's agricultural universities had developed research and extension programs. By the early 1990s, some supporters called the Green Revolution a "double-barreled blessing," because it held the potential to increase food production and diversify the rural economy.[33]

The "inflated promises" of the Green Revolution, however, had not been achieved. While increased mechanization diminished the demand for labor,

Figure 10. Handheld tractor
Farmers who can afford power technology, such as the handheld tractor, usually cultivate more acres or hectares than those who plow with bullocks. Green Revolution technologies increased yields, and farmers often solved their need for more workers with mechanized implements rather than human labor. Photo: P. Lowe / CIMMYT, CC BY-NC-SA.

it did not increase production. Farmers bought tractors for labor insurance and to gain social status. Tractors enabled them to ride rather than plow behind a bullock. Tractor ownership earned respect for the owner and increased the status of his children who could then gain higher social mobility for marriage. Mechanization with tractors, then, had ramifications far beyond cultivating fields of HYV wheat. Tractors also increased the acreage available for HYV wheat because this technology reduced the need for fodder crops.[34]

The demand for labor, however, did not keep pace with population growth, which meant more people in the countryside without employment or an adequate food supply. The planting of HYVs and the Green Revolution package could not overcome this problem. The implication that the Green Revolution caused more poverty and prevented land reform on the South Asia subcontinent, however, remained arguable, because the long-term environmental, social, and economic as well as political effects of the Green Revolution remained unknown. At best, agricultural and social scientists and farmers necessarily had to take a wait-and-see approach. Some social scientists now recognized that agricultural scientists could not realistically serve as the primary agents for social change.[35]

Indeed, by the late 1980s, agricultural and social scientists still could not agree about the benefits and consequences of the Green Revolution. Yet, India and Pakistan no longer faced famine although the food distribution system and pricing had not ended the problem of hunger. India had more than tripled its wheat and rice production between 1965, when it began Green Revolution agriculture, and 1983. Thereafter, however, grain production did not increase, water tables fell, and wells went dry. Some fields also had become waterlogged and too saline for cultivation. Irrigation in some areas proved difficult, if not impossible. At best, India only marked time with its per capita food production as the population continued to increase rapidly. Moreover, Indian farmers had run out of space. More grain could not be produced by cultivating more land; rather, more grain production had to be coaxed from the land with Green Revolution science. The Green Revolution had stalled and no new comparable agricultural developments awaited to replace it. One observer reflected that "there's no new green revolution out there."[36]

With food shortages no longer a problem by the mid-1980s, hunger on the Indian subcontinent became a matter of poverty (that is, the inability of hungry people to afford food) although inadequate food distribution, due to a failure of social and economic planning, played a role. A few opponents, however, argued that improved seeds, irrigation, fertilizer, government subsidies, and marketing faculties only created problems. The most vociferous supporters of the Green Revolution believed that it could solve all problems including those that it created.[37]

By the late twentieth century, few could deny that poverty still plagued India and Pakistan because of needed land reform, educational improvement, better transportation, and electricity in the countryside. The Green Revolution had not resolved the problems of inequity and social welfare, if not justice. The critics now did not question the benefits of increased agricultural production from the new technology. They complained, however, about the inequity issues, arguing that the Green Revolution did not support a fair distribution of the new agricultural income, although they had difficulty attacking the higher wages paid in some cases and more work available for farm laborers. For these critics, the problems of the Green Revolution did not stem directly from scientific and technological change but rather resulted from government policies (that is, political decisions regarding agricultural subsidies, taxation, and wages). Others charged that the agricultural research had not kept up with the task despite "colossal investments" by the government. Some critics contended that this failure reflected a "disturbing bankruptcy in scientific talent." They also argued, without evidence, that the population explosion, rather than a failure of agricultural science, limited the benefits of the Green Revolution and more needed to be done to prevent famine.[38]

∾

The Green Revolution came late to Bangladesh. It was not part of the Green Revolution on the subcontinent during 1960s and 1970s. Not until the 1980s and 1990s did farmers begin adopting Green Revolution technologies. Known as East Pakistan until it achieved independence in 1971 after armed conflict with both Pakistan and India, Bangladesh remained a poverty-stricken, food-deficit nation at a time when the Green Revolution measurably improved grain production in India and West Pakistan. Food disturbances, which some observers called "small riots," had occurred in several areas where shortages of wheat and rice had driven the price beyond the ability of the poor to pay. Only the comparatively rich could meet their food needs. By the spring of 1972, the food situation in Bangladesh had become "bleak and worsening." The government appealed to and depended on shipments of grain through the United Nations and India. It did not, indeed could not, depend on its farmers to feed the public. With a poverty rate of more than 70 percent of the population and a fertility rate of approximately seven children per woman, Bangladesh remained one of the most densely populated nations. By the late 1980s, little arable land remained for development beyond its 22 million acres, which fed 100 million people. With approximately 80 percent of the land cropped with rice, only an improvement in yields from the cultivated lands available would increase food production. Too many people cultivated too little land. Bangladesh needed a Green Revolution to make the land more productive and to feed this food-deficit nation. In the meantime, it necessarily imported rice.[39]

In 1971, after the Liberation War, many social scientists believed that Bangladesh's Green Revolution would contribute to land reform, social revolution, and state ownership of land based on ideological premises. Others believed that governments had created the Green Revolution to solve hunger by technology rather than by revolution. Perspectives usually differed by the way social scientists conducted village studies and interpreted their evidence, often in isolation from the nation as a whole. Consequently, some considered the decline of labor the result of land enclosure while others believed that it reflected a decline in wages. Put differently, village studies reflected "multiple realities," but they did not provide sufficient data for meaningful generalizations about the success or failure of the Green Revolution. The defenders of the Green Revolution, for example, contended that the farmers in Bangladesh needed access to the new technology, which would increase income and help reduce poverty. The critics claimed that the new technology created greater income inequality and increased poverty. Both sides argued from ideological premises and usually without sound data to prove their point. For agricultural economists who supported the Green Revolution, equity meant equal access. Other social scientists, such as sociologists and anthropologists, stressed the importance of income distribution to ensure a Green Revolution. Village studies, then, did not produce facts that both groups could use for analysis because village studies did not produce hard evidence of the benefits or failures of the Green Revolution. Neither group could prove that its findings were correct or that the other group was wrong. Moreover, social scientists could not agree whether they should evaluate the Green Revolution on matters of inequality or productivity while the agricultural scientists argued for the benefits of technology alone. In many respects, ideology trumped science for understanding the Green Revolution.[40]

Even so, between the late 1960s and the mid-1980s, the Green Revolution significantly changed agricultural practices in Bangladesh aided in part by the establishment of the Bangladesh Rice Research Institute in 1970. During that time, the area planted in rice increased from 1.6 percent of the arable land in 1967 to more than 25 percent of farmland by 1985. Moreover, farmers had planted nearly the entire wheat area with HYVs. The area under irrigation also nearly doubled from tube wells and canals. Fertilizer applications rose from 10 kg to more than 40 kg per hectare. As a result, farmers increased total food grain production by 22 percent, while rice and wheat production increased 18 percent and 140 percent respectively. These gains occurred from intensive cultivation using the components, or "inputs," of the Green Revolution. While rice and wheat production increased, however, Bangladesh farmers raised fewer fruits, vegetables, and oil seeds, among other crops, which some critics complained proved a "commodity bias" of the Green Revolution. Overall, Bangladesh's food supply became less diverse. Diets narrowed and declined in quality. Moreover, while nutritionally important crops, such as pulses, fruits, and vegetables, diminished, the price of fish, chicken, and beef increased and Bangladeshis ate less of these high-protein foods. In addition, despite increases in cereal grain production, the consumption of wheat and rice did not increase in part because people cannot eat away surplus production, even though their dietary or food choices narrow.[41]

The relatively late arrival of Green Revolution agriculture in Bangladesh resulted in part from West Pakistan ignoring it for agricultural development. After independence, Bangladesh's government also favored industrialization to finance food imports. Droughts and floods in the early 1970s and a coup in 1975 slowed agricultural development. Structural changes in the nation's politics, such as de-emphasizing the role of the state from a socialist, dictatorial government to one that supported the liberalization of free-market agriculture, however, stimulated Green Revolution agriculture. Private land-ownership and management replaced publically owned and bureaucratically managed farms. The removal of restrictions on the number of shallow tube wells that farmers could drill and the importation of cheap pumps from Korea, China, and India enabled fundamental changes. Cheaper drilling and pumping equipment helped farmers expand irrigation and adopt HYVs, and fertilizer boosted cereal production. By 1990, farmers irrigated 30 percent of the cultivable land, and by the turn of the twenty-first century, more than 50 percent of that area. As a result, farmers seeded approximately 65 percent of this land with HYVs in 2000. Not until the government began controlling grain prices through price floors and procurement along with cheaper irrigation equipment did farmers produce a surplus and seek a market. But, poor rural infrastructure of roads and electrification slowed surplus production and the marketing of grain to help feed the poor and hungry in Bangladesh.[42]

Equally important, the breakthrough for rice production came only after scientists crossed varieties bred at the International Rice Research Institute with local, improved varieties, as had been the case in India. Small-scale irrigation technology and HYVs developed in part with national germplasm made the Green Revolution possible in Bangladesh. Given the inability for farmers to acquire and cultivate new lands, the Green Revolution enabled them to cultivate their acreages more intensively, often with multiple cropping during the year. Although Bangladesh would remain a food-deficit nation into the twenty-first century, the Green Revolution helped both large- and small-scale farmers increase production despite bureaucratic constraints. Technology, however, was not the only driving force because Bangladesh's Green Revolution also relied on a market-mediated, state-driven process as proved true in India and Pakistan. Even so, cultural traditions meant that government officials and local elites favored family members for access to Green Revolution technologies, such as credit and various subsidies, which privileged the wealthier farmers.[43]

By the end of the first decade of the twenty-first century, the writing on the Green Revolution, both opinion and analysis, had continued for more than forty years. Although Bangladesh had achieved food self-sufficiency, social and agricultural scientists retained their firm convictions about the benefits and problems. Some critics began voicing second thoughts and admitted that their earlier fears had proven largely unjustified, and they began considering the Green Revolution in a more positive fashion. Other critics, however, continued arguing that HYVs only benefited large-scale farmers who had access to fertilizer and irrigation. They also continued to charge that the large-scale farmers had consolidated their holdings and forced their tenants and sharecroppers off the land, thereby exacerbating the problem of unemployment and poverty in the countryside. Still others contended that HYVs did not perform well across all of South Asia. Anyone who foolishly expected the Green Revolution to benefit small-scale farmers, they believed, rather than wealthy landowners, would also expect water to run uphill.[44]

The adoption of Green Revolution agriculture in Bangladesh proved a long and slow process and not until 2000 did it achieve self-sufficiency in rice, more than thirty years after the introduction of these HYVs. Part of the problem was that 50 percent of these early varieties did not produce to their potential in rainfed areas. Not until the 1980s did Bangladeshi scientists begin breeding rice varieties for the nation's specific environments. Given the rule of thumb that ten years are required to develop a new rice variety, these HYVs did not appear until the 1990s, but these efforts stalled when agricultural scientists had difficulty overcoming the problems of breeding rainfed HYV rice. Critics who found fault with the slowness of this research and the unintended consequences of planting HYV rice argued from a Marxian theoretical premise and did not understand the difference between biotechnology, which is scale neutral in terms of adoption, and the economy of scale associated with mechanization in a capitalist agricultural economy. By so doing, the critics could not help but conclude that those who had access to capital and credit benefited the most from the Green Revolution.[45]

By the early twenty-first century, Bangladesh remained one of the poorest and least developed nations in the world where food deficiency remained an annual concern. Agricultural production, particularly of rice, had not kept pace with the population growth. Approximate 51 percent of the population engaged in agriculture and 80 percent lived in rural areas. Although some of

Figure 11. Farmer in a wheat field in Bangladesh
The Green Revolution brought Bangladesh from the precipice of famine. Here, a farmer
has begun cutting a high-yielding wheat variety in a test field. Photo: P. Lowe / CIMMYT,
CC BY-NC-SA.

the workforce engaged in fisheries, forestry, and livestock production, Bangladeshis primarily ate HYV rice, but wheat production had become increasingly
important. They had grown accustomed to consuming it because this grain
had been the primary internationally provided relief food since the 1970s.
Bangladeshi farms had not fully integrated Green Revolution technologies
into their farming practices. They faced many constraints beyond the limits
of technology, such as landownership, environmental degradation from the
heavy use of fertilizers, lack of infrastructure, particularly roads and electrification, and access to credit and the unequal, if not inequitable, distribution
of food to the general population.[46]

In retrospect, the Green Revolution in South Asia is the result of a technological package that is part of a social system. The social system (that is, state,
culture, and class, as well as landholding institutions and political structures)
determined the use of that technological package and the distribution of the
benefits. In this context, critics can analyze and criticize the application of
Green Revolution technologies but not reject their use under the appropriate
social conditions. Critics, however, argued that because social and economic

equalities already existed, the technological package of the Green Revolution perpetuated and even created new poverty for the majority of rural people.[47]

Yet, if the Green Revolution did not create a cornucopia in India and Pakistan, neither did it create a Pandora's box as some observers had feared. Medium- and small-scale farmers adopted the HYVs, not just the large-scale farmers, partly because the components of the Green Revolution proved scale neutral; that is, even farmers with a small plot of land could plant a new high-yielding wheat or rice variety and increase production to feed their families. Landhold- ing patterns and irrigation systems supported the new agriculture. The In- dian government privileged the Green Revolution with agricultural research and extension as well as agricultural pricing policies. Moreover, advocates of the Green Revolution argued that farmers had adopted tractors only in a few states and that no large-scale eviction of tenants or displacement of agricul- tural workers occurred. In addition, the Green Revolution had made India self-sufficient in food grains, although it affected only 25 percent of its ara- ble land. In the areas where the Green Revolution proved successful (Pun- jab, Haryana, Western Uttar Pradesh, and parts of Tami Nader and Kerala) it brought not only increased productivity but also fundamental and irrever- sible economic and social changes. The most ardent supporters of the Green Revolution believed that peasant cultivators who farmed the land on a sub- sistence basis and depended on an exchange economy had become market- oriented farmers who produced a surplus, which they sold for cash. They also contended that the demand for farm labor to handle the larger crops had in- creased along with agricultural wages.[48]

Agricultural scientists did not doubt that biotechnological change signifi- cantly helped improve grain production, particularly wheat and rice, to in- crease food supplies. If large-scale and small-scale farmers had HYVs, irrigation, and chemical fertilizer, each group would profit. No minimum investment floor existed. The agricultural scientists, however, were not concerned with unintended social and economic consequences of the Green Revolution, and they never considered that they had responsibility for creating a more equi- table world. They believed that increased production of wheat and rice re- duced food costs and that more grain meant more food for hungry people. They gave less thought to the distribution of the Green Revolution benefits as long as no group suffered an absolute disadvantage because of it.[49]

Although some observers in well-fed nations believed that the Green Revo- lution would end hunger in food-deficit nations and prevent social unrest, particularly in the form of support for the Communist Party and red revolutions, this belief proved far too simplistic to explain the internal and external political affairs of food-deficit nations. India is a case in point. The Indian government accepted the premise of the Rockefeller Foundation and the United States that science could increase agricultural production to feed hungry and nutritionally food-deficient people. Nevertheless, it primarily wanted to maintain its sovereignty and ensure food security while avoiding any sense of colonialism—that is, control by a foreign nation that harkened to the days of British sovereignty over Indian affairs. India correctly blamed Great Britain for the mismanagement of agriculture and food distribution that led to the last famine in the late 1940s.[50]

The Indian government, then, used science to increase food production and the power of the state to address the social and economic changes wrought by agricultural science. Indian leaders also believed that they ultimately could use Green Revolution agricultural science not only to ensure food security for subsistence farmers and the urban poor but also to transform small-scale, backward farmers who used traditional methods and lived on the border of starvation into "risk-taking, profit-making individuals." Put differently, India would cooperate with western Green Revolution scientists but always on its own terms and for its own purposes.[51]

Overall, then, the Green Revolution in India and Pakistan was state as well as science driven. State-sponsored technological change came in the form of irrigation systems and fertilizer production, credit, transportation, and storage facilities. Government-guaranteed minimum grain price supports and subsidization of fertilizer and pesticide manufacturing and land reforms privileged small-scale family farmers. Price supporting policies encouraged commercial production not just subsistence agriculture. Government-supported research also created a scientific base for the development of high-yielding varieties, and state agricultural extension systems disseminated that knowledge to farmers. In South Asia the development of HYVs did not create a Green Revolution, and politics played the essential enabling role in India and Pakistan, two nations that epitomize the Green Revolution.[52]

The subcontinent's hungry people need more than increased food production. They need access or entitlement to it, and that depended on government pricing, distribution, and labor policies, among other factors. The HYVs are not independent agents of agricultural change. Population increase, for example, expanded the supply of unskilled labor while mechanization decreased the need for it. Still, many poor farmers in India and Pakistan would be worse off in the twenty-first century than if they did not raise HYVs of wheat and rice.[53]

Yet, while the Green Revolution in South Asia was state driven, politics and government policy also prevented it from reaching the people most in need of food assistance. By the early twenty-first century, wheat production had been so great in India's Punjab that the government rented land from farmers to store its procurement purchases. In 2002, government price supports of approximately $129 per metric ton (up from $99 in 1997) had encouraged surplus production. High government floor prices, however, drove up grain and flour prices for consumers. As wheat rotted in Punjab's storage facilities, people in neighboring Rajasthan went hungry and some starved. Across the nation, some 350 million Indians did not have enough to eat. India, under pressure from international leaders, made matters worse by reducing food subsidies for the poor to better support a free market economy. Although technically self-sufficient in food, local, state, and national governments failed to distribute the surplus to the food deficient or make it available at affordable prices. India had about 53 million metric tons of surplus wheat but could not get it to the people most in need because of economic policy, not a failure of transportation or agricultural science.[54]

India responded to this food crisis by purchasing three million tons of wheat on the world market, particularly from the United States where farmers, grain traders, and corporations sought a market for American surplus production. Many Indians remained untouched by the Green Revolution. Swaminathan believed that food should be a "legal right, just like education and information," but India had not yet achieved that goal by 2010. Increasingly, observers noted the need for a new or second Green Revolution. Union Minister of Agriculture Sharad Pawar doubted that India could provide food security for 75 percent of the population. India produced fifty million metric tons of grain but food security required sixty-five million tons annually. The Green Revolution had not kept up with need.[55]

In contrast, agricultural scientists contended that rapid population growth increased the Malthusian danger of starvation but that HYV technology would provide food for hungry people and prevent famine and want. They also continued to argue that biotechnological transformations for agriculture were scale neutral; that is, both small-scale as well as large-scale farmers could adopt HYVs. If large-scale and small-scale farmers had HYVs, irrigation, and fertilizer, each group would benefit. No minimum investment floor existed.

In this sense, of course, they ignored that the political, social, and economic power in a society determined the access to such agricultural "inputs." The agricultural scientists also argued from the premise that all farmers sought increased crop production for economic reasons (that is, profit), not for humanitarian sympathies. The goal was commercial production. They also contended that increased production would require more labor to irrigate, fertilize, and harvest new high-yielding crops. The multiplier effect of increased production meant more income for farmers and workers alike and more expenditure that would fuel the local, regional, and national economies. Moreover, they held that increased crop production of wheat and rice would reduce food costs.[56]

The Punjab State Council for Science and Technology, however, reported that the Green Revolution had become "unstainable and not profitable" because it had become too costly, particularly with the water table having fallen from ten to two hundred feet below the surface, thereby requiring farmers to sink deeper wells. Some observers considered the continued investment in Green Revolution technology a "kind of suicide" for farmers because debt hopelessly burdened them. Pumps alone cost $4,000 plus other drilling expenses, which farmers often paid on credit at interest rates as high as 24 percent annually from local and private lenders, if they did not qualify for bank loans, all of which created a "vicious cycle of debt." Deep wells also often brought up salty water, which poisoned the land and reduced production. At the same time, India's population grew faster than any other agricultural country. Critics of the Green Revolution called for a new Green Revolution that would ensure an "inclusive and sustainable agriculture." Although India produced a record 241 million tons of food grain, aided by heavy monsoon rains, during the 2010–2011 crop year for an increase of 23 million tons from the previous year, 37 percent of the 1.2 billion population lived in poverty and unable to meet their daily food needs. Some argued that genetically modified (GM) varieties would provide that new Green Revolution and end hunger and want just as others had promised that the Green Revolution's HYVs would do a half century earlier.[57]

In 2001, India had a significant grain reserve of fifty to sixty million tons, but lost 7–8 percent of that surplus due to poor storage facilities. In Pakistan, some observers accused the manufacturers of pesticides, herbicides, and chemical fertilizers that fueled the Green Revolution of having the "naked lust for private profit," and they urged farmers to return to traditional, sustainable farming methods not the adoption of genetically modified varieties developed by agribusinesses. Even so, optimists for a second Green Revolution in South Asia championed the development of seeds tailored for microenvironments and varieties with better nutritional quality, not just more calories. They also urged the replacement of inorganic with organic fertilizer, although they often failed to realize that these farmers lacked sufficient livestock and land required for that purpose. Poor farmers in the rainfed areas of India and Pakistan desperately needed a second Green Revolution.[58]

By the second decade of the twenty-first century, the first Green Revolution had not ended malnutrition and hunger, although government policy continued to emphasize self-sufficiency in cereals. Although India and Bangladesh had achieved food self-sufficiency, their governments still emphasized increased production for wheat and rice, as did food-deficit Pakistan. Agricultural and social scientists once again looked to science to solve these problems on the Indian subcontinent. The social scientists and environmentalists particularly wanted a "gentle Green Revolution" that would produce nutritious grains and vegetables with little use of petrochemical fertilizers, pesticides, and herbicides.[59]

In late 2014, Swaminathan contended that if more women became farmers and expanded crop production, hunger and malnutrition could be ended on the subcontinent, and India would not need a second Green Revolution. Women, he argued, were "great biodiversity conservers," and intellectually contributed to farming by eliminating risks and creating variety by not adopting Green Revolution science.[60]

Few could deny, however, that the Green Revolution kept many farmers from starving and the nation from famine. Yet, even in West Bengal where state-mandated land reform in the late 1970s improved the legal position of sharecroppers and guaranteed them an equitable portion of the harvests, the Green Revolution had taken an environmental toll. Although rice yields initially had increased dramatically by 2014, harvests had declined by 50 percent in many fields. The application of more fertilizer did not improve production and groundwater had significantly diminished with the falling water table. Traditional farmers still did not understand the correct applications of fertilizer and pesticides. Moreover, one observer noted, "The irony of Indian agriculture is that the educated people who understand the science of farming do not work in the fields, so they do not disseminate their knowledge to the villagers." High applications of fertilizer and intensive land use wore out the soil. Inadequate agricultural extension remained a problem. When West Bengal officials advised farmers to raise more vegetables for market and less grain, agriculturalists had difficulty understanding the policy reversal.[61]

The criticism of the Green Revolution dating to the early 1970s remained vibrant three decades later. Pakistan provides an example. Instead of recognizing that the original purpose of the Green Revolution was to increase the grain supply in food-deficit nations, some critics saw a calculated political purpose not based on food production. Rather, they contended that the government had introduced Green Revolution agricultural science "with the explicit object of eradicating rural poverty as a way out of radical land reforms." They admitted that Green Revolution agriculture provided more food, but they still argued that only the large-scale landowners profited and that it did not address "large social and economic inequities." They wanted the Green Revolution to provide "income equality," not just food for the hungry. The Green Revolution had increased wheat production from 4 million tonnes on 4.9 million hectares in 1959 and 1960 to 16.4 million tonnes on 8 million hectares in 1996 and 1997 while rice production increased from 1 million tonnes on 1.2 million hectares to 4.3 million tonnes on 2.25 million hectares during that same period. By the 1990s, however, soil exhaustion had occurred in some areas beyond the capacity of inorganic fertilizers to maintain high wheat and rice production. By 2000, Pakistan had an annual shortfall of 4 million tonnes of wheat with a negative multiplier effect on food processing industries. Still, with the average growth of grain production at 4.2 percent annually, Pakistan could feed the population, which grew at the rate of 3 percent annually.[62]

Critics also argued that the Green Revolution decreased the number of tenant farmers in Pakistan from approximately two million to one million between 1960 and 1990, because property owners dismissed them and substituted hired labor. Moreover, small-scale landowners still could not afford Green Revolution technologies and leased their land to large-scale landowners. Both groups, then, became unemployed and contributed to the poverty in the countryside. Inadequate and disingenuous government efforts at land reform failed to redistribute wealth. Without industry and manufacturing jobs to absorb the agriculturally unemployed and often landless farm workers, rural poverty became worse, despite the Green Revolution providing more but not enough farm employment. Rather than accuse the government and private enterprise for the lack of job-creating endeavors, these critics blamed agriculture for its success, which they attributed to the negative aspects of

capitalism. Certainly, capitalism has hurt many people, but it also has benefited many others. Even so, the critics contended that rather than becoming
more economically and financially secure, small-scale farmers, tenant farmers, sharecroppers, and agricultural workers became more poverty stricken in
South Asia. They, however, offered little comparative evidence that the lives
of those farmers and agricultural workers were better before the Green Revolution. Ideology often determined economic analysis. For many critics, the
Green Revolution privileged the wealthy landowners who used it to exploit
the poor who lost their land and jobs and necessarily had to look elsewhere
for employment. By contending that nearly half of Pakistan's population only
owned 6 percent of the land, the inequity seemed clear to the critics who laid
the blame with Green Revolution agriculture. Put differently, although the
Green Revolution for them was a "technical" success, it was not a "distribu-
tional" success. The Green Revolution had failed because it had not improved
"income equality."[63]

Opponents of the subcontinent's Green Revolution did not question the
benefits of increased agricultural production from the new technology. No
one argued that it was better for hungry people to starve rather than eat foods
from Green Revolution HYVs of wheat and rice. They complained about the
inequity issues. The scientists who developed the HYVs and the package of
"inputs" to increase agricultural production, maintained that they never intended to influence societies or economies other than through increased agricultural productivity to feed hungry people and, in time, improve their standard of living. Land reform, rural poverty, unemployment, and agricultural
subsidization of many sorts, they contended, remained the responsibility of
governments, not agricultural scientists. Above all, if the Green Revolution
provided any lessons, it was that agricultural transfer depended on environment and culture, not just scientific discovery, and its success relied on governmental support.[64]

Moreover, the Green Revolution was not suitable for all regions and India
provides a clear example of environmental and socioeconomic differences
that created sharp inequities. By developing widespread varieties that required
high applications of fertilizer and irrigation, Indian scientists failed to breed
wheat and rice for specific areas where geography and microclimates determined crop yields. Indian agricultural scientists who followed Borlaug's
and Swaminathan's Green Revolution research and application methods contended that HYVs bred for widespread distribution outproduced traditional
varieties even without fertilizer and irrigation. They hoped that widespread

adoption of HYVs would boost production, increase income, and promote social equity. To achieve those goals, however, they directed their research to improving wheat production in the rich lands of the Northwest (Punjab, Haryana, Western Pradesh) rather than for their country's many environmental
and agroclimatic conditions, particularly dry areas where marginal and subsistence farmers prevailed.[65]

Some Indian scientists, however, observed that Mexican HYV wheat varieties intended for widespread adoption did not meet production expectations
and that traditional Indian varieties, in the absence of fertilizer and irrigation,
produced greater yields under average or below average conditions. Mexican
HYVs produced best under favorable conditions, including irrigation at precise times. HYVs also proved most adaptable across similar agronomic conditions, including sunlight, longitude, and latitude, not in specific regions.
Variety improvements depended on the location of specific environments as
much as genetics. Yet Borlaug continued to believe that genetics trumped the
environment for crop breeders. Only by the development of wheat and rice
varieties that had the capability of widespread adoption, he contended, could
agricultural scientists make all parts of India self-sufficient in food production. By the early twenty-first century some critics charged that Borlaug and
his followers needed to breed grain varieties for local environments. Indian
wheat varieties that replaced the Mexican HYVs in the late 1960s only benefited the farmers on good lands who could afford fertilizer and irrigation.
Some observers also contended that farmers should still raise traditional varieties as a safety net in case the HYVs failed. One observer reflected, "miracle
seeds do not produce miracles unless the right combination of factors such
as fertilizers, soil management, water management and crop management
practices interact."[66]

Indeed, the positive transformations of agriculture had not been geographically uniform due in part to environmental and socioeconomic disparities as
well as population density and cultural and ethnic barriers. Punjab farmers,
for example, profited from the Green Revolution but North Arcot agriculturists did not enjoy its promises and benefits. In India, the Green Revolution
complicated regional inequities, a problem that remained one of the major
unintended consequences of the Green Revolution.[67]

In addition, HYV wheat and rice did not categorically save the Indian subcontinent from famine in the face of rapid population growth. HYVs increased
dietary calories, but not vitamins. A full stomach did not mean that the food
consumed was nutritious. Moreover, the high productivity of HYVs lasted only

a few years and then declined. As a result, scientists worked constantly to develop new varieties to replace the declining production of the old varieties. These shortcomings complicated an interpretation of the Green Revolution's unmitigated success based on production and consumption to say nothing about social and economic influences and changes. Supporters, however, usually accepted the generalization that HYVs increased food production ahead of population growth and saved India and Pakistan from imminent famine.[68]

If the Green Revolution trickled down to small-scale and subsistence farmers from India's centralized research institutions and the government, it did so slowly. In South Asia, the Green Revolution favored the Punjab and specific groups within the region. Historically, environment and space more than industry and commerce have limited agriculture. The Green Revolution in South Asia attempted to overcome the problems of environment and space by controlling the former and producing more in the latter. Agricultural science and goodwill drove both efforts, although the social and economic results often revealed ignorance and lack of forethought to possible unintended consequences. In the end, the environment and social and economic structures trumped Green Revolution science on the subcontinent.[69]

3

East and Southeast Asia

The Green Revolution in East and Southeast Asia had many agricultural antecedents in Japan, Taiwan, and Korea that predated the scientific research at the International Maize and Wheat Improvement Center in Mexico. During the late nineteenth and early twentieth centuries, for example, Japanese agricultural scientists developed high-yielding rice varieties that produced abundantly when heavily fertilized. These sturdy, short-stemmed varieties also required well-developed irrigation systems, which Japanese farmers had cultivated since the Tokugawa feudal period. By the Meiji Restoration in 1868, a demarcation for the beginning of modern Japan, farmers irrigated almost all of the paddy fields.[1]

Japanese farmers experimented in their own fields and diffused new varieties with the help of experts from the agricultural schools. In 1921, the government began buying rice to support small-scale farmers. This state intervention in agriculture became essential for the success of the Green Revolution in Asia during the late twentieth century. The introduction of inorganic or chemical fertilizers during the 1930s also kept yields high, and farmers profited if they could afford them. Those who could not purchase fertilizer or irrigate often became tenant farmers who relied on landowners to finance their agricultural operations, or they left farming for other employment. Land reform after World War II and the Agricultural Land Law of 1952 enabled greater equity in landownership and contributed to rural social stability. By the late 1960s, Japanese farmers and the government's agricultural research institutions had forged a strong relationship. The farmer-scientist cooperation, so essential to the Green Revolution, predated the Green Revolution in Latin America and South Asia by several decades. The development of small tractors with less than ten horsepower also provided affordable technology and proved necessary to offset rising labor costs. By the late 1970s, most small-scale, family farmers used tractors or power tillers.[2]

In Taiwan, the antecedents of the Green Revolution date from the early 1920s to the late 1960s. Rice production increased in part due to high Japanese demands that led to the importation of approximately 50 percent of Taiwan's rice crop in the late 1930s. At the same time, Taiwanese farmers began adopting high-yielding Japanese varieties for their subtropical environment. The Japanese colonial government had invested heavily in irrigation, and agricultural scientists produced high-yielding rice varieties by crossbreeding traditional Taiwanese and Japanese varieties. These early-maturing varieties enabled double cropping. By 1935, Taiwanese farmers planted approximately 50 percent of their paddy fields with these improved varieties. Farmers' associations kept agriculturists abreast of new technology and the importance of chemical fertilizers.[3]

In 1949, the influx of nearly two million people from the mainland created a food shortage. Kuomintang Party leadership responded quickly by instituting land reforms that benefited small-scale farmers and, along with improved irrigation facilities, enabled Taiwanese farmers to increase production. The Sino-American Joint Commission on Rural Reconstruction functioned as a *de facto* ministry of agriculture and supported and coordinated research projects and agricultural extension as well as used previously established farmers' associations to provide agricultural services in the countryside. Hybrid rice varieties, irrigation, chemical fertilizers, and government-supported research enabled Taiwanese farmers to attain prewar levels of rice production by the early 1950s.[4]

In 1956, Taiwan's agricultural scientists developed the world's first fertilizer-responsive, semidwarf rice variety that enabled farmers to increase production on irrigated paddies to approximately 4 metric tons per hectare by the mid-1960s, up from the 2.4 metric tons per hectare only twenty years earlier. Government support of agriculture by exchanging fertilizer, the production of which it monopolized, for procurement of more than 60 percent of the rice crop also encouraged farmers to achieve high productivity.[5]

The roots of Korea's Green Revolution date to the 1920s and 1930s when Japan invested heavily in irrigation and nitrogen fertilizer plants. Large-scale landowners, however, perpetuated tenancy and together with Japan's corporations controlled as much as 70 percent of the land by the late 1930s. No agricultural associations mediated between farmers and the state as was done in Taiwan. Moreover, after World War II, South Korea abolished the agricultural extension system created by Japan, and the benefits of a Green Revolution lagged until the government instituted major land reforms. Even with incentives to increase production on privately owned land and the purchase of high-yielding Japanese varieties and fertilizer, Korean farmers only slowly adopted Green Revolution technologies in part because South Korea imported large quantities of grain from the United States as authorized by Public Law 480, which established the Food For Peace program. Although these grain importations prevented famine, if not hunger, they depressed rice prices for South Korea farmers and discouraged the planting of high-yielding varieties (HYVs).[6]

During the early 1960s, however, South Korea established a new agricultural research and extension program, covered the production costs of farmers with the procurement of rice at relatively high prices, established control of fertilizer marketing, and began consolidating farmlands. In 1968, the government increased its purchase price for rice above domestic and international prices. This policy provided a profitable price support by the mid-1970s. High government prices had become a basic feature of Korean agricultural policy. Consequently, when the United States terminated Public Law 480 in 1970, the South Korean government had established the policies necessary to support a Green Revolution.[7]

On November 29, 1966, the International Rice Research Institute (IRRI), founded in 1960 by the Ford and Rockefeller Foundations in the Philippines, introduced a hybrid rice variety called IR-8, which became the foundation of the Green Revolution in Southeast Asia. IR-8 resulted from the cross of a Chinese dwarf called Dee-geo-woo-gen (DGWG) with Peta, a tall variety from Indonesia. This sturdy, short-stalked, fertilizer-responsive, fast-growing, high-yielding variety produced heavy heads of grain without toppling and permitted easier harvesting. In contrast to traditional rice varieties that reached time for harvest in 180 days, IR-8 matured in 130 to 150 days, thereby permitting double cropping with wheat on the same land. It also produced yields of six to ten tons per hectare. Essentially, it gave rice farmers an additional one to two hectares of productivity above traditional varietal yields. Science, then, could bring the benefits of the Green Revolution to farmers and nations suffering from insufficient food. Self-sufficiency, even security, in food and with it an improved standard of living seemed no longer a dream but a reality. Although some countries of the Indochinese peninsula resisted adoption of high-yield varieties because their governments considered them "American" introductions, and therefore subversive, many farmers made small-scale plantings using these improved seeds. During the 1960s, Southeast Asia began a major agricultural transformation that, by 1968, the public called the Green Revolution. It relied on intensive rice cultivation based on irrigation, large applications of fertilizer, and the seeding of HYVs. By 1968, IR-8 had made the Philippines self-sufficient in rice for the first time since 1903.[8]

Rice breeders at the IRRI enjoyed their success in the Philippines, and they hoped that IR-8 would become a miracle rice and do for Asian farmers what the Mexican wheat hybrids had done for India. These scientists had bred IR-8 for widespread adoption. They did not intend it to be a locality-specific variety. IR-8 is non-photoperiod sensitive. Its life cycle is period or date fixed, so the length of the day for maturation became unimportant. As a result, IR-8 theoretically became a high-yielding rice variety that could be adapted to a wide range of tropical environmental conditions. Farmers could raise it in any season if they had adequate water for irrigation. Farmers then could raise IR-8 across East, South East, and South Asia. Unfortunately for the Green Revolution and those who counted on it to increase rice production, IR-8 proved highly susceptible to insects and disease. It also could not tolerate submersion from heavy monsoon rains. Even so, the IRRI hailed IR-8 as "a rugged variety that could go almost anywhere in the tropics." That boast proved true in the sense that IR-8 led the way for the later development of more environment-specific varieties.[9]

By 1972, South Korean agricultural scientists also had bred a new rice variety, called *Togil*, by crossing high-yielding varieties developed at the International Rice Research Institute and at the Office of Rural Development in South Korea. Six years later, farmers planted 76 percent of South Korean rice paddies with new high-yielding, fertilizer-responsive varieties. Thus, between 1968, when the government established a remunerative pricing policy and 1978 with the near universal planting of high-yielding, fertilizer-dependent varieties, South Korean rice production increased 67 percent. By the late 1970s, South Korea had become self-sufficient in rice production and, with the exception of the mid-1980s, remained so. These scientific achievements rested on well-developed irrigation systems and government policies that reformed landholding, provided fertilizer, and set remunerative grain prices. These factors determined the success of the Green Revolution in South Korea.[10]

At the same time, Korean farmers also planted reliable, traditional, high-yielding, regional, and genetically diverse varieties for the best risk-management practices to ensure uniform and reliable long-term maximum production in time of HYV failure. The government, however, wanted maximum production, but farmers sought stable production of good tasting rice to meet the food needs of their families. Korean farmers would only produce the Green Revolution *Tongil* variety if the government paid them to do so by guaranteeing a market. By the late 1970s, the government purchased approximately 40 percent of the *Tongil* rice crop.[11]

Farmers, however, had to plant *Tongil* earlier than traditional varieties, which interrupted the spring planting of barley and other cash crops before the customary time for planting rice. As a result, most Korean farmers considered government-sponsored Green Revolution agricultural advice and encouragement as wrongheaded. In 1978, their hesitancy proved correct when disease ruined the *Tongil* crop. The government reluctantly, but necessarily, responded by reorganizing the agricultural extension service and by breeding more genetically diverse varieties to combat rice diseases, cold temperatures, and other risks. By the 1980s, Korean agricultural scientists and government officials understood that they could not impose a Green Revolution. It could not be a mandated, top-down process. The Green Revolution would not succeed until agricultural scientists and government policy met the needs of farmers, which involved more than increased production and that accounted for environmental parameters. In Japan, however, where peace, the economy, and government policy enabled farmers to adopt the principles of the Green Revolution, rice production created a 2.7 million ton surplus problem that drove prices down. For other nations, such as Thailand and Burma, change came slowly. Both nations had been traditional rice-exporting countries whose trade with food-deficit nations in Southeast Asia contributed a significant part to their national economies. Government officials in each country worried that Green Revolution surplus production in other nations would prove detrimental to their economies due to lost export markets.[12]

Despite the achievements of Green Revolution agricultural science during the 1960s, almost from the beginning social scientists criticized it for causing a host of unintended consequences. By 1970, they charged, as they had in South Asia, that new seeds would make the rich richer and the poor poorer. Only the large-scale farmers could afford Green Revolution investments, which, in turn, enabled them to produce more rice for sale on the local, national, and international markets. The agricultural scientists contended that ultimately increased production from Green Revolution science would decrease rice prices as world production increased, thereby benefiting the poor. They asserted the moral and ethical values of producing more food for hungry people. Others worried that high production of Green Revolution rice crops would displace millions of farmers and agricultural workers and force them into the already overcrowded cities. The greatest skeptics argued that a Green Revolution in

Southeast Asia without land reform would "impart into the countryside in-creased inequality, increased bitterness, with declining absolute living stan-dards for the landless laborer and the small peasant." The resulting anger in the countryside would create a "Maoist revolt" because the Green Revolution had promised many but redeemed few from poverty and want. Supporters re-sponded by saying that heavier crops and multi-crops would increase agricul-tural labor opportunities. Gunnar Myrdal, the Swedish economist and social scientist, saw things differently and urged food-deficit nations in Southeast Asia to promote high-yielding crops that required considerable hand labor. Norman Borlaug and others countered that the world's persisting food prob-lems could not be solved alone by Green Revolution science because they fun-damentally were a population problem that he called a "monster which unless tamed, will one-day wipe us from the earth's surface." The Green Revolution, not traditional crops, would buy time.[13]

Yet, state support for the Green Revolution, while essential, also could be detrimental to agricultural improvement and Indonesia provides an example. In Indonesia, the Suharto government, which came to power in September 1965, continued the agricultural improvement program of President Kusno Sukarno with the distribution of high-yielding rice varieties, pesticides, and fertilizers. By the early 1970s, however, the government coerced Indonesian farmers to adopt Green Revolution technologies and charged them for the costs. Still, the Green Revolution fostered labor savings because Indonesian farmers used more herbicides to eliminate weeds instead of hoeing them. Su-harto's Green Revolution policy, however, still favored the large-scale, wealthy farmers who could afford Green Revolution technologies. Women and poor, small-scale farmers could not afford government mandates to purchase the HYVs, pesticides, and fertilizers, and many farmers necessarily moved to mar-ginal lands. Rural elites received government subsidies and acted as the state's "agents in the countryside" by distributing agricultural development technolo-gies to loyal party followers. By so doing, they preserved traditional stability and authoritarian rule in the name of agricultural science.[14]

As Indonesian farmers resisted forced participation in the Green Revolu-tion, by 1973, crop yields lagged rather than increased. Small-scale farmers preferred to mix old and new farming methods rather than adopt expensive government-imposed technologies. Many farmers resold their high-yielding seeds, fertilizers, and pesticides. Or, the government often delivered these chemicals, fertilizers, and pesticides too late in the crop year for use. The rural governmental bureaucracy could not administer or enforce the Green

Revolution program, and the national government did not provide the education and technical training to enable farmers to apply Green Revolution techniques properly. Corrupt government officials also appropriated and sold fertilizer and pesticides for personal gain.[15]

As a result, by the early 1970s, this government-directed Green Revolution failed. Indonesia then abandoned its mandatory agricultural program and substituted a policy that permitted small-scale farmers to make choices concerning seed selection and the adoption of pesticides and fertilizers. Farmers rather than government bureaucrats became agricultural decision makers who relied on the market rather than government directives to stimulate agricultural production, although they depended on government price supports to ensure profitability and production. One Indonesian agricultural official anticipated that "After 1974 our problem will be to keep expansion down so the market is not glutted," but the government had not committed the necessary financial and marketing support to ensure the success of the Green Revolution.[16]

During the early 1970s, the Green Revolution did not quickly improve agricultural production in the Philippines. Filipino farmers also complained that they could not afford heavy applications of chemical fertilizer to gain the full benefit of high-yielding rice varieties. If the government could not provide adequate credit or subsidize the cost of fertilizers and pesticides to make them affordable, the high-yielding rice varieties would not achieve large yields. President Ferdinand E. Marcos, who had proclaimed in 1970 that "The rice revolution has been permanently won," now doubted his own proclamation and promised more credit, price supports, irrigation, rice storage facilities, and extension work. He also urged Filipinos to eat more maize and less rice.[17]

Although President Marcos ordered private banks to make loans to farmers who had the best opportunity to adopt Green Revolution technology, he also ordered the army to ensure that farmers paid back their loans. Low interest rates were crucial to encourage farmers to make an investment in the Green Revolution, particularly for the purchase of fertilizer, but small-scale Filipino farmers hesitated to participate under authoritarian directives. Moreover, crop losses to plant disease and insects would prevent them from repaying their fertilizer loans and ruin them with debt. Some critics considered the decline of agricultural labor needs a "bitter reality," noting that in Central Luzon rice production had increased 100 percent but the employment of additional labor had increased only 50 percent. The cultivation of traditional rice varieties, they contended, employed more people. In addition, the cities could not absorb the surplus labor from agriculture. Unemployed people ate less food, which also failed to solve the problems of surplus production from Green Revolution agriculture. Moreover, critics argued that large-scale farmers would reduce labor costs as soon as they could afford to purchase more machinery, and they would use their profits to expand their holdings. Furthermore, high, government-subsidized agricultural prices would hurt subsistence farmers. Agricultural income disparities then would increase social stratification and division, and class lines would harden.[18]

The unintended consequences of the Green Revolution seemed linked and nearly unlimited for critics in the Philippines. Farmers could only hope for the best, while the plant breeders worked to develop disease- and insect-resistant rice varieties. By the early 1970s, however, no one argued any longer that high-yielding varieties alone would solve the deficiency in food grains. Disease had already wiped out many of those varieties. Some plant scientists hoped to acquire new disease-resistant varieties from China. Even so, by the 1975 crop year farmers had planted more than 60 percent of the rice land with HYVs.[19]

By the early 1970s other problems occurred. Some critics contended that the Green Revolution had not improved the life of small-scale farmers or enabled them to produce a food surplus. Social scientists argued that the Green Revolution only benefited some farmers in selected areas where environmental conditions enabled increased grain production with new techniques and high-yielding varieties. Others feared the effects of heavy applications of fertilizers, herbicides, and pesticides on the environment and human health. DDT, mercury, and nitrate fertilizers caused the most concern, but Norman Borlaug and other agricultural scientists contended that science and technology could solve "pollution abuses" and that their major challenges involved the increase of grain production and limiting the growth of population. The United Nations Food and Agriculture Organization (FAO) also observed that "until cheap, safe, and efficient pesticides are produced and made easily available, there is no alternative to the judicious use of DDT."[20]

Scientists essentially contended that Southeast Asian farmers had a choice between bountiful rice harvests and crop-destroying insects and hunger. At the same time, the FAO warned that Green Revolution agricultural science was not a substitute for agrarian reform but a "necessary and natural complement." It also held that the poor, small-scale farmers who most needed increased crop production lacked the training to apply Green Revolution technologies or the ability to acquire the credit to purchase it. Consequently, they could easily "fall victim to the avarice of moneylenders and merchants who

are mainly city-based." These poor farmers easily could become landless agricultural workers despite the benefits of increased agricultural production.[21]

Moreover, war in Southeast Asia prevented efforts to achieve Green Revolution reform, particularly in Cambodia and Vietnam. Yet, in 1970, Cambodian
farmers increased their production, mainly rice, by 25 percent after recovering
from a severe drought the year before. At that same time, rice farmers in South
Vietnam increased production by 8 percent over 1969 largely due to planting
HYVs, but the country remained a major importer of rice. Optimists remained
convinced, however, that the Green Revolution would solve the problems of
food shortage and hunger in the region where half of the world's population
lived and consumed two-thirds of the grain produced there.[22]

The Green Revolution, however, could not trump nature where climatic
vagaries became, in the words of one contemporary, "a sobering reminder of
the persisting precariousness of the world's food-population balance." A. H.
Boerma, director-general of the Food and Agriculture Organization, contended that neither improved weather conditions nor Green Revolution technology would solve Southeast Asian food problems unless people made greater
efforts to achieve population control. With population growth outstripping increased food production in many areas, agricultural science could not overcome problems caused by human behavior and the inability of the social
scientists to solve them. Renewed efforts to further develop and spread the
techniques and benefits of the Green Revolution were essential, but unless
farmers in Southeast Asia's developing nations could afford improved seeds,
fertilizers, pesticides, and irrigation, and until they gained adequate purchasing power, they would not be able to afford an adequate diet. Some observers
questioned whether the Green Revolution had been successful at all, and
some agricultural experts in Southeast Asia now wondered whether their work
would have the benefits that they originally had intended.[23]

By the early 1970s, the great promise of "miracle" seeds that would enable
Southeast Asian farmers to produce surpluses and end hunger across the Philippines, Indonesia, Malaysia, Cambodia, Thailand, and Burma, among other
nations, seemed far less possible than agricultural scientists had predicted.
In Southeast Asia, the Green Revolution seemed at an end due to low rice
prices and fields ravaged by drought, floods, and war—problems that Green
Revolution technologies could not overcome. In 1972, drought caused a dras-
tic shortfall in rice production, and the Republic of Singapore necessarily imported 1.5 million tons. A rice shortage in the Cambodian capital of Phnom
Penh caused rioting and looting while the ongoing war also reduced the av-

erage grain yield and the area under cultivation by nearly 50 percent. Fore-casters expected only Burma and Malaysia to produce a rice surplus due to double cropping and increased irrigation in the best Green Revolution tradi-tion. D. S. Athwal, associate director of the IRRI, saw little alternative to the spread of Green Revolution agriculture, particularly given the continued high population increase. He responded to that problem saying that "you apply the new technology or you starve."[24]

Vietnam also provides an example of the problems and successes of the Green Revolution. Rice production in South Vietnam decreased by approxi-mately 24 percent between 1965 and 1968 because of war. Although the South Vietnamese government doubled rice prices during the winter of 1966–1967 in an attempt to increase production and bring farmers into a market economy, by that time rice land had declined by five hundred thousand acres and pro-duction by one million tons since 1963, primarily due to war. The Vietnamese Ministry of Agriculture, however, opposed the adoption of HYVs from abroad fearing the introduction of diseases, but HYVs reached farmers surrepti-tiously. In 1967, a crop-destroying flood in the Vo Dat Valley necessitated the planting of the quick-maturing IR-8 variety, but Green Revolution improve-ments necessarily awaited peace. The Green Revolution HYVs came from imports not from Vietnamese agricultural science or production. Moreover, Mekong Delta farmers, who used Green Revolution techniques, often with-held their rice from the market as a hedge against inflation, thereby contrib-uting little to solving food-deficit problems, particularly in the northern prov-inces of South Vietnam.[25]

Although South Vietnam's Long Dinh Rice Research Institute introduced IR-8 in 1966, which doubled rice production from two to four tons per acre, and while farmers in North Vietnam began using this variety in 1968, its sus-ceptibility to insects and disease limited production. In 1971, although the United Nations Food and Agriculture Organization reported that the rice-producing areas of South Vietnam were being "rapidly planted" with HYVs, the nation remained a rice importer. The aftermath of the Vietnam War also slowed the adoption of Green Revolution technologies until the 1980s, when rice production soared with an annual average increase of 5 percent from 1980 to 2000. Yet, here too, agricultural science alone was not responsible for Green Revolution success. Rather, the government encouraged a market economy, which combined with the release of high-yielding varieties enabled 90 percent of Vietnam's rice farmers to increase production to as much as 5.5 tons per hectare between 1980 and 2002.[26]

Agricultural scientists also continued to develop highly productive, disease- and pest-resistant rice varieties, thereby preventing the Green Revolution from slowing compared to the Philippines and Indonesia, where research did not keep pace with needs. Yet, in Vietnam, the Green Revolution also was not "scale neutral" as elsewhere because only the economically secure landowners could afford Green Revolution technologies. For most Vietnamese farmers the Green Revolution was beyond their reach. Moreover, where the Green Revolution increased production, it caused a rise in land values which owners used to increase rent levels to the detriment of cash-poor tenant farmers and sharecroppers. Although agricultural labor shortages occurred during harvest time due to heavy yields, land consolidations prevented increased ownership. Many Vietnamese rice farmers were women due to the high loss of the male population during the war years, but society accepted them as farmers and did not exclude them from the benefits of the Green Revolution, provided they had access to land and credit.[27]

Moreover, many South Vietnamese farmers had abandoned their paddy fields because the war had made agriculture unsafe. Observers also believed the North Vietnamese rice harvests had fallen short because of the war. In 1975, after the war ended, second-generation hybrid rice varieties and new, improved varieties drawing in part on Chinese germplasm and a national research program became available. In 1986, economic reform toward a market economy helped increase rice production and in 1989 a unified Vietnam became self-sufficient in and an exporter of rice. Further, Green Revolution improvements continued into the early twenty-first century, making Vietnam one of the world's largest rice exporters. Even so, the World Bank estimated that 13 percent of the Vietnamese population remained undernourished. Increased rice production alone based on Green Revolution agricultural technologies had not solved the problem of inadequate access to food for needy people.[28]

Before unification, North Vietnamese farmers increased their planting of high-yielding rice varieties from twenty thousand hectares in 1965 to seven hundred thousand hectares in 1972. By the early 1970s approximately 85 percent of North Vietnamese farmers worked on cooperatives (that is, collective farms of which 99 percent were organized as producer cooperatives). Even before the Vietnam or American War ended, the North Vietnamese had merged the Green Revolution with a socialist system. North Vietnamese agricultural scientists had been experimenting with crosses of rice strains from southern China and IR-8 from the Philippines. In doing so, they developed new locally specific Vietnamese rice strains. The most important feature of this rice breeding was the development of a variety that farmers could harvest in ten months and before the heavy rains or monsoon season came in November. Within this shorter growing season, the new rice varieties permitted a five-month crop that farmers could plant after the autumn harvest. The North Vietnamese planted fast-growing rice varieties in late February for harvest in June followed by a second planting for harvest in November. During the three months from November to February, farmers could plant a third crop on the dry rice lands. The February to March planting season absorbed heretofore unoccupied winter labor at a traditional slack time. American bombing of the irrigation dikes, fertilizer plants, and paddy fields, however, slowed progress with Green Revolution rice production but it did not halt it.[29]

The North Vietnamese used organic fertilizer, such as the Azolla plant that grew on the surface of rice paddies, and returned nitrogen to the water of the irrigated fields instead of chemical fertilizer. They also used hog manure. As a result, despite wartime conditions, the North Vietnamese planted HYVs with small amounts of natural fertilizer to produce fast-growing multiple crops that could utilize labor throughout the year. The North Vietnamese used Green Revolution technology to meet their own specific environmental and social conditions in contrast to the priorities of other countries. Indeed, the North Vietnamese intended to produce fast-growing rice crops, not necessarily heavy crops, because they could make up the difference with multiple crops. By 1974, farmers planted approximately 25 percent of the North Vietnamese rice crop with HYVs. Despite the war, the Green Revolution not only helped the North Vietnamese maintain rice production but it also changed the agricultural calendar to permit a third dry season crop and use of otherwise nonproductive labor. Until the war ended, however, North Vietnam had reached its limits for repairing and expanding irrigated rice lands to extend Green Revolution agriculture.[30]

Even so, the United Nations Food and Agriculture Organization reported that across Southeast Asia food production rose "at a rate comfortably ahead of the population growth." The director-general of the FAO reported, however, that slight gains in agricultural productivity did not represent a Green Revolution in Southeast Asia. Indeed, in the Philippines, where the Asian Green Revolution began, it seemed to be regressing resulting from one agricultural crisis or another. After the International Rice Research Institute began releasing high-yielding varieties in 1966, the Philippines enjoyed self-sufficiency and surplus production only until 1970. Domingo Panganiban of the National Food and Agriculture Council attributed the decline to lack of government funding and a plant virus as well as Christian-Muslim conflict in the South. As a result, the Philippines, once again, became a rice importer. Some government officials contended that the only way to revitalize the Green Revolution would be the aggressive adoption of the newly developed hybrid varieties that scientists had bred to resist the plant virus tungro, which had blighted some 140,000 acres of rice land in Luzon and Mindanao.[31]

Part of the problem for the slow adoption of Green Revolution agricultural science and application was the discrepancy between agricultural theory and reality. Scientists could produce high-yielding rice varieties that increased yields sufficiently to outstrip population growth in Southeast Asia. The early HYVs developed at the International Rice Research Institute, however, did not resist disease, insects, and drought. Moreover, the high yields produced on experimental plots proved far greater than farmers produced in their paddies. By the mid-1970s, social scientists also contended that the Green Revolution in Southeast Asia had not decreased the economic gap between rich and poor farmers because Green Revolution costs were not scale neutral. Rather, the Green Revolution privileged, as it had in Latin America and the South Asian subcontinent, the large-scale farmers who had the capital to invest in Green Revolution technologies, not the small-scale, impoverished farmers who most needed to increase grain production to feed their families. Poverty denied small-scale farmers the benefits of agricultural science, but the elimination of malnutrition was a matter of social justice. The social scientists also argued that the Green Revolution favored farmers who could afford mechanization and that it would drive labor off the land, cause the consolidation of landholdings among the few wealthy farmers, and increase social and economic inequities in the countryside, just as they had argued about India. Nutrition experts charged that plant scientists only sought to increase grain production, which they measured as an index of agricultural progress among food-deficient people. They did not concern themselves, critics argued, with ensuring the redistribution of new agricultural wealth. For these critics, the Green Revolution was not scale neutral because those most in need of it could not afford its technologies.[32]

By the autumn of 1974, however, some social scientists analyzing IRRI data found that farm size and land tenure had not changed dramatically since the introduction of modern varieties. Although farmers used more machinery, fertilizer, and pesticides, more than half of the farmers in the study area increased their use of hired labor from nearby villages, 40 percent used more family labor, and 30 percent hired more workers from beyond their villages.

Figure 12. Farmers using oxen to thresh rice in Nepal
These farmers are threshing rice by treading oxen over the cut stalks near Ghara, Nepal.
High-yielding rice varieties produced more grain and farmers sometimes used oxen rather
than flails to thresh the heavier crop. Vanessa Alberto, photographer.

Clearly, the Green Revolution had increased the need for agricultural labor.
Experts estimated that farmers planted high-yielding varieties on forty to fifty
million acres or about 40 percent of Southeast Asia's rice land. Even so, as
fertilizer prices increased due to worldwide production shortages resulting
from the Arab oil embargo, many rice farmers reverted to traditional varieties that had dependable results without the use of fertilizer. Some social scientists, however, differed with the report and the optimism of the plant scientists contending that the IRRI had conducted its survey in areas where the
Green Revolution had an optimal chance to succeed, where farmers were accustomed to using fertilizers, pesticides, and machinery, and that they had
the income to make these investments. The agricultural scientists at the IRRI
disagreed, arguing that the Green Revolution in Thailand, Malaysia, Indonesia, and the Philippines had not caused the consolidation of land and rural
unemployment due to the mechanization of farms.[33]

The plant scientists continued to argue that they had enabled farmers to
increase grain production and that their work to develop deep water varieties for Thailand, Burma's Irrawaddy River Delta, and South Vietnam's Me-

kong Delta would enable these nations to join the Green Revolution. They also contended that the development of high-yielding varieties that matured in the cold climate of South Korea would soon increase food production even further. Moreover, by 1974, IRRI scientists contended that Taiwanese farmers produced 3,500 pounds of rice per acre and that farmers had planted virtually all of the rice acreage with HYVs, which they considered a "reasonable" goal for all of Southeast Asia. Even so, expectations did not yet reveal reality.[34]

The governments of Thailand and Burma, for example, did not show "any strong sense of urgency" to expand production. Neither country confronted famine and farmers had planted only approximately 5 percent of the rice acreage in both nations with HYVs. Traditional varieties produced enough grain to keep production slightly ahead of population growth. Neither nation had the road or rail systems to transport surplus production beyond the local markets. Without a food distribution program, hungry people would still suffer despite Green Revolution production. Moreover, the monsoon season invariably flooded rice paddies and drowned the HYV varieties. Tradition and the lack of an agricultural extension system also hindered the adoption of Green Revolution science. Observers estimated that 30–40 percent of Burmese farmers sowed their rice broadcast into plowed furrows rather than by transplanting, and smaller yields resulted. Although the autocratic government of President Ne Win authorized price supports to encourage increased rice production, the traditional varieties could not provide a surplus no matter the price of rice. Environmental conditions also restricted farmers from planting HYV rice in the Mekong Delta.[35]

Others worried that the Green Revolution had stalled and that significant increases of rice and other grains might not be sufficient to prevent famine or provide surpluses for grain-poor areas, because Green Revolution techniques could not be introduced on a scale broad enough to boost production sufficiently to meet the food needs of the region. The agricultural future seemed hindered by national self-interest, the high cost of fertilizers, government bureaucracy, and cultural and religious beliefs, as well as the vagaries of weather and insufficient arable land, any one of which blocked the increase of food production. Southeast Asians could not do anything about bad weather, particularly in the form of monsoons and drought, but they agreed that the solution to food shortages in the region resided with more rice production. In the Philippines, people remained hopeful that other varieties, particularly IR-26, which reportedly increased yields by an average of 33 percent per acre and resisted insects and plant diseases, would solve their production problems from using the original high-yielding but disease-prone IR-8. Although scientists no longer spoke about "miracle rice," Arturo Tanco Jr., secretary of agriculture for the Philippines, reflected, "IR-8 was an agricultural Model T. IR-26 is by comparison a Lincoln." This new high-yielding variety also equaled traditional varieties in taste and cooking quality.[36]

At the same time, increased production in the Philippines could only come with technological improvements because farmers cultivated all arable land. No new lands remained for clearing and planting. In contrast, Indonesia had considerable lands remaining for agricultural development with only thirty million of three hundred million arable acres cultivated. Moreover, increased oil production gave Indonesia the potential to buy or manufacture fertilizers that small-scale farmers could afford. Yet, while Indonesia had the potential to expand rice production by using Green Revolution technology along with the opening of new agricultural lands, culture and religion became a major roadblock. Most subsistence farmers still used a small knife called an "ani-ani" to harvest their rice crop. One contemporary observed that "they believe rice should be treated gently and say the rice sickle angers the rice god." Only education could overcome superstitions that stifled agricultural change. Moreover, with continued rapid population growth, averaging 3 percent annually in the Philippines alone, Green Revolution technology could at best only provide minimal food security. Still, by the mid-1970s, Filipino farmers planted more than half of the nation's 3.4 million acres with high-yielding varieties, more than any other nation in Southeast Asia. The Ford Foundation, which dedicated $50 million annually, or one-fourth of its budget, to assisting developing nations, declared that "extraordinary progress" had been achieved in agricultural production and population control and noted that the Green Revolution had "radically changed the outlook" for preventing famine.[37]

~

Change came slowly but by 1980 Malaysia and Indonesia neared self-sufficiency in grain production, and the Philippines had become a rice exporter. HYVs could triple production, but most farmers did not own nor could they develop irrigated rice paddies and use heavy applications of fertilizer to produce large rice harvests. Most Southeast Asian farmers did not plant high-yield varieties because they often proved unsuitable for local environments, which often had too much or too little water or the soil was too salty, acidic, or sandy. Poor farmers planted traditional varieties and hoped for the best. At the same time, where farmers adopted Green Revolution farming technolo-

gies, such as in Lampung, Indonesia, land prices increased and made purchase and rental more difficult for poor farmers. These farmers responded by
conducting rice bartering and trade economies that improved their income
and standard of living.[38]

Still, more food is better than less food not only because it prevents hunger and want, even famine, but because it also has a multiplier effect on the
economy. In the Philippines, for example, increased rice production created
more agricultural employment and contributed to the development of local
economies. While providing for the food needs of subsistence farmers and
the poor, surplus rice production meant that extra rice became a cash crop.
Farmers became consumers and their standard of living improved. By the
early 1980s, the Green Revolution also had expanded agricultural employment rather than drive farm workers from the fields.[39]

In this sense, the Green Revolution produced more winners than losers,
although the plant scientists and social scientists still could not accept the
arguments of the other regarding scientific success or social failure. By the
mid-1980s, some optimists hoped that the efforts to develop a rainfed rice
(that is, a variety that did not require irrigation and proved drought resistant)
would create a new frontier for rice breeders. Still, regional variations prevailed. Japanese farmers, for example, planted 98 percent of their rice crop
in irrigated paddies while 80 percent of the farmers relied on irrigation in
South Korea and Taiwan. There, rice farmers produced an average of five to
six metric tons per hectare compared to nonirrigated acres that produced one
to two metric tons per hectare. With this disparity, plant scientists now focused on developing high-yield varieties of rainfed rice knowing that a systematic approach would take years to achieve success. One plant scientist remarked that "there are no real miracles in agricultural development. It is a
long, hard, step-by-step road."[40]

Between 1982 and 1986, the Green Revolution brought Southeast Asia from
the brink of serious food deficiency. Surpluses filled once empty storage facilities. During that time, agricultural scientists generally rejected the solutions of the social scientists who argued for less productivity through sustainable agriculture to protect the environment rather than feed the population.
Instead, they championed their successes contending that fast-maturing rice
varieties permitted double and triple cropping in many areas. In Thailand,
alone, rice production increased 300 percent between 1974 and 1985. Still,
intensive efforts to breed new high-yielding and pest- and drought-resistant
rice varieties increasingly depleted the germplasm available and many varie-

ties dropped from existence because farmers preferred to plant only a few elite varieties. Most farmers did not care about this danger. Near the end of the twentieth century, farmers planted high-yielding varieties on more than 60 percent of the rice area from which they harvested approximately 80 percent of the total rice production in Southeast Asia.[41]

Indonesia provides another example of a Southeast Asia nation that became self-sufficient in rice. Farmers prospered from government price supports intended to encourage their adoption of Green Revolution technology. In addition, the government heavily subsidized fertilizer prices by 50 percent or more, and it sponsored research to develop disease-resistant and better-tasting varieties. By 1985, however, surplus rice spoiled in warehouses and prices declined. Production costs, however, remained high for the government because of its fertilizer, pesticide, and rice subsidies while the quality of the Green Revolution varieties remained low. Corruption hindered the food distribution process. Some observers feared that Indonesian farmers would revert to traditional methods and forgo the new world of agricultural science and technology in part because they preferred to use cheap, government-subsidized fertilizer on higher-valued cash crops rather than rice. Overall, however, Indonesian farmers expanded Green Revolution production by using cheap, inorganic fertilizer.[42]

In 1986, the government banned the use of chemical pesticides on rice and raised the price of domestic pesticides by 500 percent. By 1990, it had banned fifty-seven pesticides and removed price subsidies. The government now encouraged farmers to rely on insects to destroy other insects, such as the brown planthopper, and to practice cultural control methods, called "integrated pest management techniques," which in this case meant removing the stem borer eggs by hand from the seedlings during transplanting. Thereafter, Indonesian agricultural scientists shifted their research emphasis from developing chemical technology to "ecological technology." This new form of the Green Revolution also increased the labor needs of farmers and thereby stimulated employment. Many Indonesian farmers, however, obtained chemical pesticides surreptitiously but cultural control practices expanded.[43]

❧

By the early 1990s, rice production had nearly doubled in Southeast Asia since the introduction of IR-8 with many farmers raising IR-64 by the early twenty-first century. They considered IR-64 better tasting and more nutritious, and they could plant two crops per year. The Green Revolution in the Philippines, however, had not kept pace with human food needs. Although the Philippines had been a leader in Southeast Asia's Green Revolution, rice production had declined from an annual growth rate of 5 percent to 2 percent by 1990. During the Green Revolution years of the Marcos regime, rice production, supported by government irrigation infrastructure, grew 3.8 percent annually. After 1983, government investment in irrigation declined and the Philippines became complacent as a producer of rice surpluses. Political turmoil diverted government attention and money from agricultural research and improvement. By the early 1990s, the Philippines had reached its limit for the development of lowland irrigated rice lands, and efforts to expand it into rainfed areas resulted in deforestation and soil erosion. The rice harvests did not meet demand, and the government covered the nation's food deficit with 240,000 tons of rice imported from Thailand, Vietnam, and the United States. By 1995, uncontrolled population growth of 2.5 percent annually translated into 1.5 million more people to feed each year. Industrial and urban housing projects continued to remove cropland from rice production. As rice production declined, reserves became "razor-thin." Many farmers also preferred to produce fruits and vegetables that brought higher prices than rice on the export market and to raise maize and grain sorghum for livestock feed. Many other farmers still did not have the technology or money to invest in Green Revolution agriculture. The country seemed adrift and the Green Revolution in the distant past.[44]

During the 1990s, however, agricultural scientists continued to reject the solutions of the social scientists who argued for less productivity through sustainable agriculture, preferring to save the environment rather than feed people, or so the agricultural scientists argued. In reality, Southeast Asia and other food-deficit regions needed both a more productive and environmentally sustainable agriculture to fend off the growing population problem plus rural and urban economic development to enable the poor to earn money to purchase food. With farmers cultivating most of the arable land in Southeast Asia, they could not increase food production by planting more acres. Instead, agricultural scientists championed their fast-maturing rice varieties that permitted double and triple cropping where traditional varieties enabled only one-crop annually. By the early 1990s, traditional varieties of multiple rice crops covered more than twenty-eight million harvested hectares in China, India, Indonesia, Vietnam, Bangladesh, Thailand, Philippines, Myanmar, Malaysia, and Sri Lanka, while double-cropped HYV rice and wheat covered an additional twenty-two million hectares in India, China, Pakistan, Bangladesh, and Nepal. Only science could further increase food production.[45]

Figure 13. Rice terraces near Tikhedhunga, Nepal
Small-scale farmers in isolated areas could participate in the Green Revolution because the costs theoretically were scale neutral; that is, they could purchase at least some improved seeds and fertilizer to increase production no matter the size of their farms. In Nepal, rice farmers near Tikhedhunga built these terraces on a steep mountainside. Vanessa Alberto, photographer.

Yet problems remained. In early 1990, the rice farmers in central Thailand planted a new HYV called Suphan-60. Disappointment soon followed when the brown planthopper destroyed the crop. Typhoons, flooding, and drought in other provinces made matters worse. The rice harvest from December to February yielded 11 percent less grain than the year before for a sixteen million ton loss. Farmers constituted two-thirds of the labor force, and they had hoped that multi-cropping with Suphan-60 would save them. Heavy applications of pesticides, however, seemed to kill everything in the fields except brown planthoppers. Multi-rice crops merely provided more food for these insects. Clearly, the Green Revolution could not solve all agricultural problems.[46]

A decade later, some observers reflected on the "sorry state" of Thai agriculture, which provided only about 12 percent of its gross national production, although it provided employment for about 54 percent of the population. Thai farmers and workers, however, pursued traditional rice farming practices that ensured food security. Poor, small-scale farmers who invested in the Green Revolution technologies often fell deeply into debt. The government also failed to provide adequate subsidized prices at the farm gate primarily because it sought rapid industrialization rather than a great investment in Green Revolution agriculture for all farmers. Most small-scale farmers believed that the Green Revolution had not improved their economic condition, and they preferred to raise their traditional, aromatic jasmine rice. Even so, Green Revolution varieties made Thailand the world's largest exporter of rice and low prices helped alleviate poverty and hunger, but small-scale rice farmers needed higher prices to compete with the large-scale producers.[47]

~

While no minister of agriculture in Southeast Asia spoke against sustainable agriculture by the twenty-first century, fertilizer companies did not support legume-based, sustainable, or organic farming that did not include cultivation with heavy applications of chemical fertilizers. Chemicals, the companies contended, helped increase food production in a world with a rapidly increasing population, particularly in food-deficit countries. Social scientists could not easily counter the economic and political arguments of the chemical companies by merely advocating the adoption of agricultural practices that would preserve the ecosystem. The Green Revolution had proven, however, that environmental damage from the application of too much fertilizer, pesticides, and herbicides polluted the soil and water and endangered human health for farmers and consumers. Environmental damage was not economically, socially, or politically neutral.[48]

By the twenty-first century, social scientists still could not agree whether increased income from Green Revolution technologies helped small-scale farmers and agricultural workers. Some contended that farmers with access to irrigation, credit, and fertilizer subsidies profited while dry land farmers did not have these advantages. While the Green Revolution increased the demand of agricultural labor for planting, harvesting, and threshing during its first phase, the greater adoption of high-yielding varieties during its second phase in the 1980s encouraged large-scale farmers to purchase labor-saving equipment, such as tractors, power tillers, and threshing machines, and thereby decreased the need for agricultural labor. Critics argued that in many regions, share tenants could not afford mechanical technology and without access to markets, improved production with high-yielding varieties served no purpose after they met the food needs of their families.[49]

At the same time, the evidence indicated that the Green Revolution had increased crop yields, intensified cultivation, and contributed to higher household farm income. In the Philippines, for example, unskilled agricultural workers enjoyed higher wages due to increased rice production. The migration of many workers to urban areas for employment also contributed to a scarcity of agricultural labor and higher agricultural wages. Without the evolution of plant breeding, which produced the second generation of high-yielding varieties that proved pest- and disease-resistant (especially IR-36 released in 1976 and which most farmers in central Philippines had adopted by 1982), however, the Green Revolution would not have been sustainable. Moreover, second-generation varieties increased production by as much as four tons per hectare between 1966 and 1986, productivity that traditional varieties could not achieve.[50]

By 2000, despite the achievements of the Green Revolution, scientists gave increasing attention to "sustainable" agriculture, by which they meant reliance on improved grain varieties that did not require great expenditures for fertilizers, herbicides, and pesticides. With an estimated 830 million people worldwide lacking sufficient nourishment, 31 percent, or 254 million, of whom resided in Southeast and South Asia, food security remained a problem. Green Revolution critics argued that sustainable agricultural practices rather than Green Revolution technologies would not only increase food production but also contribute to the development of local markets, thereby improving neighborhood economies. They advocated banning many pesticides, improving agricultural education and tillage techniques, and developing rainfed rice varieties. Hybrid varieties still proved subject to insects and plant diseases. Many farmers responded with heavier applications of pesticides, herbicides, and fertilizers, which increased operating costs, created health risks for farmers and consumers, and damaged the environment. Even so, Southeast Asia did not confront famine because the Green Revolution had increased rice production sufficiently, at least temporarily, to mitigate against it. Still, hunger remained nourished by political conflict, poorly administered and distributed grain supplies, and the lack of purchasing power of the poor to buy food.[51]

Green Revolution success fostered other problems and unintended consequences. Surplus rice production in many Southeast Asian nations caused declining interest in and support for the IRRI. Officials in many governments, philanthropic institutions, and nongovernment agencies now assumed that the Green Revolution had solved the major food shortage problems in many of the region's food-deficit nations. As a result, government support, foundation grants, and assistance from institutions, such as the Asian Development Bank, an affiliate of the World Bank, went elsewhere for other causes. Moreover, continued environmental degradation and threats to public health did not seem worth the goal of food self-sufficiency if governments could acquire cheap food imports. As a result, agricultural scientists had difficulty developing new crop varieties resistant to insects, saline water, and high temperatures for profitable distribution beyond the laboratory.[52]

By the turn of the twenty-first century, the Green Revolution had benefited many people in Southeast Asia, but not everyone. Food shortages still occurred. Few nations had become self-sufficient although many had achieved food security with acceptable increases in rice production and grain imports. The Green Revolution had done little for the poorest people who lived on the margins of society. Those with access to good land, cheap labor, and abundant capital or credit fared the best. Many observers, however, believed that food deficits could be resolved with conventional crop-breeding practices for the development of new HYVs, molecular biology, and genetic engineering, particularly to help farmers in rainfed areas.[53]

Given the differences between the agricultural scientists and the social scientists over the purpose and results of the Green Revolution in Southeast Asia, however, all agreed that without major population control its benefits would not keep pace with the food needs of an expanding population. At best, the Green Revolution had merely kept hunger from many homes; it had not eliminated the possibility of severe food shortages based on population increases in the future. By the twenty-first century, food security for both poor farm families and urban populations in Southeast Asia's developing nations remained problematic and fraught with difficulties and uncertainty.[54]

The Green Revolution in Thailand, for example, had faded. Despite rice production increases, improvements in plant breeding, and refinements in the use of chemical fertilizers and pesticides during the 1960s and 1970s, agricultural production had plateaued. Even though Thailand produced the most rice for export in the world, and enjoyed a surplus of 27 million tons per year, farmers produced only 2.7 tons per hectare. Rice breeding to improve varieties had not kept pace with need, and the government agencies responsible for the supply of rice seed could meet only about 10 percent of the demand. Despite government purchases to support rice prices, many farmers did not believe the cost of Green Revolution technologies merited the returns. Indonesia also lacked an agricultural extension system and the government lost interest in supporting agriculture as a national priority in favor of industry, which often did not have any relationship with agriculture. By 2009, the government had achieved some agricultural reform but the results lay in the future. Many agricultural policy makers and scientists also looked to biotechnology and genetically modified organisms (GMOs) to "power" a new or "second Green Revolution."[55]

By the second decade of the twenty-first century, the Green Revolution of the 1960s and 1970s had levelled off and even declined in many areas of Southeast Asia. In the Philippines population growth caught up with rice production, which remained at 1980s levels. Both agricultural and social scientists as well as farmers sought, advocated, and hoped for a second or perhaps third Green Revolution that would be nature friendly and sustainable. To achieve that goal, scientists at the IRRI worked to develop biological controls for insect infestations and to reduce the use of chemical fertilizers as much as possible to protect the soil from depletion and water from contamination. They also worked to develop rice varieties that could produce large yields with less water, particularly on rainfed rather than irrigated lands. Food specialists hoped for a new "super rice" from the laboratories of the IRRI. Higher government price supports to encourage greater rice cultivation by planting more hectares would no longer meet the food needs of food-deficit nations because farmers already cultivated nearly all of the arable land areas.[56]

By 2014, despite criticism that the Green Revolution privileged large-scale farmers, contributed to environmental degradation, encouraged the technological replacement of farm workers, caused soil salinization, and forced small-scale farmers, tenants, and sharecroppers from the land, the IRRI held that climate change posed the greatest threat to agriculture, not Green Revolution science and technology. With temperatures at the IRRI having risen two to four degrees centigrade in forty years, rice yields dropped below 1982 levels. IRRI scientists believed they had to adapt farming with modern varieties to climate change to achieve another Green Revolution. High-tech solutions, however, threatened to perpetuate the inability of poor, small-scale and subsistence farmers to participate in a new agricultural revolution. New varieties to deal with the vagaries of climate change involved breeding rice varieties that could resist drought, floods, salt water, pests, and diseases, and these varieties proved expensive. By 2015, this work had only begun.[57]

Social scientists also continued to argue that food security involved more than surplus production for a market economy. It required access to food. Indonesia proved a case in point where most of the nation's food-insecure people lived in villages. They needed access to productive land, Green Revolution technologies modified to protect the environment, credit, extension services, farm work opportunities, and market reform to permit rice surpluses to reach the urban poor at affordable prices. To help deal with these problems,

Indonesia included the right to food security, self-sufficiency, and sovereignty in new legislation. Whether these modest, even cosmetic, efforts in the absence of science and social reform would improve agriculture and food security remained unknown because the right to adequate food in the absence of political commitments to ensure it had the potential of making such legislation merely a gesture.[58]

Certainly, the Green Revolution based on hybrid rice varieties as well as the expanded use of irrigation, chemical fertilizers, pesticides, and herbicides brought dramatic improvements in food production and income to developing nations in Southeast Asia. The Green Revolution, however, also caused a major debate over its influence on the poor, with some critics claiming that it had caused greater inequality between wealthy and subsistence farmers, forced people from the land, and spawned extensive rural poverty as well as damaged the environment and upset traditional agricultural systems, perhaps for all time. Green Revolution critics had made these same arguments regarding India.[59]

In retrospect, by the early twenty-first century the Green Revolution in Southeast Asia consisted of three phases. From 1960 to 1969, agricultural scientists at the IRRI developed high-yielding varieties that substantially increased rice production and helped alleviate hunger among poor farmers and rural and urban dwellers in food-deficit, developing nations. From 1970 to 2000, agricultural scientists developed disease- and insect-resistant rice varieties that matured quickly, thereby permitting multiple crops. After 2000, scientists worked to develop genetically modified rice varieties, thereby giving a new scientific dimension to Green Revolution technologies. Farmers, however, still produced more than 75 percent of the region's rice on irrigated lands using Green Revolution technology because crop improvement for dryland or rainfed rice farming proved difficult.[60]

The Green Revolution in Southeast Asia was a combination, even a "package," of agricultural science and technology and government policies. It also was family-farm oriented—that is, intended to improve agriculture for small-scale farmers. As in South Asia, the success of the Green Revolution also depended on state assistance in the form of subsidized fertilizer, rice price supports to ensure profits, government purchases of grain, marketing assistance, credit, and infrastructures, such as roads, irrigation, drainage, and agricultural extension to educate farmers about the use of new agricultural technology and techniques. Moreover, the Green Revolution in Southeast Asia as on the South Asian subcontinent became a market-oriented as well as a state-driven, political process that utilized agricultural science in an attempt to feed people who needed more food. In many countries, the Green Revolution eventually enabled surplus production and exports far beyond the needs of self-sufficiency, but it produced unintended economic and social consequences. The gains from the Green Revolution did not affect all people equally. Any determination of whether Green Revolution agriculture and social justice were compatible or mutually exclusive depended on one's interpretation of economics, government policy, and science, as well as ideology.[61]

4

China

Hunger and famine have not been strangers to China over the centuries. Despite its long agricultural history, farmers often could not meet the food needs of the population. China's land area deceives the eye and expectations, and it offered seemingly limitless possibilities for agricultural production through the ages. By the early 1960s, however, the government considered only 15 percent or 107 million hectares, arable (that is, suitable for cultivation). Within this limited area, farmers primarily cultivated the plains and river deltas, particularly along the Yellow River in the north and northwest, in eastern and central China along the Yangtze River, and in the south along the Pearl River. In the northeast, the Manchurian plain served as a major agricultural area.[1]

As late as the 1940s, many Chinese families did not have sufficient rice to meet daily needs to prevent hunger. They did not eat rice regularly; instead they consumed sweet potatoes and taro. Although people who lived on fertile lands suitable for rice cultivation suffered less food insecurity, the poorest farmers who lived in hilly areas unsuitable for rice production often suffered hunger and want. The assumption of power by the Communist Party in 1949, however, gave agriculture a new direction. The revolution enabled China not only to pursue agricultural development based on traditional crop production but also to acquire, use, and develop modern science and technology to provide sufficient food reserves to prevent starvation and hunger. Government officials believed that science could not be separated from politics or the modernization of agriculture from revolution. Agricultural reform in China had many setbacks, but the socialist system adjusted to new developments in agricultural science and technology as well as the necessity for land and social and economic reform to enhance agricultural production to ensure food security.[2]

Chinese agricultural scientists had a long tradition of crop-breeding practices to develop high-yielding hybrid rice varieties. In 1919, soon after their founding, the Nanjing Higher Agricultural School and the Guangzhou Agricultural Specialized School supported research to improve rice breeding, but the process proved slow, and it suffered interruptions by worldwide economic depression and later civil war. In 1949, after the founding of the People's Republic of China, the government embarked on an agricultural program to eradicate hunger and starvation across the new nation. By advocating self-reliance and the Soviet model of industrialization, the government renewed rice-breeding research to help solve the problem of chronic food shortages.[3]

In 1949, the newly created People's Republic of China confronted a host of agricultural problems that required government attention. Agricultural production had decreased, inflation skyrocketed, and the food distribution system required organization. Quickly, the government established an agricultural policy that instituted land reform, established a more equitable tax, and reduced rents. It did so with the Agrarian Reform Law of 1950, which created a multi-faceted agricultural policy that ended private landownership and transferred land from local elites to the poor farmers (that is, the peasants). Government policy permitted successful farmers who cultivated half a hectare to keep their lands, because they contributed approximately 80 percent of the agricultural commodities marketed by village households, and these households comprised more than 20 percent of the households in a village. Absentee landlords, however, relinquished claims to village lands. These reforms substantially helped expand grain production during the 1950s.[4]

By late 1952, the government had completed land redistribution. Chinese agricultural policy now permitted several households to share labor during peak periods, such as planting and harvest time, and pool land. The government rewarded the eight to fifteen households that pooled their labor according to the resources that each contributed to the cooperative effort. Officials intended this policy to transfer Chinese agriculture slowly from family (that is, private) to collective farming. At the same time, 60 percent of the agricultural households farmed independently (that is, privately), not cooperatively. The other farmers worked on seasonal mutual aid teams.[5]

By the mid-1950s, however, agricultural officials debated the "peasant question," particularly regarding whether the peasants should emphasize private agriculture, or whether the government should speed the process of cooperative farming. In 1955, Mao Zedong ended this debate by rejecting gradualism and requiring all private farmers to relinquish their land. Thereafter, the government would reward farmers according to the work cooperatively performed. During the First Five Year Plan (1953–1957), Mao mandated that farmers sell their agricultural products, particularly grain, at low, arbitrary prices to the state. Cheap agricultural commodities would furnish resources to and create rural employment for light industries, such as flour milling, rice polishing, and shoe factories, while keeping urban food prices low. This policy privileged industrial development and kept surplus rural labor in the countryside. In 1955, agricultural policy now mandated grain procurement and household allocations each spring. By 1956, the government had almost completely socialized agriculture with the organization of Agricultural Production Cooperatives that superseded the Mutual Aid Teams established during the early 1950s. The government also created supply and marketing cooperatives, but it restricted private action and essentially mandated participation by farmers in its agricultural program. This policy proved successful. Farmers now saw an opportunity to improve their income and standard of living, and the more prosperous small-scale farmers did not suffer as in the Soviet system. Grain production increased substantially before declining precipitously, due in part to mismanagement during the years of the Great Leap Forward (1958–1961). The government eliminated private ownership of land, livestock, and tools. This agricultural reform policy was the most significant since the seventh century during the early T'ang period when the government seized all lands and approved agricultural plots based on need.[6]

By the late 1950s, the government had organized approximately 95 percent of China's farmers into village Agricultural Production Cooperatives. For government officials, these cooperatives seemed the best way to increase agricultural production within a socialist system. Peasant dissatisfaction about the closure of private markets and crop shortages, however, encouraged the government to provide a compromise solution for agricultural organization and production. Between 1958 and 1962, it created a new agricultural organizational unit called the People's Commune, which existed as a district in the county, comparable to a township or market town in the United States. Villages were renamed "production brigades" with teams of twenty to sixty households assigned to work the land. Each brigade and commune had production goals or targets. By 1959, the government had organized 99 percent of all households into communes. Private marketing ended and the commune confiscated individually owned land and distributed net earnings on a per capita basis rather than according to one's labor contribution.[7]

The establishment of people's communes under the policies of the Great Leap Forward, however, did not alter traditional, small-scale rice production. Government efforts to apply the Soviet farming model with large-scale mechanization also did not improve rice cultivation. Both land reform and the introduction of machinery then failed to stimulate grain production, but the population continued to increase rapidly, placing more demands on the government and farmers for food. Farmers could not increase the grain supplies by merely farming their plots more intensively. They needed government assistance for the development of irrigation, supply of fertilizer, and the development and distribution of better rice varieties.[8]

During the 1950s, while China's population grew and with it the demand for food, the rice-breeding traditions of the past began to give way to government-sponsored research. Although Chinese scientists primarily worked to improve local varieties, during mid-decade they began breeding a dwarf rice based on a Taiwan variety known as Taichung Native 1, and in 1957 produced a semi-dwarf rice variety. These rice-breeding efforts continued during the turbulent political and economic time known as the "Great Leap Forward," but which by 1960 had failed to produce major economic and agricultural improvement. Disagreement with the Soviet Union over the proper course of industrialization led Moscow to withdraw its economic and technical assistance, and bad weather and crop failure brought famine, particularly in Henan Province.[9]

The Great Leap Forward, however, included the establishment of agricultural extension services to provide scientific advice to the "production brigades." This commitment to government-sponsored agricultural research to develop high-yielding dwarf rice varieties along with land, labor, and production reforms marked the beginning of the Green Revolution in China. With these efforts to improve agriculture by dismissing traditional practices, except for political and public relations purposes to satisfy peasant farmers, by centralizing planning, and by providing local supervision, Mao sought to "conquer heaven," by which he meant to "conquer nature" with science and technology in the form of mechanization and chemicals.[10]

During the 1950s, agricultural scientists also made a concerted effort to select and disseminate the most productive local grain varieties. By 1959, farmers had planted 80 percent of China's farmland with improved varieties, an increase from 6.2 percent in 1952. Local farmers played a major role in the selection and dissemination of these seeds from superior local and imported varieties. The agricultural cooperatives in the communes allocated land for raising seed crops. This local and often traditional, even populist approach to the development of improved seed varieties soon gave way to scientific research. Many of the better varieties, however, traced to pre-1949 developments and Japanese and Korean imports. Wheat varieties from the United States, Italy,

Chile, and Mexico also contributed to the breeding program. The importation of foreign varieties declined during the 1960s, and Chinese scientists worked to breed new high-yielding varieties (HYVs) for local adoption. At the same time, Mao sought greater mechanization. He particularly wanted more tractors that would permit the cultivation of larger fields. He believed that both would help the transition from family to communal farms. Traditional crop varieties along with modern mechanization and agricultural science would provide a three-prong approach to improving Chinese agriculture.[11]

Even so, the government's exceptionally large grain procurement during 1959–1960 severely diminished seed grain stocks. During the 1960–1961 crop season, bad weather further depleted the grain reserve. Poorly engineered irrigation projects also caused salinization of fields. As a result, grain production declined from 200 million metric tons in 1958 to 170 million metric tons in 1959 for a 15 percent loss and dropped to 144 million metric tons in 1960. As grain yields plummeted, the government maintained high procurement rates without an equitable redistribution program for the public. Consequently, farmers had less seed grain, and Green Revolution technology could not make up the loss.[12]

Planning miscalculations, false reporting about the grain harvest of 1958, lack of incentives for farmers to work in the communes, insufficient agricultural extension, and government privileging of industry over agriculture during the Great Leap Forward along with bad weather contributed to serious agricultural production declines that resulted in the Great Leap famine (1959–1961). Grain production dropped approximately 30 percent and an estimated thirty million died from malnutrition and starvation. As a result, Chinese agricultural policy underwent a major change. It restored small-scale free markets, subsidized production, and allocated private plots up to 5 percent of a commune's cultivated land as a matter of necessity. These were the first private land allocations since the commune system began in the autumn of 1958. Farmers could use these plots to raise pigs, chickens, and ducks as well as crops on their own initiative. The collective, however, still owned the land and the government required farmers to meet procurement quotas, but they were otherwise free to make their own production decisions on these small plots. The government also reduced the grain tax and increased crop prices for quota procurements, and it began providing more resources, especially chemical fertilizer, to the communes to help stabilize and increase production. Research institutes, county research stations, and communes tested and purchased new seed varieties for communal farming on team agricultural plots.[13]

By 1962, a three-tier agricultural organizational system of the production team, village brigade, and commune planned, managed, and conducted all phases of Chinese agriculture. Production increased and the government helped agricultural families develop cooperative exchanges to build irrigation systems, but the population increased and kept agricultural expansion gradual and labor intensive because farmers cultivated less land per capita and planted traditional grain varieties, including rice that often did not produce great yields.[14]

During the early 1960s, as grain production fell below the level required for survival, the government responded by distributing grain from its reserves, ordering rationing, and importing food grains. This grain shortage, however, clearly indicated the need for major agricultural reform to ensure food security and affirm that agriculture remained the foundation of China's economy. Mao believed that agricultural and industrial development could occur simultaneously and that improved agricultural production would provide raw materials for industry and a market. Earlier, in 1957, Mao emphasized the symbiotic relationship between agriculture in industry when he wrote, "Without agriculture there can be no light industry. But it is not so clearly understood that agriculture provides industry with an important market." Mao did not see the competition between those who advocated agriculture and industrial development as a zero-sum game. Rather, he observed that the "technological improvement and modernization of agriculture calls for more and more machinery, fertilizers, water conservancy and electric power projects, and transport facilities for the farms, as well as fuel and building materials for rural consumers."[15]

In September 1962, China took a major step to expand agricultural research that contributed to the beginning of its own Green Revolution. It would have transnational contacts, and it would develop along a timeline similar to other nations. It also had political support in varying degrees across the political spectrum, even during the Cultural Revolution. At that time, the Tenth Plenary Session of the Eight Central Committee of the Chinese Communist Party decided to make agricultural development a policy priority and to commit to a major technical transformation for agriculture. This decision was important because until now governmental agricultural policy had emphasized social transformations, particularly the change from private landownership before the revolution to collective ownership under Mao. Thereafter, the government emphasized the "technical transformation" of agriculture. In 1965, for example, the State Science and Technology Commission intervened and demanded the continuation of agricultural research, particularly for the development of hybrid rice varieties. Extension stations and demonstration farms increased, and employees had better agricultural training.[16]

Although the government reaffirmed its commitment to collective farms, it made the production teams on these farms the accounting unit to eliminate the most inefficient features of the incentive system established during the 1950s. Improved agricultural mechanization seemingly would help consolidate the collective farms and eliminate small-scale producer approaches to agricultural improvement. At the same time, economists and agricultural scientists advocated the greater use of agricultural chemicals (that is, fertilizers and pesticides) along with improved seed varieties. Individual farmers could make these technical adoptions as well as collective farms. Although the Cultural Revolution (1966–1976) divided policy makers over the importance of mechanization, those differences involved speed and not commitment to the improvement of agriculture. The Cultural Revolution temporally slowed those efforts, but it did not ruin them.[17]

During the 1960s, China committed to major technological transformation in agriculture. Agricultural scientists developed and the government distributed their first fertilizer-responsive, semidwarf varieties before the Green Revolution became common agricultural parlance. Green Revolution technologies of high-yielding varieties, chemical fertilizers, irrigation, and mechanization transformed approximately 20 percent of China's farmland from traditional agricultural practices. Rice production increased due to the expansion of irrigation and greater availability of fertilizers, herbicides, and pesticides. In many respects, Maoist communes created China's Green Revolution.[18]

∽

By the 1970s, science-based agricultural research had produced a series of high-yielding rice varieties. Through the decade, farmers primarily produced to meet family needs and state procurement allocations. Contrary to traditional belief, agricultural production rose per commune worker and land unit. The communes supported the Green Revolution by providing the technological, educational, and managerial resources for major agricultural improvement. At the same time, rice production increased because of Deng Xiaoping's policy to let farmers retain more of their produce for sale as well as from the development of new rice strains by Chinese agricultural scientists. High-yielding rice varieties, however, required heavy applications of fertilizers, herbicides, and pesticides as well as irrigation systems, the latter often beyond the affordability of small-scale farmers. Consumers and farmers also began to question the safety of these chemicals when they consumed HYV rice and their effects on the environment. Increased grain production also depended on traditional techniques rather than crop-breeding methods of the Green Revolution, such as using natural (animal and human) excrement for an estimated 60 percent of their fertilizer needs rather than chemical fertilizers. Greater productivity, however, also stemmed from intensive farming practices and traditional methods.[19]

China now had an approximate population of 850 to 900 million with about 80–85 percent of the people engaged in some form of agriculture, or roughly 680 to 765 million people. By this time, however, Green Revolution agricultural technology had made a considerable improvement in China's agriculture and food production. In 1971, for example, China produced approximately 250 metric tons of food grain, more than a 65 million metric ton increase since 1957. This production became a baseline for future comparisons, at least for a decade, and it enabled the government to proclaim that China had achieved agricultural self-sufficiency. Green Revolution agricultural technology made this achievement of food security possible.[20]

Bolstered by these production achievements, China continued to improve high-yielding rice and wheat varieties. By 1974, in the south, HYVs grew on 6.7 million hectares, or approximately 20 percent of the rice land in southern China. There, farmers primarily raised dwarf strains of indica rice that scientists had begun breeding as early as 1956 and which farmers put into commercial production during the 1960s. These high-yielding dwarf varieties enabled multiple cropping because they matured quickly, and with heavy applications of fertilizer, triple cropping proved possible, usually by planting two rice crops and one of wheat or barley. Chinese scientists also drew upon IR-8, the dwarf rice variety released by the International Rice Institute in the Philippines in 1966 and introduced to China the next year for breeding purposes. From the late 1960s to the mid-1970s, China also imported semidwarf wheat from Mexico and Pakistan. Chinese crop-breeding programs used those varieties to develop new strains that produced heavy heads on dwarf, drought-resistant plants.[21]

In the North, high-yielding japonica dwarfs also increased the cultivated area, although the precise hectares remain uncertain. By the early 1970s, agricultural scientists also had developed dwarf HYV winter wheat varieties based on a decade of research. Hardly isolated from the West, they also drew upon spring wheat varieties developed at the International Maize and Wheat Improvement Center in Mexico. In 1973, China bought 5,000 tons of HYV wheat from Mexico and imported another 15,000 tons a year later. These varieties expanded breeding research and enabled wheat production to expand southward, particularly with quick-maturing spring wheat varieties that farmers planted after the rice harvest. Research also continued using US hybrids to develop HYV maize varieties that could grow in the colder northeast.[22]

In addition to the development of new HYV grain varieties, by the early 1970s one-third of all cropland farmers irrigated some thirty-three million hectares due to the construction of more catchment basins, diversion canals, and wells. Estimates vary but by 1965, the government perhaps added another five million hectares to China's irrigated lands. In addition, China now began a major effort to substitute chemical fertilizers for traditional organic fertilizer constituted of crop residues, vegetable and animal wastes, and human excrement. China soon became the world's largest importer of nitrogenous fertilizer, and it committed resources to build fertilizer plants that would service local areas.[23]

By the mid-1970s, the Green Revolution kept food production even with population growth, but it did not yet provide food security based on new scientific and public policy practices and reforms. Because the more successful communes were located on better lands, with the government providing them with improved access to irrigation and fertilizer, and because they could sell surplus grain, an inequality of wealth emerged among those families who produced and earned more and those who, for whatever reasons, produced less grain. The government responded not by taxing the comparatively wealthier farms to redistribute the economic gains of the Green Revolution, but rather by sending scientists and technicians to underdeveloped areas to help struggling farmers adopt Green Revolution technologies. Political revolutionaries did not necessarily consider production inequalities a problem, and the leaders of the Cultural Revolution endorsed a policy of "self-reliance," which permitted regional inequalities without efforts to redistribute agricultural income and wealth. No one anticipated an equalization of agricultural wealth generated from the Green Revolution for a long time.[24]

Still, government land reform and emphasis on agricultural science and the economy gave many peasant farmers greater access to cultivated lands from which they could earn a higher income and improve their standard of living. Compared to China's agricultural past, Green Revolution science together with land reform proved significant to help farmers meet the nation's food needs. Famine no longer remained a possibility, or a historical certainty. Most farmers supported China's agricultural policy.[25]

By the mid-1970s, the Green Revolution, though still in its early stages of development, had created an era of modern agriculture for China in which agricultural science and government policy would remain its driving force. Scientists faced the challenge to develop irrigation on arid lands in northern and western China and to breed HYV wheat for the northern region. The essential components of the Green Revolution were in place. Built on the land reforms following the revolution, a highly trained cadre of agricultural scientists who worked to produce new HYV rice and wheat varieties, local fertilizer plants that provided a needed product for the communes, and new irrigation facilities made possible with electric pumps that drew water from deep beneath the surface provided the foundation for China's Green Revolution. By 1974, farmers planted more than eighty high-yielding wheat varieties on more than 80 percent of China's wheat lands. Scientists also had bred these varieties to resist yellow rust and smut, two perennial diseases that could diminish or ruin a wheat crop.[26]

Yet problems remained. Although the land planted to HYV maize reached 1.73 million hectares with more than one hundred varieties, hybrid yields increased production only about 20 percent. Without reliable statistics, some western social scientists questioned China's claim that its grain harvests averaged about 250 million tons by the mid-1970s. Some observers, however, believed that Green Revolution technology could enable China to produce 257 million tons for a considerable improvement from 185 million tons produced in 1957 for an annual production increase of about 2 percent. Most of this increased production occurred in "high and stable yield" areas where farmers had access to Green Revolution technology, especially near urban areas such as Peking, Shanghai, and Canton as well as the Tung-t'ing Lake and Szechwan Basin areas. Improved varieties enabled the triple cropping of rice in South China, while multiple crops of rice and wheat became common in the Lower Yangtze Valley, including Hunan. Few farmers, scientists, and government officials worried about the long-term consequences of environmental pollution and exhaustion of the water supply. Moreover, by 1974 this considerable production increase proved about equal to the annual population growth so that the per capita grain production remained approximately the same as in 1957. Clearly, by the mid-1970s, Green Revolution technologies, while successfully applied in China, only kept pace with population growth. Surplus production that would provide food security over the long term had not been achieved.[27]

During the 1970s, the government continued to determine production goals for food and fiber and the prices paid by state marketing agencies. The state provided commune officials with an agricultural plan and the production brigades determined the goals. The government also distributed agricultural tools and livestock among production teams. Brigade leaders decided the fields for planting and assigned production team members' specific tasks, such as sowing, cultivating, and harvesting. After the major growing season, these farmers tended their own gardens and livestock or worked in other assigned activities, such as reclaiming land and expanding irrigation systems.[28]

Government officials recognized that although farmers accepted government agricultural policy, private gain remained an important motivation for agricultural production. Chinese farmers resented procurement and pricing policies and opposed them so strongly that the government stressed that the production teams should only increase production and income by adopting more technology through the three-tier organizational structure of the commune rather than by personal self-sacrifice. The bureaucratic structure of agricultural production, however, hindered increased productivity with Green Revolution technologies. Each brigade included production teams, which, in turn, included a number of individual households. The leader of the production teams set the reward for the productivity of each individual designated as a "work point" which determined their share of the annual income earned by the commune, less expenses including taxes, salaries, welfare fees, and a contribution to the capital investment fund. The production team paid in grain or cash for seed, fertilizer, and tools and contributed to the brigade's grain reserve. At this point, approximately 40–60 percent of the total agricultural income remained for division among team members based on their work points earned during the year.[29]

Agricultural experiment stations attached to selected production brigades introduced Green Revolution technologies to the communes. These stations trained selected farmers in the Green Revolution techniques. The government also encouraged communes and brigades to test seed varieties and develop their own fertilizers from their experiments and associational work with agricultural experts. In this case, farmers and scientists worked together to discover and develop applied agricultural improvements to increase food production and offset population growth. Agricultural scientists also provided extension services for communes that did not have local experiment stations, and they informed farmers about Green Revolution methods, much like county agents assisted farmers in the United States. By using Green Revolution technologies, farmers presumably would increase their production and earn more money. Theoretically, families also would limit births so as not to add additional members to the commune who would compete for a division of the profits. A 2 percent annual population increase by the early 1970s, meant another eighteen million people to feed. Some observers worried that the high grain yields produced with Green Revolution technology might have reached its limits. If production leveled off or stalled, even at production rates of 250 million metric tons of rice, and wheat, and other grains annually, food security might not last long for China.[30]

In contrast to free market economies, such as in India, that sometimes excluded poor farmers from adopting Green Revolution technologies because they could not afford them, the Chinese socialist system established affordable prices for the purchase of rice HYVs. It also supported the production of the required fertilizers and pesticides, provided technical assistance to farmers, and subsidized grain prices to prevent losses due to high production costs. Moreover, the commune system served as an institutional mechanism to teach new applied agricultural techniques to farmers.[31]

A limited genetic base for the development of new rice HYVs, however, posed problems that agricultural experts could not immediately solve. Many of the varieties they had developed proved susceptible to a host of insect infestations, which required higher levels of pesticide applications. Many of these chemicals did not dissipate in the soil and caused increasing environmental problems as well as health hazards for rice farmers. In time, some farmers would not eat the rice they produced because of their pesticide applications, and urban consumers questioned the safety of HYVs, thereby defeating the purpose of the Green Revolution to enable poor farmers to feed their families. Consumers also frequently complained as they had in South and Southeast Asia about their poor taste compared to traditional varieties. Equally important, HYV rice often did not produce as much as traditional varieties in some regions due to weather and soil conditions. As a result, many farmers used the new rice varieties for animal feed rather than to eat it themselves.[32]

Even so, a strong government commitment to rice-breeding research enabled Chinese farmers who used HYVs to increase rice production from 1 to 1.5 tons per hectare during the 1970s, to 2.3 tons per hectare in the 1980s, and to as much as 6.35 tons per hectare by the mid-1990s. State subsidies for

seeds, herbicides and pesticide enabled these remarkable gains in rice production. This state agricultural policy that supported research and development for new rice HYVs, however, was unique to China from the beginning
given its socialist system. By the late 1970s, Green Revolution technological
development particularly for new HYVs for rice and wheat gave Chinese agricultural scientists considerable recognition. Government officials now had
the task of developing agricultural policy that could best capitalize on sophis-
ticated crop-breeding developments.[33]

⌒

In the post-Mao period from 1978–1983 following his death in September
1976, government officials substantially changed agricultural policy. In 1978,
Deng Xiaoping terminated the commune system and introduced a new program to deemphasize collectivization and state farms and to provide farmers
greater flexibility in making their cultivating decisions. The state, however,
maintained control, but agriculture now became more "market-mediated," or
a "market-oriented communal socialism," based on Green Revolution technologies and production. It also assumed the continuation of a communal
society and a market economy directed by an authoritarian state.[34]

In 1979, Chinese leaders analyzed agriculture and concluded that farmers
lacked initiatives to increase production and that they misused the land. In a
document titled "Decisions Concerning the Rapid Development of Agriculture," leaders planned a number of major reforms, particularly implementation of greater personal responsibility for agriculture and encouragement of
diversification and specialization to increase productivity and farm income.
The planting of HYVs would be part of this plan. Officials now placed emphasis on diversification of production and decentralization of farm management. Overall, this new agricultural policy became known as the "agricultural
production responsibility system," or commonly as the "household responsibility system." Although not formally announced until 1983 when the government officially terminated the commune system, the Fourth Plenum of
the Eleventh Central Committee of the Communist Party had adopted this
reform in September 1979. Under the household responsibility system, family
farmers still paid an agricultural tax, met their mandated quota for agricultural production, and paid the fees owed to the collective. Farmers could use
agricultural production above the mandated government quota, however, as
they pleased—sold to the state at above procurement prices, sold on local markets, or consumed. Although the commune or village still controlled the land,
farmers upon assignment had the right to cultivate it for two to eight years.

In January 1984, the lease policy extended cultivation rights of fifteen years. Essentially, farmers gained the option to a permanent lease with the right to transfer it. Agricultural reformers argued that the household responsibility system was compatible with socialism because the land remained under the collective control of the state. Farmers still did not own land; they merely contracted to use it on their own terms (that is, privately). Moreover, state planning for production and procurement of grain and other farm products remained a basic feature of Chinese agricultural policy.[35]

During the 1980s, China entered the second stage of its Green Revolution. Although the state continued to coordinate agricultural production, free market forces became noticeable, because the household responsibility system transformed Mao's communal agricultural organization to a privatized, common property regime. With de-collectivization, termination of the commune, and establishment of the household responsibility policy, China returned to family-based farming. Individual remuneration now depended on production rather than work points. By the mid-1980s, more than 90 percent of rural families pursued farming based on reward for individual or family production. The farm family could raise any crop and keep all produce above the quota payment. The household then became responsible for production and distribution. Essentially, the relationship became that of the landlord-tenant system of traditional China and the share rent system of the United States. Many farmers hailed this policy as the "second land reform," referring to the distribution of land for individual (that is, private) cultivation during the early 1950s.[36]

In the mid-1980s, the government changed agricultural policy still further by ending its mandatory procurement quota (that is, the amount of crops that farmers had to sell to the government). The government would no longer serve as a monopoly for the purchase and marketing of grain and other agricultural commodities. The government announced, however, that it would purchase certain quantities of selected commodities, such as grain at contracted prices. Farmers could contract for sale to the government or sell only on private markets. At the same time, the government guaranteed the purchase of all commodities at a minimum floor price if the farmers could not find a private market. This policy reduced government expenses and provided more options for farmers, but it was fraught with difficulties because of grading and price corruption, lack of state storage space, and cost, among other problems. The government also encouraged contract grain production by providing chemical fertilizer at below market prices, tax reductions, and low interest loans to farmers who participated in the contract program.[37]

The state also relaxed price controls on many agricultural products such as meat, eggs, and vegetables, and prices rose as much as 9 percent. Essentially, these policies began the transformation of agriculture from a collective enterprise to a familial (that is, private) operation. Still, farmers worried about the return to collective principles. Officials, however, reaffirmed their commitment to the household responsibility system while assuring farmers that agricultural policy would not soon change. This agricultural policy indicated flexibility and practicality on the part of Chinese leaders. By the mid-1980s, government agricultural policy had increased production, changed cropping and land-use patterns, and boosted farming income. It also encouraged a reasonably successful union of the socialist collective system and the individual through the household responsibility system.[38]

By the mid-1980s, Green Revolution agricultural technologies and political and social reforms had gained China food security. By 1984, the household responsibility system had restored the individual farmer as the basic unit of agricultural production rather than the commune. Rural households no longer faced continual food shortages. Farmers had planted approximately 35–50 percent of the rice area in HYVs. Grain production had increased from nearly 305 million metric tons in 1978 to 407 million metric tons in 1984. Between 1979 and 1984, wheat production more than doubled, increasing from 41 million metric tons to 87 million metric tons. The Green Revolution had substantially enabled farmers to boost grain production in five years on 285 million hectares. Profitable prices for the sale of above quota grain also helped stimulate production after 1979. By essentially renting land and with income possible from market sales, farmers used Green Revolution technologies to increase production. They then met their family food needs and earned some income. Agricultural science made China's rice and wheat lands more productive per hectare than in the United States.[39]

Unintended consequences, however, began to emerge. Grain production based on Green Revolution technologies meant that the government spent more on chemical fertilizers and procurement price supports. Grain surpluses piled up and in 1985 the government responded by ending the compulsory grain procurement program. Prior to that time, free market grain prices had exceeded state procurement prices, but after bumper crops in the mid-1980s, grain prices declined. Farmers responded by raising less grain and the 1985 harvest declined by 28.2 million metric tons. In 1986, this reduction caused grain prices to increase and farmers responded by planting more grain. The government also mandated that farmers sell their surplus in free rural markets only after they had met their state procurement contract. The government enforced this dictate by closing local markets and blocking the regional grain trade to ensure deliveries to the state. In 1986, to sweeten this imposition, the government purchased 67 percent of the grain marketed and two years later raised grain prices as much as 16 percent. With only 33 percent of their grain crops to sell on the open market, farmers did not have great incentive to plant more grain.[40]

Some observers also charged that Green Revolution technologies had begun to damage the environment, particularly water pollution from excessive fertilizer applications. Farmers irrigated approximately 45 percent of China's cropland. This area used 80 percent of China's water withdrawals. Northern China farmers experienced a drawdown of the water table. Urban areas also consumed more water to serve industries and the growing population. Some agricultural and social scientists and government officials now began to use the term "sustainable" agriculture. Most farmers, however, preferred the quick and higher paying results from chemical fertilizers rather than using traditional organic fertilization of crops, such as livestock manure, night soil, and crop residues. Population pressures mandated the use of Green Revolution technologies to gain maximum production to increase the food supply.[41]

By the late 1980s, the availability of government-subsidized fertilizer intended to encourage farmers to adopt Green Revolution technologies did not meet demand, although the government distributed some 4.8 million metric tons. Unable to acquire or afford more fertilizer, many farmers reduced their grain production, which, in turn, meant that more procurement contracts went unmet. In 1989, the government responded by increasing price subsidies to a record of 25.95 billion yuan. The government also permitted greater latitude between buyer and seller to negotiate prices for grain sales after farmers had met their procurement obligation to encourage greater production. Both farmers and the government got what they wanted—increased income from larger grain crops and fulfillment of procurement contracts to ensure food security. At the same time, this agricultural policy became more expensive. By the late 1980s, the urban population reached 212 million. Food needs increased, and the number of farmers entitled to subsidized grain prices rose by 1.67 million compared to 1985. To help meet this food need, the government began paying grain prices comparable to free, local market prices, but it covered that increased expense by taxing the revenue that farmers earned from their production increases and by raising the price of chemical fertilizers. Optimists argued that if farmers produced more, they would be able to afford these increased costs and still improve their income because they would pay the tax and the government would further increase its grain reserves.[42]

Some officials, however, contended that because urbanites now had greater disposable income, they were eating less grain and more fruits, vegetables, and meat. Consequently, the government could maintain food security with reduced grain production with Green Revolution technologies. Others argued that government agricultural subsidies were necessary to keep food prices low for the poor who lived in the towns, villages, and cities. Some observers worried that as the government attempted to reduce its expenditures for agriculture, the result would mean less investment in research needed to improve and expand Green Revolution achievements to ensure food security.[43]

While these political changes occurred in Chinese agricultural policy, the government gave increased attention to fertilizer production that HYVs needed to reach maximum production as part of the Green Revolution package. Between 1978 and 1987, fertilizer applications increased 7 percent for a total application of about 1.2 million tons by the end of the period. The government suppled nitrogen fertilizer to farmer groups at reduced or subsidized prices or in exchange for grain. Large government investments to build synthetic ammonia and urea plants in the mid-1970s, plus fertilizer imports enabled large grain production from HYVs after the late 1970s.[44]

The development of electrical power stations also helped make the second phase of the Green Revolution possible by enabling the production of more chemical fertilizers, pesticides, and herbicides that were more efficient (that is, powerful). Average rice yields increased to approximately 11.2 metric tons per hectare per year. With increased rice production such as this, consumers had the security of eating rice three times per day. By 1988, however, some reports indicated that as many as two hundred million Chinese still suffered from periodic insufficient food. In that year, rice production also declined due to drought. Irrigation proved insufficient in part due to increased urban and industrial usage. Some irrigation systems also had deteriorated due to inadequate attention under the household responsibility system and loss of land to urban development.[45]

Although China increased grain production nearly 50 percent between 1976 and 1984, between 1978 and 1988 China's irrigated acreage declined by 2 percent due to overpumping from groundwater sources. No new agricultural technologies seemed poised to continue the great productivity increases of the Green Revolution. As rice production seemed to reach its limits with most arable land cultivated and with the population increasing, social scientists and government officials sought a new form of agricultural technology as well as population control.[46]

~

By 1990, China's population reached 1.2 billion. Rice production approached its limits for land area and yield. Population growth brought the old fears of hunger to the forefront, but short-term and intermediate solutions seemed impossible. The only viable solution to more people was more food, which encouraged agricultural scientists to offer biotechnology as a production safety valve. Biotechnology also could circumvent the necessity to produce expensive pesticides. Soil erosion as well as soil and water pollution from fertilizers and pesticides had become a problem. China used pesticides at twice the world average, and these chemicals polluted thirteen million hectares. Moreover, with farmers averaging only 45 percent of urban incomes, many left for employment in the cities, leaving the elderly, women, and children to till the land. Farmers now raised rice on approximately 30 percent of arable lands, and it contributed about 45 percent of the caloric intake of the nation. Biotechnology, advocates argued, could further increase food production.[47]

By the early 1990s, however, rice farmers planted HYVs, not biotech or genetically modified crops on approximately sixteen million hectares, an increase from about five million hectares during the early 1980s. HYVs contributed approximately 86 percent of the maize planted. Yet, productivity increased slowly by the mid-1990s because no new technological advancement had occurred. Some critics blamed decreases in research. With the threat of famine or even hunger no longer a problem, the government reduced its funding. More farmers, now secure with Green Revolution productivity, began producing higher-value fruits and vegetables, and total grain production declined by 6.5 percent between 1978 and 1997, although regional variations occurred. Increased production costs also encouraged farmers to raise crops other than grain now that food security no longer troubled them.[48]

Given governmental efforts to permit the commercialization of agriculture built on Green Revolution productivity, agriculture had become market driven, but it also had given China food security. The government responded by ending food rationing. At the same time, the government considered adequate grain production a matter of national security and officials wanted to maintain a self-sufficiency rate of 95 percent. Consequently, it favored continued production of Green Revolution HYVs that ensured volume rather than for farmers to produce other high-value crops drawn by the lure of profits at local markets. Chinese leaders wanted to become independent of world markets and grain imports in time of need. This policy, however, did not mean support of maximum rice production. In 1999, China had so much rice in storage that the government discouraged more cultivation.[49]

By the 1990s, the heavy use of pesticides to enhance Green Revolution production, however, had become an environmental and public health problem. Although thousands of farmers sickened or died each year because they were not sufficiently literate to read application and warning labels on pesticide containers, inadequate extension training played a role in making the fields a dangerous place for farmers. In addition, foreign investment to dump "dirty" agricultural chemicals, some banned from production in their home countries, helped China provide 2.3 million metric tons of pesticides to farmers by 1997. International conglomerates such as Ciba-Geigy, BASF, Bayer, AgrEvo, DuPont, and Zeneca eagerly sold pesticides and made plans for producing them in China, where regulations proved lax compared to western countries. Although the Ministry of Agriculture attempted to provide some control, this aspect of the Green Revolution proved increasingly deadly for Chinese farmers. Some critics wonder whether the benefits of the Green Revolution could or should be sustained given the human and environmental costs.[50]

At the same time, by the mid-1990s, HYV rice proved so productive that germplasm diversity fell because farmers preferred only a few high-yielding varieties that yielded more than 80 percent of the rice harvested. Agricultural scientists soon believed, however, that the Green Revolution package would no longer meet the needs of a growing population. They believed that only greater scientific knowledge about location-specific varieties and improved farmer use of herbicides, pesticides, and irrigation would to enable China to meet its food needs.[51]

During the mid-1990s, government officials attempted to ensure economic and social stability in the countryside by extending land contracts to thirty years and encouraging farmers to cultivate on an "optimum scale" in certain circumstances. Clearly, government officials recognized the relationship between farm income and productivity. The government also raised procurement prices to ease inflationary burdens on farmers and substantially increased its investment in agriculture. It also introduced a new policy called the "Provincial Governor Responsibility System." Provincial governors had the responsibility for grain production and supply, and grain production increased particularly for wheat and maize although decreases in rice production also prevailed. Rice production stagnated due to consumer demand for higher-quality rice rather than lower grades produced by HYVs now that an adequate rice supply ensured against food shortages. Wheat and maize production increased, however, in response to urbanites with higher incomes and who wanted more bread and meat. Yet, no major technological Green Revolution breakthrough for grain production had occurred since the late 1980s.[52]

By the late 1990s, Chinese farmers remained concerned about agricultural prices, taxes, and stability of agricultural policy. Although they did not have organized agricultural groups or associations that served as interest groups, rural deputies to the National People's Congress served as farm advocates. Supporters of Chinese agriculture also came from agricultural research institutes of the State Council and Central Committee as well as the academies and universities, and the Ministry of Agriculture, while others, such as editors and journalists, championed agricultural improvements. By the last decade of the twentieth century, party leaders also had the responsibility to help farmers achieve prosperity through the market. Agricultural policy differed considerably in principle and method from previous farm policy that promoted collectivist and egalitarian principles. By the end of the twentieth century, government officials and agricultural advocates increasingly spoke about the "legitimate rights and interests of farmers."[53]

Chinese agricultural policy, however, still required some farmers to produce a specific allocation of grain, and the government purchased more than 50 percent of that production at fixed prices. Like the United States, China still had too many farmers who could not earn a satisfactory income from the land. Indeed, by 1995, approximately 50 million more farmers worked the land than in 1978, when significant agricultural policy reform began. China's minister of agriculture believed that 33 percent of the 438 million agricultural workers were "surplus" labor whose productivity had declined. Rather than encourage them to move to the cities for other employment, the government attempted to address the income needs of farmers with administrative measures to control grain prices and reserves rather than a market economy.[54]

Put differently, between 1978 and 2001, China's cropping area increased from 1,501 to 1,557 million hectares but the area planted to cereal grains decreased from 1,205 to 1,060 million hectares. During that time, rice cultivation fell from 344.21 million hectares to 288.12 million hectares for a 16 percent decline. Wheat production dropped from 246.64 million hectares to approximately 192 million hectares by some estimates for a 15 percent decrease, but maize production increased by nearly 23 percent. Overall, however, Green Revolution technologies had increased grain production sufficiently for farmers to meet the food needs of the population and feed livestock for urban consumers who had disposable incomes to buy more meat. After 1997, the government reduced procurement prices and contract purchasing. As grain prices and government purchases declined, farmers began meeting greater demands for maize by planting as much as 90 percent of their crop in HYVs. In the main rice-producing areas farmers planted from 50 percent to 70 percent of their lands in HYVs with indica varieties predominating in the South and japonica varieties primarily planted in the north.[55]

~

By the early twenty-first century, China's Green Revolution had proved successful because politically the government had used decentralization and land reform to create an economic and social environment where nongovernment support began to replace state mandates and controls for agricultural production. China gradually loosened restrictions on trade, which encouraged western investment for the building of fertilizer plants. Grain, particularly rice, production expanded with HYVs. Fewer people went hungry and food security became a reality. The "socialist market economy" developed after the years of the Great Leap Forward and the Cultural Revolution and steamed from Deng Xiaoping's 1978 "Truth from Facts" speech that provided the basis for gradual agricultural reform beginning with the household responsibility system and ending with the termination of the commune. Decentralization of decision-making for agricultural production and the beginning of a rudimentary market economy also contributed to the success of China's Green Revolution. Nearly all farmers who planted rice, wheat, and maize seeded high-yielding varieties.[56]

These gradual economic and political reforms enabled the application of Green Revolution science to Chinese agriculture and helped ensure that the government would provide reliable encouragement and support for agriculture. In 1978, for example, the government increased procurement prices, reduced procurement quotas, and permitted collective farms more independence for managing their operations, all of which encouraged the greater adoption of Green Revolution agricultural practices. Farmers now began to receive greater rewards for individual rather than collective productivity. Food shortages declined. Green Revolution technologies enabled farmers to capitalize on land reforms, and the household responsibility system enabled better use of it.[57]

At the same time the socialist state provided greater equality in agricultural development and the adoption of Green Revolution technologies because it controlled access to land, established agricultural prices, provided a guaranteed farm market through procurement mandates, and subsidized agricultural research, fertilizer production, and the development of irrigation systems. Slowly the Green Revolution helped reduce rural poverty in China. By using the international benchmark of one dollar per day in earnings as the poverty line, China reduced rural poverty from 64 percent of the population in 1981 to 17 percent in 2001. Some of this reduction, however, can be attributed to rural, nonfarm employment, a workforce that had increased from 7 percent of the rural population in 1978 to 35 percent of the population by 1999.[58]

Green Revolution agriculture also had contributed to a reduction in soil quality and fertility due to the long-term heavy applications of fertilizer to support HYV crop production. Irrigation systems had created salinization problems on 9 percent of the land due to poorly designed and managed systems and water applications. The Green Revolution, while providing food security, particularly with rice, had contributed to major environmental pollution from the runoff and leaching of agricultural fertilizers, pesticides, and herbicides into the soil. Groundwater in some areas became contaminated, and farmers and agricultural workers exposed to these toxic chemicals suffered illness while the long-term effects remained unknown. Yet, most farmers preferred to use Green Revolution technologies to produce as much as possible to increase their earnings as well as to feed their families rather than worry about environmental degradation from Green Revolution practices. Chinese farmers had conquered nature as Mao had advocated but at an alarmingly high environmental cost.[59]

From 1980 to 2010, China's Green Revolution enabled rice farmers to increase yields by 59 percent despite the loss of arable land to industry and urbanization and increasing fertilizer costs. This production resulted from the development of HYVs suitable for three geographical and environmental areas. Scientists developed and farmers planted varieties that permitted double cropping (that is, the planting of two crops annually in the same fields) along the Yangtze River and in the south and single crop rice varieties in the southwest and north. Farmers preferred single crop rice, because double cropping required more work as well as increased costs for seed, fertilizer, and irrigation and the increase in yield from two crops did not seem worth the effort. Overall, however, between 1980 and 2010 all rice production increased from approximately four to seven tons per hectare or about 76 percent.[60]

Scientists agreed that most increases in grain production now came from crop management improvements and heavier applications of fertilizer rather than from new HYVs. In fact, fertilizer applications increased from 9.4 million tons in 1980 to 29.2 million tons thirty years later. Although nitrogen fertilizer provided the necessary nutrition for increased rice, wheat, and maize production, some critics contended that rice yields could be best improved by the development of new HYVs rather than by farmers applying more nitrogen fertilizer. Others worried that global warming would change growing cycles and reduce rice yields. Still, others argued that more irrigation and the development of new HYVs would counter global warming. In the eyes of some, it seemed that science could solve all technological problems.[61]

By 2010, China's 1.3 billion people made it the most populous nation on earth. Its Green Revolution, called the "Agricultural Miracle" in China, had stalled. Agricultural scientists and government officials, but not necessarily the public, had turned to revitalizing the Green Revolution with both science and technology in the form of genetically modified crops. With the Ministry of Science and Technology projecting a need to feed 1.6 billion people by 2050, the government continued to place its faith in agricultural science to meet the nation's food needs.[62]

Green Revolution technology had enabled China to maintain a grain reserve of approximately 150 to 180 million tons or about 35 percent of its annual production. China also had the capacity to store 200 million tons of rice and wheat. In the context of providing food alone, the Green Revolution had given China the security that it often had needed in the past. Strong governmental support for agricultural research also continued to advance, and the government provided direct subsidies to farmers to lessen the cost of fertilizer, pesticides, and herbicides. Moreover, it provided minimum price supports (that is, a floor price) below which grain prices could not fall to ensure profitability and the continued use of Green Revolution technologies. In addition, it set ceiling prices on agricultural commodities to help control inflation for food. This latter problem, however, is less attributable to Green Revolution production than to consumers with disposable income who purchased more meat, fruits, and vegetables.[63]

Although China still consumed more rice than any other nation, the public often considered it a food for poor people. Between 2001 and 2010, rice consumption declined from 135.5 million to 127 million tons respectively, primarily because consumers earned higher incomes and preferred to eat meat and vegetables, which they often substituted for rice. Green Revolution grain production, however, seemed to meet the food security needs of China, even as more land disappeared to industrial and urban expansion as well as to declining water tables. By the twenty-first century, agricultural scientists worked to improve and secure production by developing dryland and genetically modified rice varieties. At the same time, China's surplus grain production often has been diverted to livestock feed to enable consumers to eat more meat just as the Green Revolution helped them to eat more rice.[64]

By 2010, Green Revolution requirements for heavy applications of water had created the greatest threat to food security. China's water resources were not equitably developed. Southern China had 18 percent of the nation's water reserves and 65 percent of the land suitable for cultivation. As farmers drew down surface water and groundwater supplies, the share of irrigation in total water use withdrawal declined from 80 percent in the 1980s to 65 percent by 2010. Many of the wells had begun to run dry because of the heavy withdrawals that were nothing less than the equivalent of water mining to satisfy Green Revolution crop demands. This exploitation of the groundwater supply was, of course, unsustainable. Surface water could not provide the volume required for sustained crop production. Urban and industrial demands further limited the finite availability of water for crops. Some critics urged farmers to raise more maize instead of wheat because it used water more efficiently.[65]

Heavy applications of nitrogen and phosphorous fertilizers had increased greenhouse gas emissions and caused severe water pollution in many parts of China. The arable land that remained could not sustain substantial crop increases because these areas had poor soils. Green Revolution technologies had significantly reduced the quality of the soil due to the leeching of chemicals and intensive cultivation, including multiple cropping in some areas. Agricultural chemicals had polluted the drinking water for 30 percent of the population. Global warming made future productivity increases uncertain. As time passed the unintended consequences of the Green Revolution seemed to multiply.[66]

Some critics believed the Green Revolution had damaged the environment so much that China's ability to sustain high agricultural productivity had become doubtful. They also charged that even when farmers reduced their fertilizer applications, high concentrations remained in the soil and water sources for a long time. An estimated 67 percent of the farmers now applied excessive amounts of nitrogen fertilizer in pursuit of higher grain yields. With a weak extension service as late as 2010, most farmers did not know the appropriate amount of fertilizer to apply and for good measure to provide "insurance" for a large crop they applied considerably more than necessary. With low fertilizer prices and government subsidies for production and delivery, farmers could easily afford more fertilizer than they needed, all to the degradation of the environment. As crop yields plateaued or stagnated, farmers applied more fertilizer to the land to regain loss or facilitate greater yields.[67]

By the turn of the twenty-first century China also had become one of the largest pesticide manufactures, and its farmers among the largest consumers of pesticides, using some 230,000 tons per year. Green Revolution agricultural production seemed to benefit in the beginning. As farmers earned more money in a growing market economy and as family members increasingly migrated to the cities for education and employment, they substituted herbicides and pesticides for lost human labor for weeding and manual insect control. While the initial pesticide applications helped improve harvests, by the late twentieth century many insects had built up a resistance to these chemicals. Health hazards, particularly liver, kidney, nerve damage, and even death, from mixing and spraying highly toxic pesticides on their crops compounded the unintended consequences of the Green Revolution. Consumers began questioning the effects on human health from consuming pesticide-laden foods. Government regulations of pesticide manufacturers had not solved these problems partly due to weak enforcement and because agricultural extension agents earned part of their income by selling pesticides which often further encouraged their heavy application by farmers.[68]

While agricultural scientists struggled to resolve the problems of too much use of irrigation, fertilizers, and pesticides, they also began work to improve rice quality for consumers and the global marketplace. Chinese agricultural scientists now focused on "technologies of quality." Some social scientists contend that this policy had a twofold purpose—the enhancement of quality production while promoting "quality" as a part of the government's attempt to modernize Chinese society and products. Thus, after ensuring food security and confronting the problem of price depressing surpluses, China shifted the emphasis of the Green Revolution to developing better-tasting, higher-quality rice varieties, driven by the need for increased economic development and the desire to improve living standards. The government enhanced this redirection of agricultural science by subsidizing the purchase of improved seeds and farm machinery and by eliminating agricultural taxes to encourage farmer investment in the new Green Revolution technologies.[69]

By the early twenty-first century, Green Revolution technology achieved considerable success but the efforts to improve food production rapidly came at the cost of substantial environmental damage. At the same time, the Green Revolution replaced considerable traditional labor needs with mechanical and chemical technologies. Although the government periodically attempted to keep unwanted farm workers from migrating to the cities, these workers also provided cheap labor for China's industrialization. Those workers earned more than their rural counterparts and thereby created greater demand for various food products. Even so, approximately six hundred million people still relied on small-scale farming for their livelihood during the early twenty-first century.[70]

In retrospect, the Communist revolution led to a socially acceptable land reform that enabled the development and application of Green Revolution technologies that ended hunger and provided food security. After 1949, agricultural policy enabled considerable improvement in the standard of living, except the Great Leap Forward and Great Leap famine period from 1959–1961. At the end of World War II, China ranked among the worst-fed nations. Since the mid-twentieth century, its agricultural policies, particularly after 1978, have made it one of the most successful countries to reduce hunger by rapidly increasing agricultural production, particularly grain, primarily by adopting Green Revolution technologies. Agricultural extension work brought new varieties and techniques to farmers who, through demonstration, understood their benefits and adopted them. Grain production rapidly increased. At the turn of the twenty-first century, China consumed approximately 410 million tons of grain, but imported only about 2 percent of that amount. Problems of adequate food production lay in the past. Equally important, China's agricultural policy made food accessible, because officials recognized that eliminating hunger is not only a matter of increasing production but also keeping food affordable, both of which involved the formulation and execution of agricultural policy so necessary to the success of the Green Revolution. China's Green Revolution achievements are remarkable accomplishments since the famine of 1959–1961 that claimed millions of lives. Most significantly, by the early twenty-first century, one of China's major agricultural problems became surpluses, particularly grain; the second, low farm prices. Moreover, since 1979 agricultural production growth rates have exceeded population growth rates.[71]

In August 2002, the Ninth National People's Congress adopted the Law of the People's Republic of China on Land Contract in Rural Areas Act (Order of the Present No. 73). This act affirmed state ownership of the land and the right of farmers to contract land from the village collectives. The law permitted farmers to contract land for thirty years, make all production and operating decisions, and sell their produce or commodities. By 2006, however, only an estimated 40 percent of farm households had contracted or at least received land contracts. The reason for this low percentage stemmed from the reluctance of farmers to make long-term investments on their land, fearing confiscation by local or regional authorities without compensation as well as from bureaucratic inefficiency to administer the program. Despite these problems, the Land Contract in Rural Areas Act was one of the most important laws in recent years, because it addressed the rights of farmers.[72]

At the turn of the twenty-first century, some social scientists suggested that the revolution in 1949 was more important in reducing hunger in China than the Green Revolution because the political revolution provided broad-based changes in access to land that, in turn, enabled farmers to improve their standard of living. Others contended that the Green Revolution not only gave China food security but also made it the largest rice producer in the world. In 1961, when on the cusp of the Green Revolution, China produced 9.5 percent of the global grain supply. By 2009, Green Revolution technologies had boosted that production to approximately 29 percent of global rice production and 20 percent for maize and 17 percent for wheat. During that period rice production increased 3.2, wheat 8.5, and maize 4.6 times respectively, while the total area for cultivated cereal grain increased only 30 percent. Put differently, these grain increases came from greater production per hectare not by the expansion of cultivated areas. Clearly, Green Revolution technology and government policy made these productivity increases possible and gave China what it wanted and needed—food security.[73]

5

Sub-Saharan Africa

In 1985, one observer reflected, "Africa is the tragic exception" to the Green Revolution. During the past decade, total cereal production had declined 12 percent. Sub-Saharan farmers produced the lowest yield per acre per person in the world. Drought made the food situation worse. By the early twenty-first century, food production remained in crisis. The population continued to increase beyond the agricultural capacity to sustain it. Between 1960 and 1990, sub-Saharan Africa's population increased from 200 million to 450 million. Governments gave little support for Green Revolution agricultural improvement in the form of subsidies to farmers for high-yielding seed varieties and fertilizer, or for road improvements. Some people contended that Norman Borlaug's Green Revolution could not and should not be applied to African agriculture. As food supplies fell, nutrition deteriorated; hunger, particularly for the rural poor, became a daily aspect of life; and a Green Revolution remained an unrealized potential.[1]

As the population and food needs increased in sub-Saharan countries, farmers expanded onto previously uncultivated marginal lands or replanted areas where slash-and-burn techniques required longer periods for the restoration of soil fertility. Yet, with only 8 percent of the land arable, farmers could not easily increase production by cultivating more hectares. Continuous cropping further depleted organic material and nitrogen and phosphorous declined, which further diminished soil fertility and crop yields. As farmers expanded into uncultivated areas, they often contested with pastoralists who used those lands for grazing livestock. During the 1990s, this conflict over food production and the right to claim and use the land contributed to the civil wars in Burundi and Rwanda.[2]

Politics, ethnicity, civil unrest, and insufficient markets as well as education hindered the work of agricultural scientists in sub-Saharan Africa to a greater degree than in South Asia. Moreover, the region presented new problems that proved difficult to overcome. Transportation systems remained poorly developed more so than in South Asia during the 1960s. The region's subsistence farmers also had little access to irrigation, and livestock diseases, particularly East Coast fever, severely limited the use of oxen for draft power. As a result, farmers primarily relied on hand tools and human labor to plant, cultivate, harvest, and thresh their grain. Asian farmers applied twenty times and Latin American farmers ten times more fertilizer per hectare than sub-Saharan African agriculturists. Despite the benefits of fertilizer for substantially increasing crop production, few farmers could afford this essential component of the Green Revolution.[3]

Until agricultural prices increased the purchasing power of farmers and until the cost of producing and distributing inorganic, nitrogen-based fertilizer declined, sub-Saharan farmers could only rely on traditional practices to enhance soil fertility, such as planting nitrogen-fixing legumes and applying green manure (that is, organic fertilizer) to their fields. Few sub-Saharan nations had adequate extension systems to inform farmers about Green Revolution agriculture. When available, extension agents used applied, repetitive instruction about the application of irrigation, fertilizers, and pesticides to break down traditional beliefs that attributed good or bad harvests to chance or the weather. By the turn of the twenty-first century, a Green Revolution remained an unachievable goal for most sub-Saharan farmers.[4]

During the 1960s and 1970s, agricultural scientists attempted to introduce the Green Revolution to sub-Saharan Africa, but their work proved episodic and failed due to a multiplicity of causes. Overall, poverty and insufficient resources contributed the most to the lag in the implementation of the Green Revolution to the region. Inadequate agricultural education and research along with inefficient program management and government policy hindered agricultural improvement. African leaders seemed more concerned with the redistribution of wealth rather than investing in Green Revolution technologies. Still, where agricultural production increased among small-scale farmers, it did so primarily because they cultivated more land. In contrast, agricultural production increased among the large-scale farmers because they could afford to apply Green Revolution science and technology to achieve greater yields per hectare. Moreover, the large-scale farmers usually did not emphasize maize production, and they produced more profitable export crops while small-scale farmers continued to practice subsistence agriculture. Agricultural extension services also provided the most assistance to large-scale farmers who raise cash crops rather than those farmers engaged in producing staple food crops, which had a low market value. In this sense, agricultural extension became socially uneven because it did not favor poor, food-producing farmers but rather large-scale farmers who raise crops for export.[5]

East Africa provides an overview of the problems that agricultural scientists confronted with their attempts to bring the Green Revolution to sub-Saharan Africa. In 1967, for example, the Swedish International Development Agency (SIDA) embarked on a plan to foster the Green Revolution in Ethiopia. The SIDA attempted a market development program to enable farmers to receive fair prices and provide extension agents and demonstration areas to encourage them to purchase high-yielding varieties (HYVs) and fertilizers that the agency would finance with low-cost credit. The agency also planned to develop irrigation systems and improve roads. By 1971, wheat and barley production had substantially increased and household income rose by 60–90 percent in some areas largely due to the systemic development of twenty-five trade centers. These achievements convinced the traditional, conservative, elite landowners to invest heavily in HYVs and fertilizer and use their crop profits to purchase machinery and release their tenants who constituted 80 percent of Ethiopia's farmers. Land became more expensive to rent, property values increased beyond the ability of small-scale farmers to purchase it, and intermediaries skimmed earnings from the increased volume of grain sales.[6]

Change did not come quickly. Agriculture provided 55–60 percent of the gross national product. Farm commodities constituted 90 percent of Ethiopia's earnings from exports with coffee garnering 60 percent of those revenues. Subsistence farmers produced 95 percent of the agricultural output. Credit, extension, and roads, as well as commercial marketing essentially did not exist. Large-scale landowners did not want their tenants to gain a sense that they owned the land, and guerrilla activity in Eritrea turned government attention to war. Local governments proved inefficient and corrupt, often serving little more than to collect taxes and support the landowning elites. Neither national nor local governments expressed much interest in agricultural improvement for small-scale farmers. The government, however, supported large-scale farmers by providing duty-free imports of machinery and granting credit and tax waivers. These farmers were most able to capitalize on Green Revolution technology to increase production.[7]

By 1972, more than 150 landowners used some 250 tractors and 50 combines to cultivate approximately 30,000 hectares. As the large-scale farmers adopted more mechanization, they used it to cultivate the land themselves or with absentee managers. Or, they rented their lands at high rates to other commercial farmers. High rents for tenants who remained on the land discouraged investment in Green Revolution technologies, because these farmers had to pay the cost and assume the risk of failure while only retaining one-third to two-thirds of the crops harvested. By the early 1970s, eviction rates ranged between 25 percent and 75 percent of the farm population across the nation. Urban areas became destinations for displaced tenant farmers. By 1974, Ethiopia had a per capita annual income of $98, the lowest in the world. More than 90 percent of the 27.3 million people lived in rural areas, and pursued farming and livestock raising. The illiteracy rate reached 95 percent. In September, the social costs of the Green Revolution contributed to the overthrow of Emperor Haile Selassie because it further separated the rich from the poor and tenants from landowners in a society where agricultural production met only the marginal needs of the population. Critics charged that Ethiopia could not afford a Green Revolution, economically or socially. Contemporaries soon called Ethiopia the "epitome of a country incapable of feeding itself."[8]

The Swedish development specialists had failed to calculate the effects of a corrupt and dysfunctional government on Ethiopia's social order, and they thought only about the introduction of the Green Revolution agricultural package that would help elite landowners become commercial farmers. Where small-scale farmers increased production and income, local government officials took most of it through higher taxes and fees, and thereby further discouraged them from adopting Green Revolution technologies. Ethiopian politics trumpeted the goals of the agricultural and social scientists, neither of whom foresaw the social consequences of the Green Revolution on the rural population.[9]

After the military overthrow of the imperial regime of Haile Selassie, the government initiated a radical land reform program by appropriating and distributing the lands of the upper class, but not land redistribution to subsistence farmers. After replacing privately owned family farms with state and collective farms, however, the government failed to provide the resources necessary to increase agricultural production. Although the state farms received most of the chemical fertilizer and improved seeds and credit, over-centralization, few incentives, and insufficient extension services kept food production low. The government privileged military expenditures, not agricultural improvement. As a poor, socialist country, Ethiopia did not have the necessary government support to introduce Green Revolution agriculture, and farmers seemed unmotivated to make the state and collective farms productive.[10]

Figure 14. Ethiopian farmer using a sickle to harvest wheat
Across sub-Saharan Africa, most farmers rely on traditional, often primitive, handheld
implements to till, harvest, and process their crops. Photo: P. Lowe / CIMMYT, CC BY-NC-SA.

Early efforts to bring the Green Revolution to their region proved more successful in Kenya where farmers began adopting Green Revolution technology
during the 1970s, particularly maize, wheat, and rice HYVs along with chemical fertilizers. Kenya's government supported research to increase maize production over other crops, and by 1975 approximately 150,000 farmers planted
hybrid maize and used fertilizer to enhance crop yields. Although hybrid seed
required annual purchase as opposed to saving seed from the crops grown
from traditional open-pollenated varieties from one year to the next, the Kenyan extension service achieved modest success in educating farmers about
the benefits of hybrid maize. Moreover, the Kenyan Seed Company proved
instrumental in the development of hybrid maize varieties for distribution
to farmers. Farmers also found these hybrids suitable for planting in the
highlands of Ethiopia, Uganda, and Tanzania, and the Kenya Seed Company
shipped an estimated 20 percent of its hybrid maize beyond Kenyan borders.
Although the large-scale commercial farmers first adopted the hybrids, small-
scale farmers soon followed when the HYVs proved productive and profitable in the drought-prone highlands. Kenya's farmers also had the advantage
of secure land tenure, good roads, private markets, and a knowledgeable extension service.[11]

By the late 1970s, a grain surplus caused the price to fall, and farmers decreased production below the needs of the population. As a result, the government imported more grain from the United States to cover the deficit. After the 1970s, Kenyan farmers tended to ignore the acquisition of improved varieties, and they did not apply inorganic fertilizers in sufficient quantities to ensure the maximum production of maize. This crop, however, provided a most important staple for 96 percent of the population and a cash crop for small-scale and large-scale farmers. Yet, approximately 60 percent of rural households purchased maize to meet their food needs.[12]

Tanzania experienced similar problems. In 1967, the government attempted to achieve a Green Revolution by providing and encouraging the use of chemical fertilizers and expanding its agricultural extension system as well as by encouraging more land clearing for agriculture. Until the early 1970s, Tanzania enjoyed food security. Drought at mid-decade, however, caused a great decline in food crops and a major displacement of farm families from the countryside into the villages. The global oil crisis also made petroleum-based chemicals, such as fertilizers, more expensive. In 1975 the government attempted to improve food production by subsidizing the purchase of HYVs and fertilizer, but irrigation along with the credit and the marketing infrastructure remained inadequate. Government officials often proved corrupt and unable or unwilling to aid small-scale farmers. The government also dedicated most of its resources to industrial expansion. Agriculture became a marginalized contributor to the Tanzanian economy.[13]

In the southern part of East Africa, the Green Revolution began in Zimbabwe five years before India started importing HYVs from Mexico when in 1960 the government released a high-yielding maize variety called SR-52 that produced high yields in areas with heavy rainfall. White commercial farmers led the movement. When Zimbabwe gained independence in 1980, the government introduced a variety of agricultural programs to help smallholders increase food production, both subsistence and cash crop farming. It provided hybrid maize varieties, fertilizers, herbicides, and pesticides, expanded access to credit, guaranteed high maize prices, provided marketing subsidies, and expanded rural markets.[14]

For smallholders, drought and insufficient animal power prevented subsistence crop increases even with Green Revolution technologies. Green Revolution agricultural science also could not solve the problem of overall insufficient land for farming. As a result, some observers feared that intensive farming with high applications of fertilizer would ruin the land. Moreover,

only 25 percent of the farmers used HYVs and only 20 percent fertilizer because they were too expensive, and farmers preferred traditional, drought-
resistant grains, such as millet. In addition, 50 percent of the farmers lacked
oxen or tractors for draft power so hand tools prevailed for cultivation. Even
so, between 1960 and 1980, Zimbabwe began its own Green Revolution built
on strong support for public agricultural research, economic stability for commercial farmers, and an export-oriented farm policy to ensure traditional markets for surplus maize. After 1980, the government focused on small-scale
farmers by improving credit and marketing to increase maize production.[15]

In West Africa, efforts to introduce a Green Revolution also confronted
major problems. In Ghana, for example, by 1969, Yoruba traders had introduced high-yielding rice varieties to farmers in the North. Traditional farmers
cultivated only about five acres of cereal and root crops but the new rice varieties attracted investors who had wealth and credit to develop unclaimed lands
and consolidate smallholdings. The Agricultural Development Bank and the
Ghana Commercial Bank also provided credit for agricultural development
and expansion. The new rice varieties produced high yields compared to traditional varieties, and the stalks enabled machine harvesting. These rainfed
lands, however, did not provide a consistent or controlled water supply, but
fertilizer applications permitted the development of 100-to-300-acre farms.
Rice yields, however, remained relatively low and depended on the season
and soil fertility. Absentee owners hired others to plow, plant, and harvest because these rainfed lands needed labor only a few months of the year. Rich
landowners who planted HYVs and applied government-subsidized fertilizer
and who used tractors and mechanical harvesters, often purchased on credit,
created a great sense of inequality among smallholders, some of whom retali-
ated by burning the new rice lands. Many farmers saw little benefit from either traditional or Green Revolution agriculture and moved to urban areas.
Although cheap fertilizer became available to farmers in the 1960s and 1970s,
few farmers used it to raise HYV rice. By the mid-1980s, the Green Revolution had proven a failure in Ghana, and neither traditional farmers nor elite
landowners seemed to care much about it.[16]

In 1979 and 1981, political coups also slowed agricultural change. Private
credit sources did not exist for small-scale farmers, and family loans remained
the primary means for financing farm operations. Farmers preferred cheaper,
traditional practices, and few purchased HYVs or chemical fertilizers. The application rate of inorganic fertilizer also lagged. Farms remained small with
60 percent averaging 1.2 hectares or approximately three acres. Hoes and

other handheld implements remained the primary tools for cultivation and harvesting, although 57 percent of the farmers in the eastern savannah area used draft animals to prepare their fields for sorghum. Green Revolutions depend on the timely preparation, seeding, and harvesting of crops. Without mechanization, land reform, and the cultivation of larger fields, farmers could not implement agricultural intensification with Green Revolution techniques. Similar to other subcontinent nations, inadequate agricultural marketing prevented substantial increases in food production. Private traders dominated the purchases; private cooperatives and state marketing remained insignificant.[17]

Efforts to develop a Green Revolution in Nigeria proved even more difficult. There, a military dictatorship ruled from independence in 1960 until 2003. Nigeria's 350 ethnic groups, each with distinct food preferences, also hindered the increase of crop yields based on the principles of the Green Revolution. In 1960, agriculture provided proximally two-thirds of the revenue and foreign exchange for the Nigerian government and about 70 percent of the population depended on it for a living. Low productivity, inadequate markets, and insufficient government support, however, prevented increased agricultural productivity. Moreover, government policies favored export crops produced on large-scale plantations. Civil War from 1967 to 1970 also hindered agricultural production and trade and caused starvation in the state of Biafra. The government attempted to solve the food shortage problem by importing grain rather than by supporting agricultural development to ensure self-sufficiency and food security. Nigerian agricultural policy differed little from the colonial period. Government policy emphasized crops, such as cocoa, groundnuts, and palm oil, to earn international exchange. Food crop production did not concern government officials. Moreover, the government did not use revenues from taxation and foreign exchange to support small-scale agricultural production. The oil boom in the 1970s generated considerable income for Nigeria, but the government did not use it to improve agriculture. High incomes and an increasing urban population enabled the importation of necessary food products. The government did not need small-scale farmers to meet national food needs.[18]

Yet, from 1970 to 1985, Nigeria engaged in agricultural improvement through the application of Green Revolution technology. The beneficiaries of this new agricultural policy were large-scale, urban-based farmers who often held jobs in the civil service or military. Small-scale farmers received less than 20 percent of the government loans designed to enhance agricultural productivity. The state, however, provided minimum price supports and a fail-safe market if the open market collapsed. Nevertheless, government subsidies for seeds, fertilizers, herbicides, pesticides, and machinery favored the large-scale land-owners. Moreover, with subsidy levels ranging from 75 percent to 100 per-cent from 1970 to 1990, unscrupulous individuals cornered the market for these materials at government expense and resold them at higher rates to the subsistence farmers who most needed them. As a result, Nigerian farmers could not apply the "package" needed for implementation of a Green Revo-lution, because they did not have the resources to capitalize on new research that would improve their productivity. When grain production increased for subsistence and small-scale farmers, transportation and intermediary charges took most of their profit. Few "trickle down" Green Revolution benefits lifted them to an improved standard of living.[19]

∼

By 1980, farmers constituted 80 percent of sub-Saharan Africa's population, but African leaders sought industrialization and manufacturing to provide a strong economy for urbanites and they neglected agriculture other than for taxing purposes. Governments paid low agricultural prices to ensure inex-pensive food and social stability in the cities. These governments also bought cheap grain on the international market based on over-valued exchange rates. Small-scale farmers had little incentive to produce more food grains than their families could consume, and they could do it with traditional methods. State marketing and distribution agencies provided poor service and often paid farmers long after the completion of sales. Frequently, these agencies deliv-ered seeds, fertilizers, and pesticides too late for use. As the population in-creased, food production per capita declined.[20]

During the 1980s, food-deficit nations in sub-Saharan Africa suffered even more than before. The Green Revolution had not yet reached the region when famine fostered by drought and war struck the Sahel in the spring of 1983. (The Sahel is constituted of all or parts of Ethiopia, Eritrea, Sudan, Chad, northern Nigeria, Niger, Mali, Burkina Faso, Senegal, and Mauritania.) Wide-spread and acute drought had plagued the region from 1968–1973, but it now intensified. Livestock died and crops failed. Pastoralists sold their cattle for low prices on glutted markets and received little money to purchase grain. Farmers coped by planting more drought-resistant millet and sorghum and expanded onto marginal lands. Approximately 250,000 people died, cattle herds dimin-ished, and land deteriorated into desert. While drought provided the under-lying reason, it alone did not cause famine. Population growth had displaced pastoralists as farmers desperately attempted to cultivate their arid grazing lands. When catastrophic drought struck, no agricultural reserves remained to prevent starvation. Farmers could not save themselves. Observers blamed government officials for mismanaging agriculture while international aid organizations urged more support and their access to starving people. Some critics contended that Green Revolution agricultural science caused or at least made the famine worse in already food-deficit nations where the poor always suffered the most.[21]

By 1985, famine, due in part to failed agriculture, plagued the Sahel where the precipitation line necessary for crop production moves with the seasons, years, and decades. Famine means starvation but it also means a complete breakdown in the ability of farmers to produce food and governments to make it available at affordable prices. With famine comes social instability, such as the bread riots in Khartoum in April of that year. Put differently, famine is as much a political phenomenon as it is a result of natural disaster, such as drought, with the rural poor, often farmers, the chief victims who cannot be easily reached and assisted, such as those who depend on livestock raising and who migrate frequently in search of grass and water, often across political boundaries.[22]

Population growth made food shortages even worse. In addition, foreign food assistance from nations such as the United States often dumped surplus grain on food-deficit sub-Saharan nations to help American farmers unload price-depressing surpluses more than to help starving people. The grain imports contributed to low food prices and discouraged farmers from increasing food production for which they would earn a profit, even during famine. Moreover, free food in the form of foreign aid often meant wheat and rice when many sub-Saharan Africans preferred eating and raising sorghum and millet. Even if farmers in famine-stricken nations could have improved their production by acquiring high-yielding varieties from donor nations or agricultural research institutions, the infrastructure, such as roads, transport vehicles, and storage facilities, could not have supported a large increase in agricultural production.[23]

By the mid-1980s, sub-Saharan Africa contained twenty-nine of the world's thirty-six poorest nations. In these countries, chronically poor people, usually farmers, suffered food deficiencies for lack of sufficient production to feed their families during the year. Rich people, government officials, mostly urbanites, and large-scale farmers, do not starve. They have the means to purchase sufficient food. Famines are usually local more than widespread, and limited access to food by poor people worsens it. Those who have access to food do not perish.[24]

In the five years before the drought, food production increased approximately 1.6 percent per year while the population increased 3.1 percent. Yet, in the Sahel, only 24 percent of the international aid went to agriculture and forestry. Clearly, no Green Revolution could be developed and supported with such limited assistance. Moreover, 28 percent of that agricultural aid supported the development of cash crops, primarily peanuts and cotton. Before the famine, governments in the Sahel did not provide funding for agricultural research to develop dryland crops, and agricultural scientists seldom worked with local farmers and preferred to stay in their laboratories or experimental fields. Even so, poor Sahel farmers could not afford, even with credit, Green Revolution investments in HYVs, fertilizer, and pesticides. Moreover, women constituted 90 percent of the farmers in some areas, and men culturally excluded them from acquiring credit at lending institutions to finance agricultural improvements. Agricultural loans usually went to elite, wealthy, and politically connected farmers. When small-scale subsistence farmers failed during the drought, more wealthy farmers bought their lands to expand their commercial crop production for export, not for food. Exceptions, of course, occurred. Even during drought conditions, Malawi and Somalia gave increasing support for agricultural development, and subsidized price increases in Somalia led to a 40 percent increase in sorghum production. At the same time, the efforts of the United States to use food aid to counter Soviet influence in Somalia, Sudan, and Ethiopia, while providing grain to hungry people in the Sahel, did little to improve agricultural production.[25]

Migration from drought and war kept sub-Saharan farmers hungry and poor. Agricultural scientists could do little to mitigate their plight due to a lack of government commitments to Green Revolution agricultural science. At the same time, many critics blamed the Green Revolution for emphasizing the wrong kind of agricultural production because it aided farmers who needed it the least. They contended that Green Revolution agricultural science should benefit subsistence farmers and not commercial agriculture. They also advocated support for traditional farming methods based on indigenous knowledge for crop breeding and cultivation, not high-tech solutions, for the food-deficit nations in the Sahel. Other critics advocated increased credit and extension services for small-scale farmers to help them buy the seed, land, and tools and provide the training to use them efficiently and productively.

Figure 15. Ethiopian farmers harvesting maize
In sub-Saharan Africa, women constitute most of the farmers. They often are prevented
from acquiring Green Revolution technologies because they lack credit, and lending institutions discriminate against them because they are women. Photo: P. Lowe / CIMMYT,
CC BY-NC-SA.

Yet most Green Revolution agricultural scientists believed that although African farmers had skills, they had reached their limits of knowledge to improve food production significantly. By the 1980s, for the Green Revolution
to succeed in sub-Saharan Africa, agricultural scientists had to develop new
drought-resistant varieties of sorghum and millet. By 1985, they had achieved
some success breeding high-yielding sorghum, and they had begun distributing it to farmers in Sudan. Scientists had not been able to improve millet,
which one agricultural expert called a "crop consumed by the poorest people
in the poorest areas of the world." French researchers had been working more
than fifty years to make it a high-yielding Green Revolution crop. Optimistic
ventures often ended in failure, which impressed few sub-Saharan farmers,
one of whom said, "Africa has blown out a lot of flames."[26]

Many Green Revolution supporters, however, hailed the development of
disease-resistant cassava, cowpeas, and potatoes from the research laboratories of the Consultative Group for International Agricultural Research, which
replaced the work of the Ford and Rockefeller Foundations. This organization had thirteen research centers dedicated to bringing a Green Revolution

to sub-Saharan Africa. Wheat and rice strains, however, developed in other Green Revolution areas, did not adapt well to the region. One agricultural expert considered the outlook "bleak" for substantive Green Revolution transfers from other continents. Agricultural scientists did not have a good understanding of the thin, arid African soils or the interaction of soil, rainfall, climate, and temperature. No one knew much about the effects of chemical fertilizers on fragile soils in semiarid sub-Saharan Africa. Most believed that the region's agricultural problems could be solved when farmers planted high-yielding varieties, applied heavy amounts of fertilizer, and drew upon agricultural extension services for training and advice.[27]

By the late 1980s, the Green Revolution still struggled in East Africa. In 1986, Tanzania changed its policy to emphasize a market economy. The subsidization of agricultural production based on funds from the World Bank and other international institutions, however, did not foster the production gains that officials had sought. Tanzania's rice and wheat yields did not meet consumer needs, and the government resorted to imports. Between 1975 and 1985, the National Milling Corporation, a government parastatal that monopolized the procurement and distribution of grain, imported maize because it cost less to purchase on the international rather than the domestic market. Although Tanzania's government attempted to encourage greater cereal grain production by purchasing grain and storing surpluses, its intervention in the agricultural economy to control prices and marketing, including the creation of cooperatives that had monopoly purchasing power, failed due to mismanagement and corruption. Tanzania remained an importer of wheat and rice.[28]

In 1980, when Zimbabwe gained independence, approximately five thousand commercial farmers, usually white, controlled half of the farmland while some seven hundred thousand smallholders, usually black, cultivated the remaining arable land. Zimbabwe's new government, constituted of Africans, not whites, gave Green Revolution agriculture a boost when President Robert Mugabe did not pursue the appropriation of white-owned, commercial farms. This policy gained time to restructure credit, research, and extension institutions to serve the smallholders. Zimbabwe's majority-led government enabled small-scale farmers to access Green Revolution technologies and support. The previous white extension service now merged with the former black extension service and began advising small-scale farmers. The road network provided farm-to-market access for new surplus production based on Green Revolution technologies.[29]

By the mid-1980s, Zimbabwe's farm productivity became an agricultural problem. Zimbabwe had a maize surplus that resulted from the planting of new HYVs. More fertilizer and credit, higher commodity prices, and marketing subsides contributed to this grain surplus. In 1985, the maize crop totaled three million tons, or about the amount needed to meet Zimbabwe's food needs for three years. The government then instituted a policy to reduce maize production by decreasing marketing subsidies. Zimbabwe, however, experienced a Green Revolution during the 1980s because the nation sustained a pre-independence agricultural research and extension system, provided credit and marketing support, and enjoyed peace and economic stability. Zimbabwe's Green Revolution was state-based. It did not result from the outside support and leadership of donor nations and private organizations.[30]

The Green Revolution did not last. Setbacks occurred when the government ultimately sought the appropriation of white-owned lands. Acrimony grew and, in 2002, whites finally lost their farms. Zimbabwe's appropriation of white-owned lands ended commercial agriculture as a major industry. The small-scale farmers could not meet the nation's food needs, despite the increased adoption of Green Revolution technologies, and the government necessarily returned to food imports and foreign relief to feed the population. The Green Revolution died in Zimbabwe.[31]

In contrast, Malawi's estate owners also grew maize as a secondary crop in rotation with tobacco during the 1980s, but they did not seek large yields for international sale and low-yielding traditional varieties met their needs. During the late 1980s, however, Malawi committed to a research program to increase hybrid maize. In 1990, researchers drawing on germplasm from Malawi and the International Maize and Wheat Improvement Center (CIMMYT) released semi-flint hybrids known as MH17 and MH18. These varieties produced the flour quality desired and resisted insect damage due to their hard kernels. By 1992, Malawi's smallholders had increased the area planted to hybrid maize from 7 percent to 24 percent. They primarily produced HYV maize for home consumption or sold green maize on local and urban markets. Green Revolution maize varieties proved successful because they met the taste, texture, and flour needs of the farmers who raised, stored, and consumed them. Moreover, Malawi's soils did not vary significantly and the few Green Revolution varieties available made widespread adoption easier than in other sub-Sahara nations. In addition, the government had supported seed research and marketing, provided extension services, and improved credit opportunities. Malawi's Green Revolution clients became the smallholding subsistence farmers. Contemporaries in other sub-Saharan nations hoped for a similar smallholder Green Revolution.[32]

Malawi's Green Revolution success, however, did not come quickly. Women made the major economic contribution to agriculture by owning lands and producing crops. They also conducted most of the farm work. In this comparatively heavily populated country where 85 percent worked in agriculture, maize served as the major grain crop. Often they attributed good and poor harvests to rainfall and "God's will." Malawi's female farmers primarily planted local maize varieties because they could not afford HYVs or fertilizer. They knew about Green Revolution agriculture, but they rejected it because it did not meet their needs and circumstances. When Malawi's women applied fertilizer, they did so to increase the yield of traditional maize varieties. Moreover, Malawi women said that they needed credit to improve maize production, but they feared it because any investment in Green Revolution agriculture might fail. Then, they would be unable to pay their loans and lose their land. They seldom received advice from extension agents which went to the men of the household for cultural reasons, and because they only dealt with large-scale commercial farmers, not small-scale, subsistence maize farmers.[33]

Government efforts to improve irrigation during the 1980s also met resistance because farmers resented the loss of land, village displacement, and disruption of rural economies. Irrigation systems also fostered waterborne disease, such as malaria, cholera, and typhoid fever. Still, these new irrigation farmers began planting rice rather than maize, thereby moving from subsistence to commercial agriculture with government-required Green Revolution technologies and mandates to raise two crops annually rather than one maize crop under rainfed conditions. Subsistence farmers, however, criticized officials for allocating irrigation plots and water based on favoritism. Moreover, the government intended to shift irrigation farms from maize to rice production, but farmers resented the extra labor required to cultivate rice and resisted the agricultural improvement program.[34]

By the mid-1980s, government and nongovernmental organizations (NGOs) also introduced Green Revolution rice cultivation to West Africa, particularly in The Gambia and Mali. This effort failed because scientists and government officials did not consider and accommodate traditional agricultural practices, which women conducted. By expecting men to adopt Green Revolution technologies and raise rice without sharing the benefits with their farmer wives, they reaped failure. In these nations, rice is a "woman's crop." Mali's isolated and landlocked location protected its farmers from cheap rice imports and consumers preferred traditional varieties. Female farmers who had a long tradition of raising rainfed rice could not easily increase production with HYVs because they could neither afford the expensive seeds nor get surplus grain to urban markets due to inadequate road and marketing systems. Price subsidies to make their grain competitive with imports did not exist. Côte d' Ivorie farmers confronted similar problems that stifled Green Revolution agriculture. By the early twenty-first century, little had changed.[35]

During the 1980s, the Nigerian economy disintegrated due to foreign debt, low manufacturing production, and a stagnating agricultural economy. By 1981, the population increased about 3.5 percent while agricultural production increased about 1 percent annually. The oil boom lured many young men to the cities from the countryside. The majority of Nigeria's small-scale farmers cultivated fewer than five acres and could not produce enough food using traditional methods. Insufficient extension, roads, seed, and fertilizer as well as an inadequate marketing system kept farmers ignorant and poor and the public, if not hungry, malnourished. Nigeria's farmers had no incentive to increase production beyond subsistence, particularly staple crops, such as maize, given unprofitable market prices. One observer, speaking for sub-Saharan Africa, including Nigeria, remarked, "There is no substitute for encouraging farmers to grow food and sell it." Encouragement required a supportive government policy. One farmer reflected, "It's useless talking about Nigeria's green revolution."[36]

In 1986, the government further decreased its support for agriculture, including eliminating subsidies for fertilizers and pesticides and by reducing support for agricultural research. Small-scale farmers now had even less access to these components of the Green Revolution. By 1990, Nigeria had an annual per capita income of approximately $300. Despite the oil-dominated economy, it remained one of the poorest nations in the world. Malnutrition plagued the countryside. The state responded by importing more wheat, rice, and barley, a policy that remained when the twentieth-century ended. Even so, small-scale farmers produced approximately 90 percent of the food consumed at home. They also planted new maize and soybean varieties and applied subsidized fertilizer, when available. Still, agricultural scientists could not guarantee a Green Revolution in Nigeria and the theoretical accruements of universal prosperity, social equality, and economic equity. The effects of the Green Revolution suffered limitations, but it benefited some farmers in limited areas.[37]

A renewed government attempt to introduce Green Revolution agriculture to Ghana came in the late 1980s when smallholders used traditional methods to produce 80 percent of the nation's food supplies. In 1986, the government worked with the Global 2000/Sasakawa Africa Association to establish one-acre demonstration plots where farmers applied Green Revolution technologies to let other farmers compare the results with traditional agricultural practices. Extension services improved, but a road network that had "deteriorated almost beyond repair" hindered mobility and marketing. Moreover, the government still emphasized agriculture for export such as pineapples and bananas to earn foreign exchange.[38]

Even so, by 1991, five years after the initial experiment to transfer Green Revolution agriculture to farmers, Ghana had become a self-sufficient food producer. Former US president Jimmy Carter, who had assisted this work, expressed satisfaction with the results saying that "now Ghana is a food-exporting country instead of being dependent on others and starving to death." The distribution of Quality Protein Maize, developed at CIMMYT thirty years earlier, made this achievement possible. Compared to other varieties bred for widespread adoption, it proved easy to grow. This high protein maize quickly made a difference in productivity and nutrition. Carter believed that it was a "key to Africa's future." By 1993, Ghanaian farmers planted 93,000 acres with this improved variety. The government now sought foreign assistance to build grain silos and elevators to house the surplus maize that farmers produced each year.[39]

Liberia however, still struggled to launch a Green Revolution. By 1980 more than 70 percent of the Liberian population, about 1.2 million, lived in rural areas and depended on agriculture as a way of life. After one or two crops, however, soil exhaustion substantially diminished yields of cassava, manioc, eddoes, maize, banana, plantain, and various vegetables. Small-scale farmers then cleared more land by slash-and-burn techniques, and let their depleted fields lie fallow. These farmers produced for subsistence and largely met their own food needs. Opportunities to earn more money in iron ore and rubber production also limited agricultural expansion. The government of President William R. Tolbert Jr. initiated a Four-Year Development Plan (July 1976–June 1980) that was intended to achieve self-sufficiency in agriculture, especially rice production. In 1979, however, civil unrest resulting from escalating rice prices that the government hoped would encourage farmers to increase production failed to achieve that goal. In 1980, a military coup led by Samuel K. Doe deposed Tolbert and committed the government to achieving a Green Revolution that would make Liberia self-sufficient in food, produce crops for export to grow the national economy, and improve the standard of living for farmers. The government planned to achieve its goals by allocating each county two thousand to three thousand acres of land, called Estates, and to selected individuals to raise crops. After four years, the farmer would receive a deed to the land if productivity was evident. No one said anything about the displacement of small-scale farmers or peasants whose lands the government might take for redistribution.[40]

Women, who conducted most of the agricultural work, were not included in this land distribution plan. Moreover, it did not address the use of technology other than the adoption of the rice variety LAC-23, which the Liberia Agricultural Corporation tested in 1979 to increase the production of food crops for domestic consumption or export. The plan urged crop diversity but nothing more. As such, the government only sought increased production, not the implementation of Green Revolution technologies. In 1986 the minister of agriculture blamed nonparticipating farmers for the failure of the government's agricultural plan. With a debt of $1.3 billion, Liberia did not have the financial resources to support a Green Revolution with price supports and other incentives. The government essentially proved dysfunctional and the nation's economic condition became worse than before the coup. In order to achieve a Green Revolution in Liberia, social and political change had to accompany or precede the introduction of science-based agriculture.[41]

By the 1990s, East Africa continued struggling to start a Green Revolution. Although Kenya contributed more than 45 percent of its revenue through taxation to agriculture, state expenditures declined from 7.5 percent during the 1980s to 3.6 percent from 1994 to 2000 for various agricultural programs. The government only allocated about 40 percent of that expenditure for agricultural development, which included Green Revolution technologies. Agricultural research declined and seed and agricultural companies, not the state, often provided extension services. Moreover, banks proved reluctant to grant credit to farmers despite legal requirements that they loan as much as 20 percent of their reserves to them, and loans tended to go to farmers averaging 7.7 hectares rather than those farming the national average of 1.7 hectares. In addition, 73 percent of all borrowers during the late 1990s had off-the-farm income. Many Kenyan farmers, as in other sub-Saharan nations, feared that bank loans would mean the loss their land if they could not make their payments. As a result, farmers who needed money had to sell at harvest time when prices were the lowest. Generally, the government did not purchase maize or provide price supports. The local markets drove the agricultural economy, and little storage capacity existed to enable farmers to hold their surpluses from the market until prices improved.[42]

In 1994, the government ended production, pricing, and marketing controls. Thereafter, farmers had less access to affordable HYVs, fertilizers, pesticides, and machinery. Farmers compensated by recycling HYV seed, which lost productive capability, or they opted to forgo the purchase of these seeds, which required heavy applications of expensive fertilizer and irrigation. Moreover, small-scale farmers had little access to markets due to the road system and inadequate marketing information. A few traders dominated local markets, and they offered low prices that farmers necessarily accepted to sell their grain. Increasingly, small-scale farmers reverted to subsistence agriculture, which did not bode well for Kenya's food self-sufficiency and security.[43]

In East Africa, by the 1990s, Malawi's government favored "estate-based" agriculture and marginalized small-scale farmers. Large-scale farmers expressed little interest in maize production, traditional or Green Revolution. Agricultural researchers also lacked sufficient germplasm to develop new high-yielding maize varieties. Although subsistence farmers planted 80 percent of Malawi's arable land, they did not practice fallowing or crop rotation. Annual plantings diminished production, which farmers attempted to increase by cultivating new lands. European, large-scale farmers emphasized tobacco, tea, and cotton for export. Native sharecroppers and tenants raised their own food, and they preferred safety-first production with traditional maize varieties rather than expensive HYVs.[44]

Overall, by the mid-1990s, sub-Saharan Africa suffered nearly catastrophic agricultural failure and food shortages even though farming employed most of the population. Hunger and rural poverty prevailed. The region imported one-third of the rice and two-thirds of the wheat needed for consumption. The population increased rapidly, which posed the threat of famine. In nations where all lands that merited cultivation based on the environment, soil conditions, and geography, such as Burundi, Rwanda, Kenya, Malawi, and Senegal, the prospect of food scarcity and higher food prices became an ever-present possibility.[45]

By the mid-1990s, most agricultural experts, if not government officials, recognized that they could not seamlessly transfer the Asian Green Revolution to sub-Saharan Africa because most farmers depended on annual rainfall, not irrigation, for the production of stable food crops. Moreover, most Afri-

can nations remained at an early stage of the scientific and institutional development needed to implement and sustain a Green Revolution, compared to
India and Pakistan during the 1960s. Despite problems, a maize-based Green
Revolution had begun in Zimbabwe, Malawi, Zambia, Kenya, Nigeria, Ghana,
and Southern Burkina Faso.[46]

Sub-Saharan Africa, however, remained an agricultural region with 538
million people; more than 70 percent lived in rural areas and depended on
farming for their livelihood. An estimated 50 million households tilled more
than 130 million hectares, and they used 740 million hectares for grazing
lands. These small-scale farmers seldom cultivated more than ten hectares
each and most farmed fewer than five hectares, usually with handheld tools,
although they sometimes used cattle for plowing. Few farmers had the financial ability to purchase hybrid seeds and fertilizer. Even fewer farmers had access to irrigation. These farmers irrigated only five million hectares, mostly
in Madagascar and Sudan where they watered more than three million hectares. Few farmers had access to mechanized equipment, such as tractors.[47]

In the absence of markets, agricultural development remained restricted at
best. Good markets depended on access to large urban areas that had a population density of more than three hundred persons per kilometer. Without
accessible and profitable markets, sub-Saharan farmers could not use Green
Revolution agricultural science to expand production, improve their income,
and ensure national food security. Most sub-Saharan farmers depended on
financing from family and friends or relied on off-farm jobs to provide the
savings for Green Revolution investments. Formal credit institutions did not
have the resources to provide loans to so many small-scale farmers. Moreover, those institutions did not exist in the needed areas, or they did not make
loans to these farmers because they judged them credit risks, primarily because most were women. The rudimentary efforts to introduce Green Revolution agriculture to sub-Saharan Africa during the 1990s often failed because
it bypassed the poor. It also failed because agricultural scientists assumed that
high-yielding varieties developed on other continents would easily transfer to
sub-Saharan Africa. Norman Borlaug's legacy of assuming that HYVs developed elsewhere would have widespread application no matter the environmental limitations failed in sub-Saharan Africa.[48]

~

By the twenty-first century, most agricultural commodities still reached market via footpaths and local roads, often in baskets balanced on the heads or
carried on the backs of women. With the least developed road network in

Figure 16. Transporting maize in Zambia
The Green Revolution has lagged in sub-Saharan Africa because of inadequate transportation systems that make transporting the harvest to market difficult. This photograph depicts
a cartload of maize, pulled by two bullocks down a narrow dirt road in Zambia, leaving the
harvest field for storage or market. A farmer follows behind balancing the day's necessities on
her head. Photo: P. Lowe / CIMMYT, CC BY-NC-SA.

the world, farmers had great difficulty getting their produce to market, particularly in large quantities. Without improved roads and access to transport
vehicles, such as trucks or other motorized vehicles, increased production
would not benefit subsistence farmers if they could not market their crops.
At the same time, much of sub-Saharan Africa had a low population density,
which made investment in roads costlier and easier for governments to ignore compared to the densely populated Green Revolution areas in Asia. Irrigation remained "relatively scarce."[49]

In Ghana, Kenya, Nigeria, and Zambia, 60 percent of the people lived in
the countryside and 70 percent in Tanzania, while 85 percent of the population in Malawi, Uganda, and Ethiopia resided in rural areas. As a result, farms
became smaller as the competition for land increased. In order to meet food
needs, cereal grain imports increased ten times in these countries (excluding
Zambia for which the data is incomplete). Since 1970, international food aid
to sub-Saharan African countries had become an annual necessity. Drought,
floods, and refugee movements created and compounded the need for more

food and agricultural production. At same time, markets depended on governmental policies regarding production incentives, credit, and land reform. Moreover, with extensive cultivation reaching its limits in some areas, only government-supported intensive agriculture with Green Revolution technologies could solve the growing food problem. Yet agricultural intensification and a Green Revolution are not synonymous. Agricultural intensification means increased farm production, often by traditional methods, over time. In contrast, a Green Revolution involves considerable outside scientific and government support over a comparatively brief period.[50]

Overall, political problems as well as natural disasters, such as drought, slowed government support for the Green Revolution in sub-Saharan Africa. Political turmoil also invariably led to the redirection of resources from agricultural subsidization in various forms. In some countries, such as Malawi and Uganda, government policy encouraged the development of commercial agriculture, not small-scale subsistence farming, thereby circumventing the purposes of the Green Revolution. In contrast to the Green Revolution in Asia, which was based on state support and market mediation to aid subsistence farmers, sub-Saharan states largely neglected smallholders. Moreover, nongovernmental organizations had a long history of assisting Asian agriculture, but support from these institutions in sub-Saharan Africa only became relatively important during the last two decades of the twentieth century. NGOs, whether internal or international, worked with lower-level, grassroots, and community-based organizations to improve agricultural production through extension services, seed banks, and agro-processing businesses as well as credit-granting institutions. Some large-scale NGOs, such as Global 2000/ Sasakawa Africa Association, worked directly with governments to introduce the "classic" packages of high-yielding seed varieties and fertilizer that created the Asian Green Revolution, while others emphasized agricultural diversification and the production of high-value export crops. Some international NGOs, however, supported agricultural improvement among small-scale, poor farmers, but overall the NGOs worked with governments and imposed a top-down approach to agricultural development.[51]

The NGOs, however, had not replaced the state in providing agricultural assistance, particularly regarding market control. During the early twenty-first century, Ethiopia monopolized the grain trade while Kenya, Nigeria, and Zambia served as the buyer of last resort for food staples. Zambia instituted a price floor for maize, Kenya had marketing boards for all major crops, and Nigeria prohibited the importation of many crops that farmers could produce domestically to encourage production while Tanzania subsidized fertilizer to help maintain or increase production and thereby ensure food security.[52]

In retrospect, while maize production increased after 1960, quadrupling in Ghana, Malawi, Tanzania, and Uganda, population growth exceeded food production. Few sub-Saharan nations achieved food security or self-sufficiency. Governments sought greater food production by expanding the hectares cultivated. They emphasized extensive rather than intensive production with science-based agriculture. In contrast to the science-based Asian Green Revolution, which improved production by small-scale farmers, the sub-Saharan Green Revolution offered little for most farmers. Instead, states often channeled the technological packages designed to increase productivity to large-scale farmers, who often had political connections to the state, to help them produce high-valued export crops. As a result, a Green Revolution in sub-Saharan African had not been achieved by the early twenty-first century.[53]

The failure of Green Revolutions to develop in sub-Saharan Africa resulted from political miscalculation and lack of commitment. During the 1960s and 1970s, few governments recognized that food self-sufficiency would become national problems. Agricultural production could still expand horizontally by the more extensive cultivation of unoccupied and unused lands. Grasslands and forests remained for clearing. Moreover, African governments did not have the political stability comparable to Asian nations. Frequent changes in governments prevented the implementation of consistent policies designed to expand agricultural development. Reduced foreign aid and the inability of governments to provide agricultural assistance to small-scale producers kept about half of the rural population in poverty. Markets remained inadequate and underdeveloped and transportation limited; crop yields remained low because farmers did not use HYVs and fertilizer due to cost. Few farmers had access to credit, and farmers, often women, relied on traditional hand tools to cultivate their fields. Agriculture remained subsistent, and it did not enhance national food security or prevent family or widespread hunger in times of drought or civil war.[54]

Still, by the turn of the twenty-first century, science-based agriculture remained a potential for sub-Saharan Africa. Many governments, however, preferred to purchase cheap food on the international market rather than invest in costly Green Revolution technologies and polices required to support it. Production of high-valued exportable crops drove agricultural policy, not farming for self-sufficiency. As long as surplus-producing nations subsidized crop production and dumped grain on the world market, thereby driving down prices, investments in Green Revolution agricultural technology in sub-Saharan Africa were not realistic, unless the international market changed drastically for some reason such as massive crop failures. Politics, then, prevented the development of a Green Revolution in sub-Saharan Africa. Only high-level political commitments could ensure the acquisition and distribution of the necessary HYVs, fertilizer, pesticides, and mechanical hardware necessary to implement and sustain a Green Revolution.[55]

By 2003, sub-Saharan nations confronted many problems when attempting to initiate a Green Revolution. In Ethiopia, for example, the Green Revolution collapsed due to overproduction, which brought famine. Ethiopian farmers produced more grain with Green Revolution technologies than domestic consumers could eat or competitively sell on the world market. As a result, grain prices fell below production costs. Storage capacity proved inadequate and an estimated three hundred thousand tons of grain spoiled. In Tanzania, only a third of the farmers used oxen to plow their fields. Tanzanian farmers also planted traditional maize varieties not HYVs, and they used more organic than inorganic fertilizer because it was cheaper. Without access to or the ability to afford HYVs, fertilizers, and pesticides, crop production remained low, usually less than one ton of maize per hectare. Moreover, the Tanzania extension service provided little technical assistance, and farmers seldom sought advice. Most farmers sold their crops directly to traders at their farm site or at local markets, when the traders arrived with their trucks on an irregular basis and negotiated prices. Overall, sub-Saharan African countries did not have a systematic and orderly marketing system for agricultural commodities.[56]

Rice production remained low in Tanzania for similar reasons. Only 10 percent of the farmers used inorganic fertilizer, and they preferred traditional, not HYV, varieties because of consumer tastes. Government and other institutional limitations prevented improvements in tillage practices, mechanization, seed varieties, chemical fertilizers, and irrigation. Still, food production kept pace with population growth, and Tanzanian farmers sold food crops for cash as well as used them for subsistence, but malnutrition plagued many households due to inadequate food supplies and low income. Credit regulations set minimal borrowing rates and lending institutions charged high interest rates, thereby making repayment difficult, if not impossible. Government efforts to encourage farmers to purchase power tillers and tractors frightened these farmers given the cost. Green Revolution investments meant the possibility, if not probability, of large-scale farmers buying out debt-ridden smallholders.[57]

Malawi fared better and, by the early twenty-first century, it had earned the sobriquet of the "Cradle of Africa's Green Revolution." The "Malawi Miracle" set the bar for many sub-Saharan nations, proving that a traditional Green Revolution could provide food security for hungry people. Even so, Malawi still relied on maize imports to feed its people. More than 50 percent of the population remained trapped in poverty, 25 percent of the "ultra poor" could not afford a diet with a minimum recommended caloric intake, 50 percent of the children suffered acute malnutrition. Credit for investment in Green Revolution technologies remained nearly nonexistent. Few farmers' cooperatives provided that service and the semiliterate farmers did not have the collateral to acquire loans for agricultural improvement. At best, they came to creditors as supplicants, gambling that they could apply Green Revolution technology to their land, reap high yields, earn a profit, and pay off their loans. Many critics charged that the "fertilizer led" Green Revolution had failed. Indeed, if some hailed Malawi as a Green Revolution success story, others considered it an abysmal failure.[58]

In 2007, however, Malawi introduced a subsidy policy to reduce the costs of HYV maize and chemical fertilizer with the goal of eliminating widespread hunger. Known as the Agricultural Impact Subsidy Programme (ISP) it targeted small-scale subsistence farmers. Malawi's farmers took advantage of the ISP program, which helped boost production from 38 percent to 55 percent, depending on local conditions. Grain sales increased 60–90 percent across the country. The Green Revolution package increased food security, created demands for more labor, and improved agricultural wages. Erratic precipitation, however, made maize gains variable, but the Green Revolution gave Malawi a grain reserve of 9.25 months in 2008, thereby reducing the hungry season by as much as four months. The Green Revolution package of HYVs and fertilizer also buffered the effects of crop failure due to bad weather in the years that followed, particularly for the more economically and financially secure farmers.[59]

Yet, as late as 2011, the Food and Agriculture Organization (FAO) estimated that 26 percent of sub-Saharan Africa's population remained undernourished. Drought had ruined many efforts to introduce the Green Revolution to the region, and many commercial farmers emphasized biofuel rather than food crops. Some scientists worried that climate change that increased temperatures and fostered drought along with rapid population growth would further increase food insecurity. With most of sub-Saharan Africa's thirty-three million farms constituted of fewer than two hectares of good land,

some agricultural scientists argued again that only Green Revolution technologies could feed the region's people. Others championed crop diversification to end the reliance of smallholders on maize as a buffer against climate
change and drought. Still others urged a return to traditional but improved
open-pollinated maize varieties whose seeds could be planted the next year
rather than HYVs. The major HYV seed producers such as Monsanto, however, fought the use of open-pollinated varieties and aggressively advocated
the production of HYVs to save sub-Saharan Africa. Many regional governments wanted food security and supported the Green Revolution package approach at least in theory to increase food production. Yet, critics charged that
the international seed companies forced out local seed companies, decreased
genetic diversity, and convinced farmers to forgo planting traditional open-
pollinated varieties.[60]

Other problems remained. In Ghana, agricultural experts considered the
Green Revolution as the most important opportunity to end poverty, but cocoa had become Ghana's most important export crop, and government policy
supported this agricultural endeavor at the expense of grain, cassava, yam,
plantain, and other food crops. At the same time, Ghana's households spent
between 40 percent and 50 percent of income on food and imported 60 percent of the required rice. Green Revolution advocates argued that science
would increase food production and farm income while greater agricultural
production would reduce urban food prices. They urged Ghana's policy makers to support Green Revolution agricultural science because it was pro-poor.
The old argument for a Green Revolution similar to that in Mexico and Asia
still held an allure for some Africans despite decades of evidence that it could
not seamlessly transfer to sub-Saharan Africa.[61]

Little success also marked Ethiopia's attempt to spread Green Revolution
technology to subsistence farmers. This effort primarily failed because the
government used the agricultural extension service to aid farmers who supported it. The government deemed the farmers who did not accept this assistance as disloyal and they suffered political intimidation and repressive treat-
ment. In Ethiopia, politics and cultural expectations not science determined
agricultural success. The government used the Green Revolution to reinforce
its authoritarian presence while maintaining the dominant political culture.
Green Revolution technologies went to those who supported the government,
and the farmers, usually young, who accepted it, considered the Green Revolution technologies a way to gain social and political favoritism rather than
to increase agricultural production.[62]

Moreover, the Food and Agriculture Organization, World Bank, and various NGOs had rejected Norman Borlaug's package of HYV seeds, fertilizer, and irrigation to increase agricultural production, particularly for cereal grains. These institutions pressured many sub-Saharan African governments to eliminate fertilizer subsidies and price supports. In Ghana, land banks charged as much as 30 percent interest on agricultural loans. Ghanaian farmers responded by reducing fertilizer applications. Maize production declined, and two million Ghanaians became malnourished. World Bank officials, however, preferred the free market and private sources, not government aid, to improve agriculture and provide food security. The private sector, however, proved too underdeveloped to supply seed, fertilizer, transport, and markets. The World Bank responded by urging governments to expand agricultural exports so that impoverished, food-deficit nations could buy cheap grain on the world market to feed their people. For the World Bank, Green Revolution arguments that agricultural science would help poor, hungry farmers no longer resonated.[63]

The old critics of the Green Revolution now became the new critics of the efforts of multi-national corporations, African states, multi-lateral institutions, such as the World Bank, and some nongovernmental organizations among others, which supported "private sector" agricultural development. This meant that these institutions provided financing for the purchase of seeds and agrochemicals, land acquisitions, and consolidations as well as supported processing, storage, trading, and distribution companies for the export of high-value crops and biofuels. Multinationals, such as Yara, Monsanto, Syngenta, and Cargill, insisted on the control and distribution of new agricultural science and technology as well as control of their intellectual property. They did not intend to distribute it freely or cheaply to small-scale farmers. The multi-national corporations proved more interested in profits than improving the lives of small-scale farmers and hungry rural and urban people. These entities used government-friendly policies to support corporate agriculture, which the critics called a "new wave of colonialism." If the Green Revolution was bad for small-scale farmers, the critics contended that the new biotech, multinational corporate agriculture was worse, because it further marginalized poor farmers who constituted 50–90 percent of the sub-Saharan population, half being women. Food security became corporate driven not state or farmer driven. Many observers now lessened their criticism of the Green Revolution and advocated that governments subsidize agricultural science and farm prices to achieve household food security. They also demanded open access to new agricultural technologies, particularly germplasm. The Alliance for a Green Revolution in Africa (AGRA) countered, saying that the public-private agricultural relationships would enhance food security by providing the development and distribution of new grain varieties enabled by outside investment. The US Agency for International Development supported this strategy because it allegedly would promote peace and security through agricultural economic growth rather than political turbulence by hungry people, or so it seemed. American investors also would benefit even if small-scale farmers would not.[64]

Moreover, agricultural policies that provided subsidies, marketing guarantees, and tariff protection had been erratic, and many farmers preferred traditional methods than adjustments to ever changing agricultural policies that ranged from socialism to free-market economies. Without markets, farmers had little opportunity to sell their crops for fair prices and accumulate the capital to invest in Green Revolution technology, and many governments did not provide essential leadership in market development. As late as 2010, more than 70 percent of rural households in sub-Saharan Africa did not have access to urban markets. The farmers in these households lived more than a thirty-minute walk from an all-weather road. In addition, without major governmental commitments to increase agricultural production to achieve food security, rather than the enhancement of export marketing, the outlook for a Green Revolution in sub-Saharan African remained doubtful.[65]

Yet, some agricultural experts, usually the hard scientists, such as Norman Borlaug, and donor nation specialists, argued that the Asian Green Revolution provided a model for Africa, even though not all of its components could be immediately transferred to the sub-continent. Others, however, contend that the agricultural conditions in sub-Saharan Africa were different from Asia, which had large irrigated areas suitable for hybrid varieties of wheat and rice. In contrast, sub-Saharan Africa had a variety of climates and nearly all farmers relied on erratic rainfall, not dependable irrigation systems, to water their crops. Moreover, Africa had many staple crops, not just wheat and rice, with different technical requirements for efficient production. In addition, Asian governments provided more systematic structure and supportive agricultural policies than sub-Saharan governments.[66]

Agricultural scientists, however, maintained that the technology was available for a sub-Saharan Green Revolution. Social scientists countered that it was not affordable, that farmers did not know how to use it because of weak extension systems, and that without reliable markets farmers had no reason to increase production beyond household needs, which did not solve the prob-

lem of food self-sufficiency or security for their respective nations. These critics used Mozambique as an example of the failure of the Green Revolution
in sub-Saharan Africa.[67]

Mozambique remained one of the poorest nations in the world with 54
percent of the population living in poverty. Agricultural production did not
meet subsistence standards and food riots occurred in 2008 and 2010. Farmers constituted approximately 80 percent of the population. The Ministry of
Agriculture and extension service had become underfunded and unmotivated.
Agricultural production declined and cultivation with hoes prevailed. The government lacked funds to purchase Green Revolution technologies and establish an efficient distribution system. Less than 3 percent of Mozambique's
farmers used fertilizer and only 5 percent planted improved maize varieties
for their most important food crop. Few markets existed for the sale of surplus grain. Poor roads made matters worse. Mozambique's participation in
the Green Revolution remained as distant as ever.[68]

Other problems prevailed. In 2002, the National Agricultural Research
Center and the seed company NASECO introduced the HYV rice variety called
NERICA (New Rice for Africa). The West Africa Rice Development Association crossed Asian and African rice varieties to produce this strain, and it intended to spread rice farming to rainfed uplands. It aggressively competed
with weeds, resisted major diseases, and responded to fertilizer as well as produced high yields. NERICA seemed a perfect solution to bringing the Green
Revolution to Uganda. Uganda's extension agents, however, knew little about
rice production, and they could not provide the necessary advice to farmers for
its cultivation. Farmers planted their fields with seed saved from the previous
crop because the extension service failed to convey that they could not plant
the harvested HYV seeds from one crop year to the next. When production
fell, farmers abandoned this HYV rice variety, because they could not raise
it without irrigation, fertilizer, and pesticides on drylands, and it had a short
growing season. NERICA also required more water than traditional rainfed
varieties as well as more labor for planting, cultivating, and harvesting. A rain
shortfall further reduced the yield and profits, and farmers returned to traditional varieties. Agricultural scientists believed that a Green Revolution for
Uganda remained a possibility but no one could say when that might occur.
Some observers hoped that a new indigenous science for indigenous people
would bring an "African Green Revolution."[69]

Too much had been expected of sub-Saharan agricultural scientists who
contended with many microenvironments and soil types, and who needed

five to ten years of plant breeding to develop indigenous varieties rather than make seed introductions from another continent, which usually failed. Sub-Saharan plant breeders also dealt with water and drought problems not confronted in other food-deficit regions. Subsistence farmers often preferred traditional sorghums and millets because they could replant the harvested seeds from these plants, and these crops proved less risky for investment, particularly without government price floors for grain.[70]

Only increased agricultural production could provide food security in sub-Saharan Africa, but that goal proved difficult to achieve. Some critics asked, "How come the Green Revolution eluded Africa?" Two answers were offered. First, too many African agricultural scientists and politicians believed that the Green Revolution in Asia could be seamlessly transferred to sub-Saharan Africa. Second, sub-Saharan African governments lacked the political will to establish agricultural policies that would have supported the Green Revolution, such as providing seed and fertilizer subsidies, cheap credit, agricultural research programs, extension services, infrastructure, and markets.[71]

Others looked to the past and took a more traditional approach to creating a Green Revolution in sub-Saharan Africa. In 2007, Kofi Annan, former secretary-general of the United Nations, agreed to head the Alliance for a Green Revolution in Africa (AGRA). It had the goal to provide new seed varieties and tools as well as techniques to develop a productive and profitable sustainable agriculture for small-scale farmers through public and private partnerships. AGRA supported technological innovation, including the adoption of genetically modified seeds. It wanted to increase planted acreage by 50 percent with HYVs in twenty countries, eliminate hunger by 40 percent, and reduce poverty by 20 percent, all funded by the Bill and Melinda Gates Foundation and the Rockefeller Foundation. Some observers challenged its purpose and argued that the variety of soils and microclimates across sub-Saharan Africa prevented a Green Revolution, even with private foundation investments, and contended that there was "no single magic technological bullet . . . for radically improving African agriculture." Rather than propose a single Green Revolution, as in Asia, they recommended "rainbow evolutions"—that is, environmentally friendly methods locally developed by technicians and female farmers to improve agricultural production. Biodiversity, not monoculture, they contended, would provide a sustainable agriculture and achieve food security. They rejected creating a Green Revolution based on expensive, patented seed varieties purchased from foreign, usually western companies. Moreover, they argued that a Green Revolution should be based on crops adapted to local and regional ecological conditions and suitable for sub-Saharan markets. Agriculture based on indigenous knowledge would establish a functional Green Revolution in sub-Saharan Africa. Or so the critics argued.[72]

In 2014, the African Union lamented that sub-Saharan Africa largely missed out on the Green Revolution. Some looked to the past and advocated a second Green Revolution for the region with the increased application of "underused technologies," such as irrigation and chemical fertilizers. Some contemporaries, however, thought that the solution to sub-Saharan Africa's food deficiency lay with the development of genetically modified seed varieties. Earlier in 2009, Bingu wa Mutharika, president of Malawi and chair of the African Union, put it differently. He said, "Africa must feed Africa," by whatever means possible.[73]

In retrospect, sub-Saharan Africa missed the Green Revolution because it had low population densities, weak financial systems, poor roads, few markets, little irrigated land, and inadequate government support, including research. By the early twenty-first century, agricultural production remained stagnant. Governments had not developed approximately 80 percent of sub-Saharan Africa's irrigation capacity nor had farmers efficiently utilized 40–70 percent of the irrigation available, depending on the area. As a result, farmers could not efficiently use HYVs and fertilizer to increase crop yields. In addition, sub-Saharan farmers preferred maize and root crops, such as cassava, not wheat and rice. Government corruption and inefficiency further slowed the adoption of Green Revolution technologies. Great climatic and soil diversity also complicated agricultural improvement. Rather than develop Green Revolution technologies appropriate for microclimates and soil conditions, particularly in rainfed areas, many sub-Saharan African nations chose to rely on food imports rather than agricultural developments to help feed hungry people, if not gain food security. During the early twentieth-first century, sub-Saharan countries still played catch-up to Green Revolution in Asia.[74]

Although the Green Revolution still floundered during the early twenty-first century, optimists remained hopeful that there was a "moral imperative to provide an African agricultural revolution." That revolution was at best in the distant future, even though many observers recognized that agriculture in sub-Saharan Africa had become the fundamental humanitarian problem of the time. Realists recognized that if a Green Revolution ever occurred in sub-Saharan Africa, it would be constituted from many Green Revolutions given the region's ecological diversity. A Green Revolution for sub-Saharan Africa also depended on the improvement of transportation in the form of railroads

and roads and communicating systems to bridge the vast distances of the region to enable market development and encourage subsistence farmers to produce surpluses for a market economy. The "tyranny of distance" remained a
major challenge. Rapid population growth, however, also threatened to out-
pace food production. Moreover, a Green Revolution for sub-Saharan Africa
depended on the inclusion of female farmers. Governments needed to end
their marginalization, extend credit, provide extension services, and secure
their land rights. Evidence indicated that female farmers proved good credit
risks and seldom defaulted on loans. Climate change also provided new and
unknown influences on Green Revolution agricultural development, except
that it threatened to create even greater agricultural and migration problems.
Moreover, many agricultural officials and the public realized that modernization did not necessarily mean westernization.[75]

By the turn of the twenty-first century, the Green Revolution had not been
achieved in sub-Saharan Africa. It remained a possibility, but a limited one at
best. The history of the efforts, or lack of them, to implement a Green Revolution in sub-Saharan Africa did not bode well for the future.[76]

6

Green or Gene Revolution

The antecedents of the Green Revolution originated with the experiments of farmers in breeding new seed varieties in many regions over the ages. In the public mind, however, the Green Revolution dates from the 1940s and 1950s and it achieved the greatest success boosting agricultural productivity in food-deficit nations during the 1970s and 1980s. As production peaked and as scientists failed to produce new hybrid varieties that could replace older and less productive strains, they increasingly turned their attention from hybrid development that used crossbreeding techniques to the genetic engineering of new varieties. During the 1980s, plant breeders began inserting the molecules of deoxyribonucleic acid (DNA) from the genes of selected plants into traditional and Green Revolution varieties to create new strains that did not exist in nature. Put differently, scientists engineered new crop varieties in laboratories rather than by breeding for specific characteristics in open-air fields. The scientific community referred to these crops as genetically modified organisms, GMOs, or GM varieties. Many agricultural scientists believed that GM crop varieties would solve the hybrid seed problems of the Green Revolution and create a Gene Revolution that would help farmers (not necessarily subsistence farmers) improve production to meet the food needs of ever increasing populations in food-deficit nations. Optimists also believed that GM crops that reduced the need for herbicides and pesticides would help preserve the environment and reduce soil exhaustion, water pollution, and health hazards for farmers and consumers. GM crops also had the potential to resist drought and use water more efficiently.[1]

⁓

By the early twentieth century, China, which had achieved food security with Green Revolution hybrid crop varieties for wheat, rice, and maize, still sought improved and increased agricultural production as a matter of national priority. By 2014, Chinese farmers fed 1.3 billion people or 20 percent of the world's population from 7 percent of the world's arable land and used 5 percent of its water resources. Green Revolution technologies of hybrid varieties, fertilizers, pesticides, and irrigation, however, enabled sufficient grain production to feed the population. This agricultural success primarily occurred after the establishment of the household responsibility policy in 1978 and during the early twentieth-first century with Green Revolution technologies. Yet, Green Revolution hybridization did not solve the problem of increased insect damage or diseases for rice plants, and it often made the situation worse, because new insect infestations required heavier pesticide applications. Moreover, large application of fertilizers and pesticides to boost the productivity of hybrid varieties proved expensive, and the environmental and human health problems generated caused increasing public concern.[2]

By the early twentieth-first century, China had a goal to produce 95 percent of its annual food needs. Government officials believed that this productivity would ensure food security and that they easily could cover the remaining deficit by importation (that is, trade). Yet, they understood that food security meant building grain reserves and increasing production to meet the food needs of a growing population. Maize became an increasingly important crop; indeed, in 2012, it became the most widely planted cereal grain. Farmers primarily used it for livestock feed.[3]

Although Green Revolution technologies substantially increased grain production in China, during the 1980s, agricultural scientists began work to ensure food security by developing GM crop varieties. Specifically they worked to develop new transgenetic (that is, GM) lines of japonica and indica rice in the laboratory that would resist disease and insects. By 2009, they had developed GM rice varieties Huahui 1 and Bt Shanyou that produced from 6 percent to 9 percent more than conventional hybrid varieties and they used 80 percent less pesticides. Some varieties resisted bacterial leaf blight, and others proved tolerant to herbicides. Agricultural scientists and farmers anticipated approval of these new GM varieties for the commercial release to some 440 million farmers. In August, the Ministry of Agriculture (MOA) approved five-year certificates that permitted planting of these rice varieties on a commercial scale but not for sale, pending completion of further regulatory requirements.[4]

At the same time, agricultural scientists made significant progress to develop GM maize to resist drought, cold, saline soils, and pests, such as the stem borer. They also wanted to engineer wheat varieties that resisted diseases such as the barley yellow mosaic, powdery mildew, and sharp eyespot as well as boost the nutritional quality and dough strength to improve processing and baking qualities. In addition, they worked to engineer herbicide-resistant soybean varieties. Although Chinese scientists met with GM plant breeders in the United States, at the International Rice Research Institute in the Philippines, and at the International Maize and Wheat Improvement Center in Mexico to acquire germplasm and consult about engineering techniques, national and international political difficulties prevented commercial success. The problems ranged from consumer health fears over consumption to nationalism to international trade regulations.[5]

Outside of China, GM research also changed. Critics countered that private corporations, not public institutions, controlled GM research. As a result, these firms patented their seeds and charged high prices that poor farmers around the world could not afford. They also criticized private companies, such as Monsanto and Syngenta, for ignoring the development of GM subsistence crops, such as cassava, sorghum, and pearl millet, that would help subsistence farmers feed their families because these crops would not return a sufficient profit. Many critics warned that GM crop varieties had the potential to let a new genie out of the bottle by enabling certain genetic characteristics to transfer via windblown pollen and create weeds resistant to herbicides.[6]

GM crops did not present a magic solution for increasing food production. The potential dangers were many. GM critics, outside of the United States, argued that caution and government regulation should guide agricultural scientists in this new crop-breeding endeavor. The dangers of a Gene Revolution rivaled those of the Green Revolution, perhaps more so. Naturally, agricultural scientists disagreed. They contended that genetic modifications in food plants would only increase agricultural production. They argued, as they had with their Green Revolution critics, that food distribution, not scientifically based food production, had created problems of malnutrition and hunger.[7]

During the 1990s, China exerted increasing control of the research and publicity agenda for GM crop development. By the early twenty-first century, China had become the leading nation for publically supported (that is, government-funded) biotechnological research for food crops outside the western world. Most GM research occurred in the private sector of industrialized nations. Developing, food-deficit nations spent little or no money for GM agricultural research. China and India proved exceptions given their strong scientific base and commitment to GM agricultural research essential for economic development. Chinese scientists took a fast-track approach to developing rice, maize, wheat, and soybeans, among other crops. China, however, did not have any biosafety regulations to guide its GM research until 1993, and agricultural scientists became the first to raise a GM disease-resistant tobacco and cotton in commercial quantities. Scientists and government officials preferred to pursue "promotional" and "permissive" policies to achieve the rapid development and commercialization of GM crops while downplaying potential environmental and health risks.[8]

In order to create a Gene Revolution, agricultural and social scientists, politicians, and consumers had to resolve a host of complicated technical, social, economic, environmental, and political issues, many of which had no solution by the early twenty-first century. China's past success with Green Revolution technologies that increased cereal production and ended the periodic danger of famine did not guarantee absolute food security in the decades beyond the early twenty-first century. Many problems slowed efforts of agricultural scientists to put GM cereal grains in commercial production to provide that food security. Moreover, as the population continued to increase rapidly, farmers planted more commercially remunerative biofuel rather than food grain crops. Consumer fears about food safety at home and abroad also gave authorities pause and prevented authorization for commercial production of GM crops, particularly rice. Yet, while agricultural scientists generally believed that biotechnology could meet new and growing demands for food, by the early twenty-first century, the government took a "precautionary" approach to the commercial authorization of GM food crops. It had only approved the production of GM industrial crops, such as cotton, yellow maize, and soybeans, the latter two for livestock feed. It had not approved any GM crop for direct consumption as human food.[9]

Despite uncertainty about the long-term safety of GM crops, scientists in China and India conducted field trials on insect- and disease-resistant GM rice varieties, but China has not approved a GM crop for commercial production since 1997. Outside of China, however, they encountered increasing difficulty acquiring land for field trials of GM crops. Government scientists in India had problems locating test sites, because opponents charged that the pollen of GM varieties could blow with the wind and contaminate traditional hybrid Green Revolution varieties and because of public opposition to commercial firms developing and controlling new GM varieties. By the early twenty-first century, Spanish farmers grew GM maize, Iran had become the only country that had approved the commercial production of GM rice, and only in South Africa did farmers, usually wealthy and large-scale, raise GM white maize for the commercial market. In China, GM food crop adoption lagged in part due to insufficient evidence that GM varieties would increase productivity beyond Green Revolution hybrids and techniques, especially for poor farmers. In field trials, rice bred for insect resistance proved that it reduced the need for pesticides, thereby suggesting less environmental degradation and risks to human health for farmers and consumers.[10]

By the late twentieth century, the Green Revolution had taken a new technical direction. During the 1980s, China began increasing its support of biological agricultural research as part of its attempt to modernize and secure adequate supplies of the nation's major food crop—rice. Scientists had based much of the Green Revolution genetic research on improved varieties received from the International Rice Research Institute (IRRI), some 3,335 varieties between 1971 and 1981. In contrast to the United States, the government, rather than private seed companies, funded this research. The work of Chinese agricultural scientists departed from traditional plant breeding as it had in the US because they did not use natural cross-pollination techniques but manipulated plant genes mechanically in the laboratory to create new varieties.[11]

Chinese agricultural scientists and government officials soon confronted unintended consequences from their research, as did their American counterparts. Quickly, social scientists, environmentalists, and public critics began charging that such manmade plant varieties endangered human health and the environment. The government responded by establishing a committee to study the problem of bio-food safety. Since 2004, a high-level committee charged with this responsibility has made it a matter of policy to deny approval for the distribution of western transgenetic seeds to farmers for commercial production. Some Chinese farmers, however, who have been concerned about increasing their yields and income, have surreptitiously acquired GM rice varieties for their fields and paddies.[12]

In 2001, China approved an environmental release (a stage before commercial scale planting and testing) of drought- and herbicide-resistant GM rice varieties to farmers in Zhejiang province. Between 1997 and 2001, it also approved several GM rice, maize, soybean, rape, and potato varieties for field experiments, particularly in Jiangsu Province. American officials watched the development of China's agricultural policy for signs that it would approve the commercialization of GM rice production. Such a decision would have great influence in other countries about whether to permit the flow of GM grains into the human food supply.[13]

By 2011, many public officials, scientists, and consumers in China contended that genetically modified plant research would enable the nation to become independent of foreign grain for human and livestock food. Nationalists, neo-Leftists, and the military became the most critical of foreign GM grain imports. They opposed the introduction of "foreign technology" in the form of GM rice as a threat to Chinese independence and civilization. Instead, they championed the development of GM maize and rice varieties by Chinese scientists to ensure food security, but they ignored that rice and processed foods in Mainland China and Hong Kong tested positive for GM rice not approved for production. Some GM rice also contained genetic material already patented in other countries, thereby undermining the argument that China could be independent of foreign agricultural science. These critics essentially expressed a "cultural nationalism" for agricultural development, particularly advocating "conventional" plant breeding to ensure public health, independence, and high crop yields, because GM rice varieties often did not produce greater harvests than Green Revolution varieties.[14]

Early in 2012, the Beijing-based seed company Agritech Limited expected the government to approve production of a GM maize variety for commercial production but only for use as livestock feed, particularly for hogs. As the largest consumer of pork in the world and the second largest consumer of maize through pork, China had a great need for more maize. Some consumers welcomed the news because the increasingly urban, well-educated population had more disposable income and they intended to spend some of it for meat. Other observers believed the new GM maize planted by Chinese farmers would increase production and eventually decrease imports of this grain.[15]

These hopes proved premature, because the desire for greater yields from GM crops to increase farmer income and food production had moved from the realm of biological science to domestic politics and international relations, where it had become a matter of acute debate. In 2013, Peng Guangqian, a major general in the People's Liberation Army and deputy secretary-general of China's National Security Policy Committee, criticized the government for permitting the increased importation of GM grain from the United States because it indicated a hidden American agenda to harm China with transgenetic technology and endangered China's security. GM crop imports from the United States would make China food dependent on the Americans. Critics charged that the introduction of American GM crops was nothing less than biological imperialism and the launching of the equivalent of a "new Opium War." Only traitors would support such a policy. Instead, China needed its own independent GM research and crop development. Emotions rather than science drove this attack.[16]

The Ministry of Agriculture, which exercised authority over policy for the creation of genetically modified crops, responded through Lin Min, director of the Biotechnology Research Institute of the Chinese Academy of Agricultural Sciences. Min contended that GM crops were not only safe for human consumption but also that China's limited arable land and growing population meant that foreign grain imports were "inevitable." He also wanted China to increase cereal grain production with GM varieties. Min rejected Peng's "Cold War thinking." Nevertheless, biological science to improve crop yields became a matter of the "national interest" and defense policy. Agricultural scientists who pursued GM crop research and had degrees from the United States and professional contacts with western scientists confronted charges that they were "American agents."[17]

Agricultural science had become political. At this time, China imported three varieties of GM insect- and herbicide-resistant soybeans from Monsanto in the United States and the German chemical producer BASF, and the government had approved GM maize shipments from Argentina. By 2017, China had imported more than 9.5 million metric tons of GM soybeans from Argentina, Brazil, and the United States. The MOA also supported extensive GM research designed to reach commercial production, and China had imported GM soybeans for more than a decade. With this news, the MOA also came under attack by consumers who worried about food safety. Liberals wanted restriction or prohibition of US GM grain to ensure public health, while conservatives considered it a threat to national food security and an attempt of the US to control China's agricultural production. The MOA fought back, arguing that foods processed from GM grain that it had approved for import were safe for consumption. Moreover, the MOA contended that matters of nationalism and fear for the public health, not science, dominated the debate.[18]

Economic and national pressures no doubt combined temporarily to halt the importation of American maize to China. The MOA, however, had difficulty combatting nonscientific reports that GM crops, no matter whether produced in the United States or China, caused health problems, including cancer and infertility. Yet, China had developed its own GM tomatoes, papaya, and sweet potatoes, which consumers unknowingly consumed. By 2014, China had quietly approved fifteen other strains of GM maize for importation. Although maize still could be used for livestock feed only, the MOA had a political problem that it could not solve by agricultural science alone.[19]

In late 2013, authorities at ports in Fuzhow, Shenzhen, and Shandong, discovered that maize shipments from the United States contained an unapproved insect-resistant variety known as MIR162. China had not approved this GM variety for import, and it rejected more than 180,000 tons of the grain. In November, China banned all imports of US maize. This market loss proved significant for American maize producers, buyers, and shippers. By 2014, American grain producers had lost as much as $2.9 billion due to the Chinese rejection of American grain contaminated with MIR162, including "distillers grain"—that is, the dried grain byproduct from the production of ethanol for a gasoline additive, used for livestock feed. They anticipated greater marketing losses in the future as GM varieties contaminated traditional Green Revolution varieties from their pollen when grown in nearby fields. By April 2014, China had rejected approximately 1.45 million tons of maize with a loss to American shippers Cargill, Incorporated and Archer Daniels Midland Company of approximately $225 million. American observers charged that this rejection did not involve food safety but rather China's desire to keep American grain off the market to raise domestic prices for its own farmers. Other American observers contended that the ban essentially served as a calculated nontariff barrier (that is, vailed protectionism) that China imposed to benefit domestic production and prices. At this time, the European Union (EU) discovered that some Chinese rice and rice products exported to its member nations contained GM ingredients. As a result, the EU required China to report all rice consignments before export to the EU and to segregate GM rice to prevent it from reaching countries that had not approved it for human consumption. Lax enforcement of biosafety regulations caused this mistake, and China rushed to prevent recurrence.[20]

Considering that the United States supplied approximately 94 percent of China's maize imports during the first ten months of 2013, the loss of China's market for American maize caused considerable concern for producers, and exporters bore the loss of the rejected shipments. The American exporters demanded that the seed companies pay part of the loss, and they argued that those companies should not develop GM grain varieties that exporters could not sell on international markets. In the United States, the National Grain and Feed Association estimated the loss of $1 billion alone from rejection of the maize variety Viptera produced by Syngenta AG. American maize farmers also saw prices drop eleven cents per bushel and projected losses of $1.14 billion from January through August 2014. Agricultural observers estimated another loss ranging from $1.2 to $3.4 billion during the next trading year beginning September 1, 2014. Farmers, seed companies, and exporters looked for someone to blame while yearning for a means to earn more money.[21]

While the MOA worked to convince the public that GM foods were safe, it also supported the development of its own GM crops to ensure food security through Chinese agricultural science and thereby avoid dependence on the United States. In order to meet its food needs, China had no choice. GM advocates contended that agricultural science was essential to help farmers meet the nation's food needs. Some observers, however, believed the government would ban all GM grain imports by 2018 to end the criticism from nationalists and food safety critics. Others saw GM crops as a method to boost food crop production and thereby lessen the effect of the increasing loss of land for industry. Agricultural scientists contended that they needed strong support for their GM crop research and development to keep China competitive if bans on crop production for commercial purposes ended.[22]

～

During the early twenty-first century, consumer concerns over health and international trade implications regarding GM crops and foods encouraged China to transform its agricultural policy regarding the development and release of GM food crops for commercial production. It did so primarily because international political and economic relationships mandated change for China to compete on a world market and reach biosafety and regulatory agreements with other nations. China's increasing expansion in world trade required changing its rapid development of GM food crops to a slower, conservative approach for authorizing the commercial production of those crops. By so doing, China could better gauge the future of GM crops in international trade and avoid commercial risks. This change occurred not only in response to consumer demands and military nationalism but also from the reality that if China intended to be a leader in agricultural science and world trade it had to accommodate GM crop regulations in other nations.[23]

China confronted the problem that many countries had higher standards for the production and importation of GM food crops. If it did not pursue a careful approach to GM food crop development to meet the importation standards and production regulations of other countries, it would lose considerable income from agricultural trade on international markets because it would be unable to sell its unapproved and internationally regulated GM products. China had enthusiastically supported the development of GM crops to help provide food security, but other nations often blocked the importation of these foods from other countries because they did not meet the importing country's standards for consumer and environmental safety. China had no alternative but to join the international community by imposing stringent regulations for the development and use of GM crops in order to gain a prosperous international agricultural trade.[24]

In 1998, the European Union placed a moratorium on the development of GM crops, a regulation that occurred on the eve of the January 2000 Cartagena Protocol on Biosafety. This protocol permitted the signatory nations to set their own GM regulations as well as determine the conditions under which they would accept GM commodities and foods from other countries when confronted with scientific uncertainty about food safety. No strict international standards existed for regulating the development and trade of GM crops and foods, a problem made more difficult because the United States government considered GM foods as merely containing additives and subject to minimal regulations by the United States Department of Agriculture. In contrast, the EU considered GM commodities a potential health hazard and made them subject to extensive review, regulation, and prohibition from importation if any "uncertainty" existed about a food's safety.[25]

In 1999, China imposed its own moratorium on the importation, consumption, and development of GM food crops. The State Council, a cabinet-level body, became responsible for all GM regulatory activities, and it watched the GM regulatory process in Europe, Japan, and Korea, where China wanted to develop important trade relations. A year later, China also studied the Cartagena Protocol on Biosafety, which did not provide a time limit for GM crop and food review and regulatory decision-making. As a result, an importing country could reject GM foods and seeds if it determined that the scientific risk or damage to the environment or human health might result from that importation.[26]

China's agricultural scientists also interacted with western scientists whose increasing environmental sensitivity, biosafety concerns, and responsibilities to help ensure human health influenced their GM policy advice to the Ministry of Agriculture and other government agencies. Chinese delegates to international conferences and exchanges helped convince the government to establish a risk assessment policy for the development of GM crops and regulations for importations of transgenetic seeds.[27]

In 2001, China joined the World Trade Organization (WTO) and increasingly sought to open its agricultural market to foreign imports as well as expand its agricultural export trade. The WTO worked to facilitate international trade, but the liberalization of China's agricultural trade policy meant that it might lose markets to other nations with stricter GM food crop regulations. In 2003, the European Union mandated a comprehensive labeling requirement for all GM foods so that consumers could have a choice between GM or non-GM products. Japan and Korea, major agricultural customers of China, also imposed restrictions on the importation of GM foods, particularly soybeans for the manufacturing of tofu and soybean sauce. EU, Japanese, and Korean regulations created a major roadblock for the further development of GM food crops in China. China met this challenge by selling Green Revolution rather than GM soybeans to Japan and South Korea. Moreover, in 2000, the Europe Union had already prohibited the importation of Chinese soy sauce after inspectors discovered GM content. Although this sauce probably had been manufactured from soybeans purchased from the United States, it caused considerable concern about the protection of China's export market. Moreover, Chinese authorities suspected that farmers had been planting illegally imported GM soybeans or domestic GM varieties that had not been released for commercial production. In response, China placed a ban on the commercial production of GM soybeans. China feared the loss of international markets for its agricultural commodities so it prohibited production for trade. It did not prohibit, however, the importation of soybeans in order to meet growing demand and acquire higher-quality beans from other nations.[28]

Government officials recognized that they needed to adjust GM agriculture policy to meet international norms and expectations. Prohibition on the development of GM commercial crops also had the benefit of easing growing consumer concerns by eliminating to the extent possible the consumption of GM food grains whether domestic or foreign. Moreover, it also had the advantage of emphasizing national sovereignty for the development and regulation of GM crops. This policy readjustment enabled China to address an environmental, a public health, and a protectionist constituency while expanding its participation in the global economy, particularly with countries that had GM importation restrictions. Strict regulations regarding food safety meant that China could satisfy the regulations of the Cartagena Protocol and the World Trade Organization, all to the benefit of its agricultural export and import markets.[29]

This agricultural policy change, however, did not mean that many agricultural scientists and government officials abandoned their desire for a strong research and development program for GM crops. It meant that politics, not scientists, determined China's GM policy. China made the calculated decision to follow EU policy for dealing with GM risks by establishing a cautious, long-term process for risk assessment. This procedure contrasted with its earlier science-based approach with limited time to make risk assessment and management decisions about the potential for serious or irreversible harm to the environment and public health from GM crops.[30]

The government's desire to restrict the development of GM research to protect its agricultural export market in food grains, however, remained contested by agricultural scientists who pressed for greater support for GM crop developments, particularly rice. China did not want to lose its competitive edge in the development of GM crop varieties that would help meet its need for food security. Even so, China essentially adopted a compromise solution to the development and importation of GM crops. While it practiced the wait-and-see policy of the European Union before authorizing the development and importation of GM crops for humans, it permitted the importation of GM crops, such as soybeans and maize, for livestock feed.[31]

Essentially, China and other nations have concluded that there is a difference between food security and food safety. While the Green Revolution increased cereal grain production to meet daily needs and provide a surplus, genetically modified grain crops caused public fear about food safety. While many Chinese proved willing to buy GM foods and while farmers showed eagerness to raise GM crops, other consumers at home and abroad remained unwilling to consume them. Moreover, the government cannot guarantee the segregation of GM rice, wheat, and maize throughout the trade system at home or abroad. China would have difficulty controlling the shipment of GM grain varieties from producer to port, because it does not have the bureaucracy to identify and track a crop, such as wheat, from the farm to export.[32]

In 2000, for example, more than two hundred million families engaged in farming and, if each farmer produced a ton of GM wheat, the problem of maintaining segregation from traditional or Green Revolution varieties would prove immense, expensive, and impossible to control, particularly if exporters at home and importers abroad required identification or certification of GM or non-GM varieties. If China or any other nation could not identify GM grain for export, its reputation would suffer when it attempted to sell non-GM grain. By refusing to authorize the commercial production of GM food grains, China minimized the danger of GM varieties entering the global market and causing an international trade problem. Until the agricultural science proved the safety of GM foods for human consumption or until officials can track such foods and grains in international trade, China has preferred to follow a cautionary course to ensure access of its agricultural commodities on the global market.[33]

At the same time, China imported considerable tonnage of GM soybeans and maize, particularly from the United States, Brazil, and Argentina. China requires the licensing of exporters and importers as well as the testing of all shipments arriving at its ports. Because millers crush soybeans into meal and oil at nearby plants, little chance occurs of these GM varieties transferring to the private market place or farm for planting. Moreover, licensing and test-ing costs increased the expense of imported grains, thereby providing a form of tariff protection to Chinese farmers who raised Green Revolution varieties because domestic prices were lower for livestock raisers and food processors. In this sense, China's concern for biosafety regulations for GM crops guar-antees an economic advantage on the domestic agricultural market. Regula-tory diversity has had its merits.[34]

∽

Genetically modified crop problems also occurred beyond China, particularly in sub-Saharan Africa. In 2002, the United States sent a considerable amount of food aid to the drought-stricken regions of southern Africa. It provided this food aid in the form of whole kernel maize. Grain shippers had not notified the recipient nations that it was a GM crop, and many, such as Zambia, Zim-babwe, Mozambique, and Malawi, refused to accept it when they learned about this maize. They did so based on three reasons: (1) they distrusted its safety regarding human health; (2) they believed that if planted the new crops would contaminate their traditional varieties and prevent sales on the European mar-ket; and, (3) it represented a new colonialism whereby major western agricul-tural corporations attempted to impose their own science on unsuspecting farmers and at a high cost. Zambian President Levy Mwanawasa consid-ered GM food grains nothing less than "poison," and said, "We would rather starve than get something toxic." Ultimately, some of these food-deficit na-tions agreed to accept GM maize if the donor companies and countries milled it first, thereby preventing it from entering the planting cycle. The donors usually refused to incur that cost and blamed the EU for preventing the distri-bution of food to famine-stricken sub-Saharan Africa. By 2003, two-thirds of the maize and one-third of the soybeans produced in the United States came from GM varieties, and shippers did not segregate it into GM and non-GM crops in storage facilities. Zambia eventually accepted milled GM maize from the United States but only to feed Angolan refugees, not its own people.[35]

As a result, Tanzania and South Africa provided most of the needed maize for relief. Some social scientists, however, argued that the inability of subsis-tence farmers in sub-Saharan Africa to raise GM grain would keep them pov-erty stricken because traditional varieties could not provide sufficient food for their families and a surplus for income. They needed drought- and insect-resistant and nitrogen-fixing food crops. EU political influence supported by European NGOs and European importers determined GM agricultural policy in sub-Saharan Africa, or so the critics charged.[36]

Some of the arguments against Green Revolution technologies transferred to the science of genetic modification and the effect it had on small-scale farmers and consumers. Critics added that the "oligopoly capitalist firms," such as Monsanto, Pioneer Hybrid, Syngenta, and DuPont, licensed and patented their GM seeds. In addition, critics charged that the profit-based Alliance for a Green Revolution in Africa (AGRA) of the Bill and Melinda Gates Foundation worked to develop large-scale corporate farming, not improve the lives of poor, hungry subsistence farmers. These seeds would not be easily or affordably available to subsistence farmers and only the wealthy would benefit. Moreover, subsistence farmers might become dependent on relatively limited seed varieties because few suppliers engaged in this research and production. The international seed companies also could force farmers to abandon traditional varieties by denying them seed choices. AGRA and other private companies would use native germplasm for their own benefit, the critics charged. They equated seed patents with exploitation. At the same time, genetic diversity would plunge and cross-contamination would make matters worse. Even so, the critics acknowledged that GM varieties would increase yields and target particular problems, such as drought, disease, and insects, while reducing pesticide and herbicide use.[37]

Many sub-Saharan African nations, however, preferred to err on the side of caution regarding potential health risks or failed to embrace GM agriculture because they did not have the research and extension infrastructure to develop this new form of crop production among poor farmers. Malawi, South Africa, Burkina Faso, and Egypt being exceptions with commercial production of some GM crops, mostly cotton, while Kenya, Nigeria, and Uganda field tested some GM crops, such as cowpeas, tomato, cabbage, and eggplant, to determine commercial viability. In July 2011, Kenya also imported GM food crops from necessity to combat famine and food shortages. These countries had strong government support for GM research. South Africa and Kenya provided regulatory legislation governing the commercial development of GM crops, but most sub-Saharan nations did not have the scientific commitment to agricultural modernization or bureaucratic infrastructure to provide it.[38]

Supporters of GM research in sub-Saharan Africa argued the inevitability of GM technology applied on a commercial scale. Extensive lands, low traditional production, and high birth rates made the adoption of GM crop varieties a foregone conclusion. Perhaps so but as late as 2013, one reporter termed the GM debate "controversial and polarizing." Food grain increases came from the planting of traditional crops. Some critics advocated "indigenous solutions" to solve the food shortage problem in sub-Saharan Africa, particularly since GM crops had failed to significantly outproduce Green Revolution crop varieties. They also charged that GM crops "favored high-input industrial farming methods." Small-scale farmers with capital and credit who tried to keep up with GM developments would suffer indebtedness and the loss of their lands to large-scale farmers.[39]

Many scientific dangers loomed, critics charged. A Gene Revolution might end with no winners and only losers. Some supporters of GM agriculture in sub-Saharan Africa, however, held that no one forced farmers to raise GM crops. Still others argued that the losers in the failure to adopt GM technology would be small-scale subsistence farmers who would never be able to produce enough to feed themselves and the rural and urban poor as well as earn some disposable income. These critics blamed NGOs for poisoning relations between seed companies, governments, and needy farmers. Others granted that sub-Saharan nations might develop GM crops, but they contended that research would be limited to foods for domestic consumption rather than trade to Europe. The Gene Revolution then created complex issues that divided agricultural scientists from the public, with farmers often forgotten. Efforts to expand, regulate, and stop GM crop production continued into the early twenty-first century with no solutions in sight.[40]

~

In Latin America, Guatemala provides another example of the contest between supporters of the Gene Revolution and their opponents. By the early twentieth century, the evidence indicated that the Green Revolution primarily befitted the nation's expanding plantation elite. As new lands opened for large-scale cultivation, small-scale subsistence farmers remained closed out of the benefits of Green Revolution technologies. They could not raise enough maize to buy fertilizer, the cost of which escalated during the late twentieth century. Farmers who borrowed to purchase fertilizer often became indebted beyond their means to pay. Green Revolution production gains went to the medium- and large-scale farmers. During the early 1980s and 1990s, civil war further hindered the expansion of Green Revolution agriculture.[41]

During the early twenty-first century, Gene Revolution critics also warned as they had on other continents that pollen from transgenetic seeds would contaminate traditional varieties unless companies, such as Monsanto, placed a terminator gene in the seed varieties to prevent germination of newly raised seed the next year. Moreover, they warned that patented transgenetic seeds gave corporations control of the agricultural economy because small-scale and subsistent farmers could not afford them. They also warned that the private seed companies might prosecute farmers for planting the seeds from transgenetic-patented seed the following year.[42]

In 2012, Semillas Cristiani Burkard, the largest seed company in Latin America and headquartered in Guatemala, wanted the government to legalize GM seeds, arguing that they fostered biodiversity and reduced the need for chemical pesticides. Although the government has not yet acceded, the company pressed hard to commercialize GM agriculture in the region. Critics charged that the company fostered an inequitable plantation system and that it did not have an infrastructure to manage the risks of transgenetic biotechnology. The big international biotech companies wanted minimal regulations, while Guatemala's authorities did not want to approve anything that would damage the environment, perhaps permanently, with the creation of super weeds. Mayan farmers also voiced loud opposition to GM maize for cultural reasons to protect the environment and their traditional agricultural way of life and fears about their health. The issues of seed patenting and the corporate control of technology directly linked to the public concerns about the Green Revolution. A Gene Revolution further threatened Guatemala's farmers with a technological treadmill that had more potential to ruin than to help them, particularly because traditional varieties planted without fertilizer sometimes outproduced GM varieties with fertilizer. Supporters of GM varieties argued that the production increases overall merited investment in biotechnological science by farmers and governments. Critics of GM maize, however, charged that it would only feed ethanol plants rather than hungry, poor farmers. The desires of elite plantation owners who wanted to plant GM maize were "not to stop hunger but fill gas tanks." GM maize agriculture they contended would force small-scale farmers from the land. This debate also re-energized the Mayan movement for the protection of their indigenous rights. GM science, then contributed to a new social movement that included environmentalists. By 2012, in Central America only Honduras and El Salvador permitted growing GM maize. As late as 2015, Guatemala did not permit its legal cultivation.[43]

~

While many people remained reluctant to eat GM foods, perception remained part of the problem. Some Chinese consumers asked, "Why should people eat Bt [GM] rice that even insects do not eat?" Once the negative public opposition to, even fear of, GM crops changed, however, many consumers would readily adopt them. Rice, for example, which plant molecular biologists genetically modified to increase its nutritional level of vitamin A, proved beneficial to fighting blindness in children who did not consume enough vitamin A in food-deficit nations. By 2008, vitamin A deficiency took the lives of an estimated 670,000 children, ages five and under, annually in these areas. Moreover, since publically employed scientists, not corporate scientists, developed this "Golden Rice," they could not patent it for private sale and deny its benefits to the poor. GM optimists considered golden rice a continuation of the Green Revolution, because it offered the potential for a crop to aid poor subsistence farmers at little cost in food-deficit nations. Greenpeace, the international environmental organization, charged that Chinese scientists had violated discipline-based research ethics and made children "guinea pigs" and their research a "scandal of international proportions." GM opponents quickly blocked production, arguing that cultivation would be nothing less than a "Trojan horse" leading to the approval of other GM crop varieties. In addition, they contended that golden rice had a bad taste, that vitamin A could be easily acquired (although poor people often cannot afford vitamins), and that it would cause the loss of hair and sex drive. Norman Borlaug called the opposition, whether opposing the Green or Gene Revolution, the "antiscience crowd." Certainly, both groups blamed the other for not working in the best interests of people worldwide.[44]

In 2004, the United Nations Food and Agriculture Organization proclaimed GM crops safe, but once again, this new agricultural development favored large-scale commercial farmers who produced for a market economy and cared little about helping local, poor farmers improve their accessibility to food grains. Agribusiness, not poor farmers, benefited from the newly developing "gene revolution" that agricultural scientists and others hoped would launch a new Green Revolution. Private seed companies did not distribute new GM varieties free of charge as the publically supported research institutions, such as the International Rice Research Institute, had done with high-yielding varieties (HYVs).[45]

By the early twentieth-first century, a grain of wheat, maize, and rice, or a soybean, was not merely a seed to improve agricultural production and to generate more farm income and food for hungry people. Biological science had made GM crop breeding a contentious matter of national sovereignty, domestic food security, and public health as well as troubled international trade. The creation of new GM grains brought unintended consequences, both domestic and global. Although no evidence existed that GM crops proved unsafe to eat, no evidence indicated that they are safe for consumption. As long as the European Union and many Asian and sub-Saharan African nations prohibited the importation and development of GM grains to protect the public health and gain political trade advantages, GM agricultural science would remain in limbo with strong supporters and opponents. Matters of toxicity, allergenicity, lack of nutritional content, and the safety of newly developed GM varieties in the long term for public health remained major concerns—all unintended consequences of biological agricultural research. If anything, GM foods and agricultural science are political and, as such, they are not neutral.[46]

7

Reflections

Essentially, the Green Revolution involved the transfer of fertilizer-responsive, high-yielding grain varieties to less developed countries, assisted by national public research institutions, extension networks, and international agricultural research centers, such as the International Maize and Wheat Improvement Center and the International Rice Research Institute. The Ford and Rockefeller Foundations and the Food and Agriculture Organization of the United Nations also provided support. The Green Revolution did not end world hunger or lead to food self-sufficiency in all of the underdeveloped nations. It did not cause or eliminate widespread unemployment or income inequality and poverty. It increased the yields of food grains and helped keep crop and food prices lower than might have been possible without Green Revolution technologies. At the same time, landowners benefited more than tenants and agricultural workers, although some farm laborers improved their economic condition beyond their circumstances prior to the Green Revolution. Even so, the demand for agricultural labor has not kept up with population growth and the Green Revolution cannot reverse that trend. Many agricultural workers have left the land. Moreover, neither farm size nor tenancy determined the adoption of the Green Revolution technology package. Long-term environmental changes remained uncertain, particularly regarding water pollution from chemical fertilizers, herbicides, and pesticides along with corresponding health hazards as well as soil salinization from irrigation and aquifer depletion. Moreover, the loss of genetic diversity became an increasingly threatening problem.[1]

Supporters of the Green Revolution contended during the mid-twentieth century that it would stay the threat of a Malthusian catastrophe among food-deficit nations with science-based agriculture that subsistence farmers would use to produce high-yielding crops of wheat, rice, and maize. Along with the application of irrigation, fertilizer, pesticides, and agricultural machinery,

Green Revolution agriculture would make countries, such as Mexico, India, and Pakistan, as well as many Southeast Asian and sub-Saharan African nations, free from hunger and want. A host of political, social, and cultural, as well as environmental problems, however, prevented unqualified achievement of these goals in food-deficit areas. Some scholars reject rapid population growth in the absence of adequate food production as a cause of hunger. They prefer ideological interpretations that emphasize historical social and economic inequalities and gender and class differences as causes of inadequate agricultural production. They neither consider rapid population growth as a threat to food security for individuals or nations, nor the need for agricultural science to help farmers produce more food, primarily because of environmental degradation. Yet, where the Green Revolution proved most successful, agricultural science slowed or delayed the food problems that unchecked population growth could potentially cause. By the turn of the twenty-first century, the number of undernourished people worldwide remained relatively stable at approximately one billion out of a total population of six billion, but many scientists, politicians, and various publics worried about the effects of continued rapid population growth, natural disasters, and global warming on agricultural production.[2]

Agricultural scientists, such as Norman Borlaug, who succeeded in breeding new varieties of wheat, rice, and maize, and disseminated technical information to underdeveloped, poverty-stricken, hungry nations, deserve recognition as benefactors of humankind. Without question, they were skillful geneticists and plant breeders whose commitment to applied research helped reduce hunger and possibly famine in many countries and revolutionized world agriculture. Yet, a host of related issues marred the unbridled success of the Green Revolution and prevented science from solving agricultural and food problems on a global scale among food-deficit nations during the late twentieth and early twenty-first centuries.

Above all, any assessment of the Green Revolution should recognize that it resulted from a long, continuous process of agricultural experimentation over generations, first by farmers and later by scientists, to improve crop production by breeding new wheat, maize, and rice varieties to increase yields and resist diseases and pests. Increased agricultural productivity resulted from many individual and institutional efforts. Agricultural scientists around the world contributed their expertise. No one person can legitimately claim credit for the Green Revolution. At the same time, the Green Revolution would not have occurred without a complex variety of institutional and government supports that provided the infrastructure, such as roads and irrigation systems, and the economic policies that authorized the credit and price supports to facilitate agricultural expansion with the adoption of Green Revolution technologies. Where the Green Revolution increased agricultural production, most of the people benefited as the result of more food and higher incomes, while areas that have not experienced a Green Revolution continue mired in persistent poverty, hunger, and want.[3]

The unintended social and economic consequences of the Green Revolution never concerned most agricultural scientists. They never believed that they had responsibility for creating a more equitable world. They also contended that increased production of wheat, maize, and rice would markedly improve the availability of food and reduce its costs to the greatest number of people. In contrast, social science critics focused on the inequities of the Green Revolution in Latin America, Asia, and sub-Saharan Africa. They contended that the new biotechnology only favored regions where the environment and infrastructure offered the greatest possibilities of success. The high-yielding wheat, maize, and rice varieties favored irrigated regions, but most of Asia and sub-Saharan Africa did not have water control systems. Moreover, high-yielding variety (HYV) technology proved best suited for regions with good soils and cheap transportation to urban markets. Farmers without access to irrigation or transportation and favorable environments did not benefit, and income disparities increased among farmers who had or did not have access to Green Revolution technologies. Supporters claimed that increased production meant more hours of work for agricultural laborers. At the same time, critics contended that mechanical technology in the form of tractors and grain harvesting and threshing machines displaced human labor and forced people from the land as owners consolidated properties into even larger farms. The displaced tenant farmers and agricultural workers then migrated to the cities where they complicated the social and economic problems of urban areas. Only a relatively few landowners profited from the Green Revolution, they argued.[4]

The critics of the Green Revolution also contended that the introduction of HYVs decreased the genetic base because farmers stopped cultivating traditional strains. If disease ruined those varieties, the results would be catastrophic because other varieties that could have taken their place would no longer exist. They also argued that intensive and heavy applications of fertilizers, herbicides, and pesticides polluted water supplies, ruined the soil, and endangered the health of farmers, agricultural workers, and consumers.[5]

~

When governments introduced the high-yielding seed varieties of wheat, rice, and maize during the late 1960s, agricultural observers and scientists believed that the threat of Malthusian famine and hunger loomed and underdeveloped countries seemed unable to meet their food needs because of rapidly increasing population and traditional, low-productive agriculture. Although they overestimated the danger of famine caused by rapid population growth, the dissemination and planting of the HYVs seemingly promised a cornucopia of agricultural productivity that would ensure an abundant food supply. Advocates hailed the benefits of scale neutrality and labor intensity, which would enable small-scale farmers and agricultural workers to profit from the Green Revolution and thereby help mitigate poverty and unemployment, the basic problems of Mexican, Asian, and sub-Saharan agriculture. The benefits seemed nearly miraculous and the scope of the Green Revolution unlimited.[6]

After the 1960s, the Green Revolution dramatically transformed wheat, maize, and rice production in some areas. In Asia, increased production benefited farmers and consumers, particularly when governments subsidized the purchase of high-yielding grain varieties, fertilizer production, and irrigation. By the second decade of the twenty-first century, farmers planted modern wheat varieties in about 90 percent of that grain area in developing countries where the environment and infrastructure permitted. At the same time, rice provided daily subsistence for 520 million Asians who lived in poverty, and it served as the major source of income and employment for more than 200 million farm families in the developing world. Continued population growth, however, still threatened to exceed the production of wheat, maize, and rice in many countries. In some areas, productivity diminished, thereby mandating the development of new varieties to meet the future demands for food as well as to create a sustainable and environmentally sensitive or protective agriculture. Sustainable adjustments to improve agricultural production required the development of varieties that resisted diseases and pests without the use of chemical herbicides and pesticides and produced heavy yields without irrigation in semi-arid environments. This research, however, caused new consumer fears about food safety.[7]

The Green Revolution particularly contributed to an unprecedented growth in the production of wheat, which, by 2013, had become the most widely cultivated grain worldwide with some 220 million hectares planted annually. Wheat production based on Green Revolution agricultural science particularly benefited farmers and consumers in South Asia, East Asia, and Latin

America. Wheat deservedly became the "miracle crop," because the breeding of high-yielding, semidwarf varieties and government support in various forms ensured that increased yields would reduce hunger and poverty. Similar developments that produced short-straw, fertilizer-responsive varieties of rice subsidized by high price supports and market development helped provide food security for subsistence and small-scale farmers as well as urban populations. Surplus production of wheat and rice meant improved income and a better standard of living. Both crops depended on publically funded agricultural research and government extension systems that took Green Revolution agricultural technologies to the farmers in food-deficit areas. In sub-Saharan Africa alone, the demand for wheat increased by 2–3 percent annually from 1961 to 2010, largely due to population growth and increased disposable income by urbanites. Yet, the nations of sub-Saharan Africa remain wheat importers because the Green Revolution had not significantly met all food needs.[8]

The Green Revolution also created new problems such as soil salinity and waterlogging on heavily irrigated lands. Water tables declined, and crop diseases and insects built immunity to fungicides and pesticides, thereby requiring the development of new highly toxic agricultural chemicals as well as disease-resistant varieties. Some nations preferred to purchase comparatively cheap grain on the international market to feed consumers and keep food prices low rather than invest heavily in agricultural science to develop Green Revolution technologies. Nor did many governments, particularly in sub-Saharan Africa, invest in the infrastructure required for transportation to market or provide credit opportunities. The negative effects of global warming remained unknown but agricultural scientists knew that new crop varieties necessarily had to respond to climate change.[9]

Governments made decisions to adopt Green Revolution technologies based on food needs and politics. In 1965, United States terminated food aid to India and Pakistan, who had gone to war. This termination convinced each nation that it had to become independent of international food suppliers and to develop its own agriculture for food security. During the 1960s, India and Pakistan began importing HYV wheat from Mexico. They also imported HYV rice from the International Rice Research Institute and Taiwan in hope of establishing food security. The Ford Foundation and the Rockefeller Foundation also provided financial support for the development of agricultural research centers. The United States government did not directly support these efforts until 1967, when it gave assistance to the International Maize and Wheat Improvement Center. Essentially, the US produced surpluses of wheat and rice

Figure 17. A woman clears a maize patch in Chiapas, Mexico
The maize breeders in the Mexican Agriculture Program at first ignored the small-scale
subsistence farmers. Today, however, the plant breeders at the International Maize and Wheat
Improvement Center are working to breed high-yielding maize varieties for rainfed areas
where irrigation is not possible given the terrain or the resources of the farmers. Photo:
P. Lowe / CIMMYT, CC BY-NC-SA.

and preferred to sell it to food-deficit nations rather than help those countries
develop highly productive agricultural programs of their own. In the meantime, Indian agricultural universities played a major role in disseminating
HYV wheat and developing new varieties while the India Fertilizer Association
popularized the benefits of chemical fertilizer to farmers. By the late 1960s,
for some observers the substantial increases in Asian wheat and rice yields
promised to end world hunger. Traditional food importing nations, such as
India, Pakistan, and the Philippines, had nearly reached food self-sufficiency.[10]

A host of "second-generation problems" emerged with the application of
Green Revolution agricultural science. Some observers warned that Green
Revolution technology would not spread as quickly as it had during the 1960s.
Irrigation, for example, covered only one-fourth to one-half of all land in Asia.
In addition, Green Revolution high-yielding rice varieties proved unsuitable
for rainfed lands. Irrigation often remained prohibitively expensive for small-
scale farmers unless governments subsidized well drilling and land leveling.
Some observers worried that Green Revolution agriculture would produce

too much surplus. Storage facilities often proved deficient and the marketing system inefficient. Farmers also would need more fertilizers, pesticides,
and insecticides, which became expensive without government subsidization
of production and prices.[11]

Consumers also rejected many of the new hybrid varieties because they
did not like the taste. In addition, many poor, small-scale (that is, subsistence farmers) also remained distrustful of the HYVs. They only reluctantly
risked planting the new varieties because they knew that traditional varieties would give them a safe, calculated return. Farmers are not willing to risk
crop failure when they live on the margin of hunger and want. They pursued
their farming practices with the adage that it was better to be safe than sorry.
Last, Green Revolution agricultural science required improved knowledge
and better farming skills than traditional cultivation regarding new planting
dates and depths, application rates for fertilizers, pesticides, and insecticides,
as well as irrigation.[12]

The Green Revolution also had the greatest effect in parallel latitudes of
seed development that facilitated the successful transfer of new wheat varieties from Mexico to India and Pakistan and rice varieties from the Philippines. Early Green Revolution adopters also were more literate and progressive in their farming practices regarding cultivation and water management,
and they had better access to roads and markets than subsistence farmers.
The large-scale property owners produced more and became even wealthier.
In India, for example, by the late 1960s, only 20 percent of the land planted
in wheat consisted of the new dwarf, high-yielding varieties, but these grain
crops contributed 34 percent of the total wheat production. As a result, some
critics charged that such large-scale production would lead to a net income
reduction by the small-scale subsistence farmers that would cause problems
of welfare and inequity. Equally important, some observers warned that the
introduction of high-yielding varieties alone would not guarantee improved
production. Governments and private enterprises had to provide fertilizer
plants, processing and storage facilities, markets, distribution, subsidized
prices, and affordable credit, as well as technology in the form of irrigation
wells and mechanized equipment.[13]

With Filipino farmers spending $20 per hectare to seed traditional rice
varieties and HYVs costing them $220 per hectare to raise during the late
1960s, a threefold production increase and a monetary return of 400 percent
meant nothing if farmers could not acquire the credit to purchase the HYVs
and fertilizer and apply irrigation. Often modern credit institutions proved

lacking. If traditional varieties outproduced Green Revolution HYVs, subsistence farmers would not adopt the new varieties. Overproduction also had the tendency to drive down grain prices unless governments kept prices high enough to merit continued production by farmers. At the same time, urban consumers wanted lower food prices. In addition, as food-deficit nations became self-sufficient, or nearly so, they needed less importation of rice from surplus-producing nations, such as Burma and Thailand, whose economies depended on the exportation of rice. Consequently, another unintended consequence was the dislocation of traditional trading patterns and dependencies.[14]

By the 1970s, the Green Revolution had gained a number of critics as well as supporters. Both sides argued their case in absolutist terms. They saw no gray areas concerning the benefits or problems of the Green Revolution. The supporters argued that a billion and a half people suffered malnutrition, hunger, and want in developing nations. They contended that the dramatic increases in wheat, maize, and rice yields during the 1960s had to be maintained. Scientists had to extend Green Revolution technologies to other food crops, otherwise population growth would guarantee famine in the near future. The critics of the Green Revolution, however, found fault with them on economic, political, and social grounds. They contended that improved productivity harmed rather than helped rural workers. The application of Green Revolution technology, they held, favored those farmers who had the financial resources, including credit, to purchase high-yielding seed varieties and fertilizer as well as irrigate their fields with the aid of newly drilled tube wells. As a result, the already prosperous farmers received the most benefits of the Green Revolution, which further widened the gap between the affluent and the poor. The critics also contended that the large-scale landowners used Green Revolution science to increase their productivity by consolidating the lands of the small-scale farmers to whom they rented a few hectares, and by replacing them with mechanized implements, thereby driving them from the land into even greater rural or urban poverty.

During the 1970s, however, Green Revolution supporters countered and contended that high-yielding wheat and rice varieties enabled both large- and small-scale farmers to benefit from increased production to feed their families as well as earn a profit from the sale of surplus grain. They also argued that HYVs often permitted multi-cropping, which increased the need for agricultural labor. Critics responded by saying that government policies favored the wealthy farmers because special tax concessions enabled them to purchase tractors and lenient trade policies permitted the importation of equipment that reduced labor needs and increased income for the large-scale farmers. All could agree, however, that the goal of the Green Revolution should be increased agricultural production, higher and more widely distributed agricultural income, and greater employment opportunities for farm workers. To achieve those goals, agricultural and social scientists necessarily had to work together. During the 1970s, critics saw more failure than success. Only select areas benefited based on the availability of irrigation as well as suitable environmental and agronomic conditions for the new HYVs. Although the Green Revolution increased the demand for labor and improved wages in some areas, where irrigation did not exist, few benefits from the new agriculture developed.[15]

~

By the 1980s, the Green Revolution had not eliminated world hunger but it had substantially increased the food supply of wheat, maize, and rice in some food-deficit nations and surplus production helped lower consumer prices. Landowners still benefited more than agricultural workers did but compared to the past many of these laborers had improved their lives because they had more work and higher rates of pay. Surplus workers continued their migration to urban areas, and their economic situation may not have improved. Critics now reached a consensus that HYVs increased the need for agricultural labor, but the labor supply grew faster, therefore the real income of farm workers declined because employers could hire workers more cheaply from a larger labor pool. In many cases, agricultural workers earned lower wages but they had more work because multiple cropping increased the demand for labor. Large-scale landowners still benefited more than small-scale farmers did because they had access to capital to invest in HYVs, fertilizer, and irrigation. The pros and cons of the Green Revolution had become matters of interpretation shaped by economic and social ideology. The statistical evidence supporting each argument remained imprecise and based on limited case studies.[16]

The Green Revolution also appeared as scale neutral, but large-scale landowners had an advantage over small-scale farmers because they could plant more land with HYVs and secure larger harvests for commercial sale. Sharecroppers and tenants, however, often adopted HYVs as rapidly as large-scale landowners did. Inequality in production and earnings resulted from unequal access to HYV seeds, fertilizers, and irrigation that were limited or controlled by political considerations. Where governments provided roads, markets, and subsidies for fertilizers and price supports, Green Revolution farmers of all sizes benefited. Still, no one knew the environmental effects of the Green Revolution. Some critics suspected that the heavy use of fertilizers, pesticides, and water would cause chemical pollution of the land and water supplies, but little solid evidence existed to confirm the reality of these dangers. Critics of the Green Revolution continued to worry about the loss of genetic diversity as plant breeders increasingly used only a few varieties for the development of new varieties.[17]

Despite these criticisms, by the mid-1980s, traditional rice importing nations such as India, Indonesia, Bangladesh, and the Philippines had roughly achieved self-sufficiency. Farmers in some of these densely populated nations even produced enough rice for export primarily due to the adoption of hybrid varieties. In approximately two decades, Asian rice production nearly doubled. At the same time, the introduction of high-yielding wheat varieties in India and Pakistan also substantially increased per capita food production by more than 25 percent. Grain yields also grew faster than populations and the public demands for food. Asia became a region of food security rather than food crisis.[18]

≈

During the 1990s, scholars remained divided regarding the success of the Green Revolution. Agricultural scientists argued that technological (that is, biological) change significantly helped improve grain production, particularly wheat and rice, to feed hungry people. In contrast, social scientists, public intellectuals, and others continued to argue that the Green Revolution caused many economic, social, and environmental problems. In this respect, the Green Revolution involved more than the introduction of new high-yielding seeds. Rather, biological agricultural change became inextricably linked to the availability of hardware and chemical technology, capital and credit, landownership and use patterns, labor, and the environment. It gave some farmers the opportunity to produce more grain, earn greater profits, and substantially improve food supplies through agricultural intensification and expansion of crops lands. Simply put, the Green Revolution was state and market, not population, driven. It also situated on a class-based agricultural technology intended to increase commercial production and not just provide food for hungry people. Opportunities for commercial agriculture encouraged farmers to adopt the new high-yielding seed varieties rather than altruistic desires to increase the food supply. Where market demand encouraged farmers to expand production and where good roads enabled them to reach markets, production increased.[19]

Figure 18. Contract worker using a combine to harvest wheat in Ethiopia
Relatively few farmers in food-deficit nations can afford mechanized implements. They are
large-scale farmers who have the financial resources and access to credit to purchase the
equipment and thereby take the best advantage of Green Revolution technologies. The
owner of this wheat land in Ethiopia preferred to hire a contract worker who had a combine
and other implements to harvest the wheat crop. Photo: P. Lowe / CIMMYT, CC BY-NC-SA.

In India and Pakistan, for example, the British had built the railroad system into the countryside to facilitate the shipment of cotton and other agricultural products. As a result, wheat and rice farmers had the means to ship seed, fertilizer, and grain. Where market demand for the new high-yielding crops existed, farm household income increased, and this income and corresponding government support, often in terms of price supporting policies and subsidies for fertilizer, stimulated other agricultural improvements including higher wages for farm labor. In contrast, the Green Revolution had less influence on agricultural practices in remote areas.[20]

By the late twentieth century, some scholars contended that rapid population growth increased the Malthusian danger of starvation. Green Revolution technology, however, would provide more food and prevent famine and want. They also continued to argue that biotechnological transformations for agriculture were scale neutral; that is, small-scale as well as large-scale farmers could adopt HYVs. If large-scale and small-scale farmers had HYVs, irrigation, and fertilizer, each group would benefit. No minimum investment floor existed. The multiplier effect seemed destined to increase yields and income for farmers and workers alike. In this sense, of course, they ignored that governmental political, social, and economic power determined the access to these "inputs." They also ignored that bad weather and politics caused famine not overpopulation or inadequate agricultural production. Since the beginning of Green Revolution plant breeding in the mid-twentieth century, famine had occurred only in China and sub-Saharan Africa. In China, the cause was not the failure of agriculture but government policy that negatively reoriented land use and failed in the distribution of grain to those who needed it. In sub-Saharan Africa, drought ruined crops and created food deficits for many people across time and space. In addition, as in the case of Ethiopia and Somalia, government policy and ethnic and religious war prevented both adequate crop production and the distribution of food to the hungry.[21]

∽

Hungry people need more than increased food production. They need access or entitlement to it, and this depends on government pricing, distribution, and labor policies, among other factors. One can judge the success of the Green and Gene Revolutions with considerations given to the equitable distribution of wealth created from increased cereal grain production. If the Green and Gene Revolutions are judged by increased productivity alone, they were a remarkable success. If, however, one judges both on the premise that they eliminated hunger, then both failed because people in the food-deficit nations discussed here often did not have access to the Green and Gene Revolution technology, adequate land, or access to food. Since governments promoted Green Revolution technologies and policies that increased wheat, rice, and maize production for large-scale farmers, they failed to meet the needs of subsistence farmers and left them without sufficient food, inadequately nourished, and poor. Still, no one has presented evidence that traditional varieties would have met the food needs of growing populations in these nations.[22]

Moreover, no one has provided evidence beyond supposition and assertion to prove that Green Revolution agriculture kept food-deficit nations from red revolutions and the imposition of Communist regimes in place of democratic governments. Counter opinions cannot move those who believe in the Malthusian threat of population growth and famine, particularly in food-deficit nations. Certainly, population increases require more food, particularly in areas where agricultural productivity has failed to meet those needs. Supporters of the Green Revolution do not consider, however, the economic, social, and cultural aspects of grain distribution. Nor do they consider the complications of wealth, land use, and labor patterns based on tradition and political power. Fundamentally, the supporters of the Green and Gene Revolutions have failed to understand that the mere increase in cereal production could not end hunger and want because both historically had been matters of distribution (that is, access to adequate food).[23]

At the same time, one must recognize that traditional agricultural practices did not and do not guarantee equity between producers and consumers. By the early twenty-first century, the world economic crisis also threatened continued research at the international agricultural research centers, and private sector research did not permit the sharing of knowledge. By 2009 in India, for example, the water table declined at the rate of three feet per year in some areas. Wells now reached two hundred feet where thirty years earlier pumps pulled water from ten feet below the surface. As a result, the cost of new powerful pumps necessitated borrowing, and credit proved expensive, often usurious, from nonbank, private lenders. Soil salinity also plagued many farmers, but without groundwater for irrigation, the future of the Green Revolution seemed unsustainable and unprofitable. If the wells went dry or irrigation became too expensive, these farmers would return to dry land farming. Whether HYVs would meet that challenge remained unknown.[24]

In retrospect, the Green Revolution became a global success only in part due to scientific achievement. Nationalism, Communist expansionism, and fear of Malthusian famine and societal collapse together with the development of irrigation and transportation infrastructures, and adaptive national research programs, made the Green Revolution possible along with the combined intellectual ability of agricultural scientists in many nations. At the same time, neither technology nor demography served as the singular driving force of the Green Revolution, although both were necessary factors that enabled and encouraged scientific success, but always in the context of agriculturally favorable environments.[25]

At the same time, genetic improvements to develop new disease-resistant wheat, rice, and maize varieties caused many consumers to worry about the safety (that is, health risks) of consuming genetically modified (GM) foods. Genetic crop engineering even though designed to increase food production became too dangerous for many consumers who feared potential health risks from consuming food grains that scientists had developed in the laboratory. Consumers either welcomed or feared GM crops depending on their perspective. Generally commercial farmers in the United States and other export-producing nations favored GM crop varieties while many food-deficit nations in sub-Saharan Africa often opposed them for purchase, development, and trade for health and political reasons. Many counties banned these grains for human consumption, thereby relegating them to livestock feed.[26]

Some critics remained convinced that the Green Revolution benefited large-scale farmers more than small-scale farmers, but the evidence remained inconclusive regarding its effects on inequality. They also did not consider the Green Revolution as socially appropriate. Part of the problem is the definition of a large- or a small-scale farmer for determining the benefits of Green Revolution science on productivity and the multiplier effects that it has on families, workers, landholding, and government policy. Historically, agricultural development has been a "tried and true" strategy to fight hunger and poverty. While the Green Revolution provided benefits that helped alleviate hunger among the poor in many developing countries, it also benefited commercial not subsistence farmers in some areas such as Mexico and India. Despite the successes and problems of the Green Revolution, it required continuous adaptation, or rather change, to meet new population and environmental challenges, particularly regarding diminishing land and water resources, plant diseases, and global warming.[27]

The problems and unintended consequences of the Green Revolution differed among countries and regions. Part of the difficulty was that agricultural scientists did not plan on long-range consequences of their research beyond economic improvement for subsistence and commercial farmers. Instead, a host of social and political changes occurred that social scientists often interpreted as problems. Yet, neither agricultural nor social scientists had given much thought to long-term consequences and no one could predict unintended consequences with much precision. No one seemed to have thought in terms of contingency planning—that is, about the implementation of policies and procedures if unintended consequences occurred. Plant breeders and other hard scientists, such as Norman Borlaug, resented the social scientists, particularly economists, for their criticism of the unintended social and economic consequences of Green Revolutions.[28]

By the turn of the twenty-first century, Borlaug lamented the lack of success in implementing a Green Revolution in sub-Saharan Africa where its effects had been geographically uneven with marginal agricultural improvements. Outsiders with good intentions spoke of sub-Saharan Africa as "technologically deficient," not food deficient. Infusions of science and technology, or the lack of such, had not yet brought a Green Revolution to many countries in sub-Saharan Africa. South Africa provides an example. Beginning in 2002, the

South African government initiated the Massive Food Production Program to address food insecurity among communal farmers. It provided farmers with subsidies to purchase GM seeds, fertilizers, and pesticides. The participating farmers, however, did not have the training to apply Green Revolution technology to their best advantage. When the government ended the subsidies program, many farmers could not pay their debts incurred from acquiring GM technologies. Local elites then acquired their lands, consolidated farms, and applied more GM technology, which also expanded the market for GM seed varieties and agrochemicals. Only the commercial farmers and agribusinesses profited from the program.[29]

Norman Borlaug recognized that the food crisis resulted from the long-term political neglect of agriculture in sub-Saharan Africa and he complained that governments had not done more to improve food production to sustain the rapidly growing populations. In 2002, he wrote, "More than any other region of the world, food production south of the Sahara is in crisis." Few farmers used the improved Green Revolution technologies. National food deficits escalated and nutritional levels plunged, especially among the rural poor. Social unrest, insufficient agricultural extension systems, lagging research, and inadequate transportation and marketing infrastructures kept food production below the levels needed for subsistence in many areas. Although 75–85 percent of the people relied on agriculture for their living, their governments gave little financial commitment to the policy requirements needed to improve agricultural production and the rural standard of living.[30]

No one can doubt that Borlaug's work in Mexico at what became the International Maize and Wheat Improvement Center proved instrumental in developing new wheat varieties that helped increase yields and that the principles of his research influenced similar work in India and Pakistan. Borlaug's commitment, however, to developing wheat varieties that would have the widest application (that is, planting) did not meet the needs of all small-scale farmers. He knew, however, that the new wheat varieties that he and his colleagues developed needed extensive applications of fertilizer and irrigation, which proved costly. He believed, nevertheless, that his HYVs could produce bountiful harvests everywhere even without fertilizer and irrigation. The development of wheat varieties that farmers could raise over broad areas, however, did not perform satisfactorily on low fertility soils and where farmers could not afford fertilizer and irrigation. Green Revolution varieties performed on only fertile soils with considerable applications of fertilizer and water. Traditional varieties often produced greater yields in local areas. In retrospect, most Indian and other agricultural scientists accepted Borlaug's approach to plant breeding rather than develop high-yielding wheat and other grain varieties that farmers could plant on a variety of local and regional soils with varying microclimates. Borlaug's approach to the development of high-yielding wheat varieties for widespread planting remained the lingua franca of the agricultural community.[31]

Borlaug's Green Revolution "package" indicates the fallacy of his attempts to develop wheat varieties that had widespread application. By the early twenty-first century, some critics charged that Borlaug gave too much attention to the importance of genetics and photoperiod insensitivity that affected the way that new varieties performed across geographical areas. Simply put, Borlaug expected Green Revolution wheat varieties to produce large yields everywhere without consideration of longitude and latitude, periods of light, or varying soil types. As a result, much of his work and that of his followers failed in sub-Saharan Africa, the South Asian subcontinent, and East Asia. The Green Revolution, for example, did not spread across India. It only occurred in the Punjab where fertile soils, irrigation, and access to fertilizer and high-yielding varieties enabled farmers to produce large harvests under optimal conditions. Although some Indian scientists attempted to break away from Borlaug's approach to develop varieties that farmers could plant across wide areas and instead develop HYVs for local soils or specific regions, the path has proven difficult, and they have not achieved much success so powerful remained Borlaug's methodological influence, even from the grave. For these critics, Borlaug's obstinacy prevented adjustment and limited his effectiveness, but most of the scientific agricultural community does not want to hear it.[32]

Some observers have reminded that agricultural change does not guarantee universal prosperity, more equitable distribution of wealth, and greater social equality. Adequate food, however, ensures personal, domestic, and national security. Food security in part depends on agricultural science, which creates political, economic, and social power. Agricultural science that is technically possible is not always economically profitable. The cost of HYVs or GM seeds, fertilizer and irrigation can prevent farmers from acquiring the new technology. Few farmers with low incomes can participate in Green and Gene Revolutions. Both revolutions consider hunger as a technical, agricultural problem. Hunger, however, is a political and social problem that involves access and entitlement to food.[33]

Often the arguments and claims of success and charges of failure became little more than polemical and ideological arguments with fluid facts used to justify the claims of both groups. No one argued against improving agricultural production, particularly food grains, but critics found fault with almost every social change that the Green Revolution fostered. Often they used narrow case studies to generalize the problems of the Green Revolution. In turn, the agricultural scientists either rebuffed them because they did not understand science or ignored them. This confrontation continued into the late twentieth century until a "Gene Revolution brought new production increases and problems." When the twenty-first century began the old arguments for and against the Green Revolution remained, although increasingly more people knew little about it. Some people even confused it with the urban environmental movement.

The Green Revolution was neither an unmitigated success nor an abject failure. It increased grain (that is, food) production, but the Green Revolution did not prove as damaging to economic and social structures as critics charged. The Green Revolution changed agriculture in many nations. It benefited some farmers and urbanites more than it did others. It changed the lives of some people based on gender, access to capital, and need for labor. The agricultural science of the Green Revolution proved productive but unneutral concerning economic and social ramifications, but that is not to say that it was detrimental.

If anything, the contentions of the agricultural and social scientists, environmentalists, and others should encourage an informed public to consider the Green and Gene Revolutions as processes of continuing agricultural change, not a single event. GM research and crop development divided the agricultural and social scientists, the public, and governments, particularly regarding food safety, environmental or biosafety, and trade, as well as intellectual property rights, among other concerns. With the Gene Revolution supported and attacked by many of the same arguments for and against the Green Revolution, no one can precisely say where the contention might end, but acceptance of GM crops in food-deficit and many other skeptical nations would only come when the public no longer feared their potential danger. Only the future would tell.[34]

Notes

Chapter One

1. Joseph E. Cotter, *Troubled Harvest: Agronomy and Revolution in Mexico, 1880–2002* (Westport, CT: Praeger, 2003), 252; Norman E. Borlaug, "A Choice for Mankind: Adequate Food Production with Equitable Distribution or Hunger and Poverty for Millions" (Sterling B. Hendricks Memorial Lectureship Award, sponsored by the Agricultural Research Service, US Department of Agriculture, presented on August 24, 1981, at the American Chemical Society Meeting in New York), 15; Don Paarlberg, *Norman Borlaug—Hunger Fighter*, PA 969 (Washington, DC: Foreign Economic Development Service, US Department of Agriculture, cooperating with the US Agency for International Development, 1970), 1, 3; Nicholas Wade, "Green Revolution (I): A Just Technology, Often Unjust in Use," *Science* 186 (December 20, 1974): 1093; Nick Cullather, *The Hungry World: America's Cold War Battle against Poverty in Asia* (Cambridge, MA: Harvard University Press, 2010), 7–8.

2. Cynthia Hewitt De Alcántara, "The 'Green Revolution' as History: The Mexican Experience," *Development and Change* 5 (May 1974): 25–27; Lakshman Yapa, "What Are Improved Seeds? An Epistemology of the Green Revolution," *Economic Geography* 69 (July 1993): 269; Richard D. Hanson, *The Politics of Mexican Development* (Baltimore, MD: Johns Hopkins University Press, 1971), 41.

3. Tore C. Olsson, *Agrarian Crossings: Reformers and the Remaking of the U.S. and Mexican Countryside* (Princeton, NJ: Princeton University Press, 2017), 98, 119–22. Olsson contends that Secretary of Agriculture Henry A. Wallace did not purse or support agricultural assistance to Mexico after his return in December 1940. He also argues for the antecedents of the Green Revolution in the American South.

4. Olsson, *Agrarian Crossings*, 124; Kenneth Thompson, "The Green Revolution: Leadership and Partnership in Agriculture," *Review of Politics* 34 (April 1972): 175; E. C. Stakman, Ricard Bradfield, and Paul C. Mangelsdorf, *Campaigns against Hunger* (Cambridge, MA: Harvard University Press, 1967), 20–25; Yapa, "What Are Improved Seeds?," 269; John H. Perkins, *Geopolitics and the Green Revolution: Wheat, Genes, and the Cold War* (New York: Oxford University Press, 1997), 105–7; Alcántara, "'Green Revolution' as History," 31–32.

5. Deborah Fitzgerald, "Exporting American Agriculture: The Rockefeller Foundation in Mexico, 1943–53," *Social Studies Science* 16 (August 1986): 463–64; Olsson, *Agrarian Crossings*, 151–52; Perkins, *Geopolitics and the Green Revolution*, 105–7.

6. Alan Anderson Jr., "The Green Revolution Lives," *New York Times*, April 27, 1975; Olsson, *Agrarian Crossings*, 99; Stakman, Bradfield, and Mangelsdorf, *Campaigns against Hunger*, 222–38, 266, 273–74; Edwin J. Wellhausen, "The Agriculture of Mexico," *Scientific American* 235 (September 1976): 129–30; John H. Perkins, "The Rockefeller Foundation and the Green Revolution, 1941–1956," *Agriculture and Human Values* 7, no. 3–4 (1990): 8; Perkins, *Geopolitics and the Green Revolution*, 106–7.

7. Thompson, "Green Revolution," 176; Stakman, Bradfield, and Mangelsdorf, *Campaigns against Hunger*, 15, 39, 266, 273; Fitzgerald, "Exporting American Agriculture," 464–65; Perkins, *Geopolitics and the Green Revolution*, 108, 113–15.

8. Karen Matchett, "At Odds Over Inbreeding: An Abandoned Attempt at Mexico / United States Collaboration to 'Improve' Mexican Corn, 1940–1950," *Journal of the History of Biology*, no. 2 (2006): 345–46, 360–62.

9. Fitzgerald, "Exporting American Agriculture," 463, 466–67.

10. Matchett, "At Odds Over Inbreeding," 345–46, 360, 362, 368; Olsson, *Agrarian Crossings*, 142; Gordon Conway, *The Doubly Green Revolution: Food for All in the 21st Century* (Ithaca, NY: Cornell University Press, 1998), 47–48; Fitzgerald, "Exporting American Agriculture," 465–67; Stakman, Bradfield, and Mangelsdorf, *Campaigns against Hunger*, 58–59, 65–66, 68.

11. Matchett, "At Odds Over Inbreeding," 363–66; Jonathan Harwood, "Peasant Friendly Plant Breeding and the Early Years of the Green Revolution in Mexico," *Agricultural History* 83 (Summer 2009): 387.

12. Matchett, "At Odds Over Inbreeding," 368–69; Harwood, "Peasant Friendly Plant Breeding," 384–86, 397; Olsson, *Agrarian Crossings*, 147–49.

13. Wellhausen, "Agriculture of Mexico," 130, 132, 134, 147.

14. Anderson, "The Green Revolution Lives"; Harwood, "Peasant Friendly Plant Breeding," 398, 400–401.

15. Perkins, *Geopolitics and the Green Revolution*, 108–13.

16. Perkins, *Geopolitics and the Green Revolution*, 108, 113–15; Michael D. Wolfe, *Watering the Revolution: An Environmental and Technological History of Agrarian Reform in Mexico* (Durham, NC: Duke University Press, 2017), 189. See Olsson, *Agrarian Crossings*, for an elaboration of this theme.

17. Norman E. Borlaug, "The Impact of Agricultural Research on Mexican Wheat Production," *Transactions of the New York Academy of Sciences*, ser. 2, 20, no. 3 (January 1958): 278–80, 287; Norman E. Borlaug, "The Green Revolution, Peace and Humanity" (speech delivered upon receipt of the 1970 Nobel Peace Prize, Oslo, Norway, December 11, 1970); Wellhausen, "Agriculture of Mexico," 130; Stakman, Bradfield, and Mangelsdorf, *Campaigns against Hunger*, 73, 75.

18. "Living History Interview with Dr. Norman E. Borlaug," *Transnational Law &*

Contemporary Problems 1 (Fall 1991): 541; Borlaug, "Impact of Agricultural Research," 281; Olsson, *Agrarian Crossings*, 151; Stakman, Bradfield, and Mangelsdorf, *Campaigns against Hunger*, 80.

19. Perkins, *Geopolitics and the Green Revolution*, 226–28; Israel Shenker, "Peace Prize Goes to Leader of the 'Green Revolution,'" *New York Times*, October 25, 1970; Conway, *Doubly Green Revolution*, 49; Olsson, *Agrarian Crossings*, 151–52.

20. Borlaug, "Impact of Agricultural Research," 281, 284, 288–89, 291–93; Boyce Rensberger, "Science Gives New Life to the Green Revolution," *New York Times*, September 3, 1974; Conway, *Doubly Green Revolution*, 48.

21. Borlaug, "Impact of Agricultural Research," 281, 284, 288–89, 291–93; Conway, *Doubly Green Revolution*, 48; Fitzgerald, "Exporting American Agriculture," 468; Borlaug, "Choice for Mankind," 15; "Living History Interview," 542; Stakman, Bradfield, and Mangelsdorf, *Campaigns against Hunger*, 89–90; Homer E. Socolofsky, "The World Food Crisis and Progress in Wheat Breeding," *Agricultural History* 43 (October 1969): 432; Dana G. Dalrymple, "Changes in Wheat Varieties and Yields in the United States, 1919–1984," *Agricultural History* 62 (Autumn 1988): 33–34; Perkins, *Geopolitics and the Green Revolution*, 229–31; Stakman, Bradfield, and Mangelsdorf, *Campaigns against Hunger*, 90–91.

22. Borlaug, "Impact of Agricultural Research," 281–84, 288–89, 291–93; Conway, *Doubly Green Revolution*, 49; Fitzgerald, "Exporting American Agriculture," 468.

23. Borlaug, "Green Revolution, Peace and Humanity."

24. Wellhausen, "Agriculture of Mexico," 129, 134.

25. Joseph Cotter, *Troubled Harvest: Agronomy and Revolution in Mexico, 1880–2002* (Westport, CT: Praeger, 2003), 209, 234–36.

26. Perkins, *Geopolitics and the Green Revolution*, 115.

27. Stakman, Bradfield, and Mangelsdorf, *Campaigns against Hunger*, 24, 51, 321; Cotter, *Troubled Harvest*, 251–55.

28. Stakman, Bradfield, and Mangelsdorf, *Campaigns against Hunger*, 24; Cotter, *Troubled Harvest*, 251–55.

29. Gary Vocke, *The Green Revolution for Wheat in Developing Countries*, Economic Research Service, Staff Report No. AGES 860911 (Washington, DC: US Department of Agriculture, Economic Research Service, International Division, 1986), 7; William C. Thiesenhusen, "Green Revolution in Latin America: Income Effects, Policy Decisions," *Monthly Labor Review* 95 (March 1972): 21–22; Cotter, *Troubled Harvest*, 257; Wellhausen, "Agriculture of Mexico," 129, 134.

30. Cotter, *Troubled Harvest*, 257–63.

31. Cotter, *Troubled Harvest*, 257–63.

32. Wade, "Green Revolution (I)," 1094–95.

33. Cotter, *Troubled Harvest*, 263–64, 281; Philip Russell, "On Mexico," *New York Times*, July 20, 1978.

34. Wellhausen, "Agriculture of Mexico," 134.

35. Wellhausen, "Agriculture of Mexico," 136, 139.

36. Wellhausen, "Agriculture of Mexico," 139.

37. Wellhausen, "Agriculture of Mexico," 140; Michael K. Roberts, C. Michael Schwartz, Michael S. Stohl, and Harry R. Targ, "The Policy Consequences of the Green Revolution: The Latin American Case," *Policy Studies Review* 4 (November 1984): 321.

38. Wellhausen, "Agriculture of Mexico," 139, 143–44, 146–48.

39. Wellhausen, "Agriculture of Mexico," 143–44, 146–48.

40. Alcántara, "'Green Revolution' as History," 25, 33–34, 38–40.

41. Alcántara, "'Green Revolution' as History," 40–41.

42. Alcántara, "'Green Revolution' as History," 40–41.

43. Roberts et al., "Policy Consequences of the Green Revolution," 321; Alcántara, "'Green Revolution' as History," 41–44; Fitzgerald, "Exporting American Agriculture," 459; David L. Clawson and Don R. Hoy, "Nealtican, Mexico: A Peasant Community That Rejected the 'Green Revolution,'" *American Journal of Economics and Sociology* 38 (October 1979): 371–87.

44. Billie R. DeWalt, "Mexico's Green Revolution: Food for Feed," *Mexican Studies / Estudios Mexicanos* 1 (Winter 1985): 29–31.

45. DeWalt, "Mexico's Green Revolution," 32–33, 35–38, 41–42.

46. Cotter, *Troubled Harvest*, 281–84, 286–87; Norman Borlaug, "The Green Revolution: For Peace and Bread," *Bulletin of the Atomic Scientists* 27 (June 1971): 6–9, 42–48; Norman Borlaug, "In Defense of DDT and Other Pesticides," *UNESCO Courier*, February 1972, 6; Roberts et al., "Policy Consequences of the Green Revolution," 321.

47. Cotter, *Troubled Harvest*, 281–84, 286–87; Borlaug, "Green Revolution," 6–7, 42–45; Borlaug, "In Defense of DDT and Other Pesticides," 6.

48. Wellhausen, "Agriculture of Mexico," 134; Cotter, *Troubled Harvest*, 287–88, 290.

49. Cotter, *Troubled Harvest*, 292.

50. David A. Sonnenfeld, "Mexico's 'Green Revolution,' 1940–1980: Towards an Environmental History," *Environmental History Review* 16 (Winter 1992): 46–47.

51. John Walsh, "Mexican Agriculture: Crisis within Crisis," *Science* 219 (February 18, 1983): 825.

52. Walsh, "Mexican Agriculture," 825–26.

53. DeWalt, "Mexico's Green Revolution," 44–45, 47, 49–50.

54. DeWalt, "Mexico's Green Revolution," 43–45, 47, 49, 52–55; Steven E. Sanderson, *The Transformation of Mexican Agriculture: International Structure and the Politics of Rural Change* (Princeton, NJ: Princeton University Press, 1986), 191, 220–21.

55. Sanderson, *Transformation of Mexican Agriculture*, 191, 220–21; DeWalt, "Mexico's Green Revolution," 52–55; "Environmental Neglect That Fuels Migration," *People & the Planet* 3, no. 4 (1994): 14.

56. "Corn and Mexico Evolve Together," *New York Times*, July 12, 1993.

57. Cotter, *Troubled Harvest*, 292–300, 303, 306.

58. Cotter, *Troubled Harvest*, 307–8.

59. Cotter, *Troubled Harvest*, 329–31.

60. Anthony DePalma, "The 'Slippery Slope' of Patenting Farmers' Crops," *New York Times*, May 24, 2000.

61. Stakman, Bradfield, and Mangelsdorf, *Campaigns against Hunger*, 216–17, 219, 221–23; Fitzgerald, "Exporting American Agriculture," 476–77; Ann Crittenden, "In Colombia, Science Sows Seeds of Hope for the Hungry," *New York Times*, May 17, 1981.

62. Conway, *Doubly Green Revolution*, 56.

63. Jonathan Kendell, "'Green Revolution' Now Stressing Help for Impoverished Farmers," *New York Times*, March 16, 1977; Peter R. Jennings, "Rice Breeding and World Food Production," *Science* 186 (December 20, 1974): 1086; Conway, *Doubly Green Revolution*, 56; David M. Jones, "The Green Revolution in Latin America: Success or Failure," *International Aspects of Development in Latin America: Geographic Aspects* 6 (1977): 60.

64. Kendell, "'Green Revolution' Now Stressing Help"; Crittenden, "In Colombia."

65. Crittenden, "In Colombia."

66. Ann Crittenden, "Gains for Latin American Crops Called No Help to Small Farmers," *New York Times*, May 4, 1981.

67. A conversation with Michael Conlon, Counselor of the Foreign Agricultural Service, USDA, Bogotá, Colombia, at Purdue University, March 8, 2016.

68. Kendell, "'Green Revolution' Now Stressing Help."

69. Jonathan Kendell, "New Stress on Agriculture Aiding Latin America," *New York Times*, March 23, 1977.

70. David Carey Jr., "Guatemala's Green Revolution: Synthetic Fertilizer, Public Health, and Economic Autonomy in the Mayan Highland," *Agricultural History* 83, no. 3 (2009): 284–85, 289–91, 295, 297, 304.

71. Carey, "Guatemala's Green Revolution," 292–95, 297, 299.

72. Carey, "Guatemala's Green Revolution," 305–6, 310–11. For the health effects of synthetic pesticides on nontraditional crops, see Sonia I. Arbona, "Commercial Agriculture and Agrochemicals in Almolonga, Guatemala," *Geographical Review* 88 (January 1998): 47–63; and Angus Wright, "Rethinking the Circle of Poison: The Politics of Pesticide Poisoning among Mexican Farm Workers," *Latin American Perspectives* 13 (Autumn 1986): 26–59.

73. Sonnenfeld, "Mexico's 'Green Revolution,'" 28, 32–33.

74. Sonnenfeld, "Mexico's 'Green Revolution,'" 34–38.

75. Irma Lorena Acosta Reveles, "The Limits and Contradictions of Agricultural Technology in Latin America: Lessons from Mexico and Argentina," *Perspectives on Global Development Technology* 11, no. 3 (2012): 391–93.

76. Sonnenfeld, "Mexico's 'Green Revolution,'" 39–40, 42–43.

77. Barbara H. Tuckman, "The Green Revolution and the Distribution of Agricultural Income in Mexico," *World Development* 4, no. 1 (1976): 17–18, 21–22; Hanson, *Politics of Mexican Development*, 60, 81–83; Clark W. Reynolds, *The Mexican Economy:*

Twentieth Century Structure and Growth (New Haven, CT: Yale University Press, 1970), 97, 107, 142–44.

78. Hanson, *Politics of Mexican Development*, 41, 58, 77; Reynolds, *Mexican Economy*, 97; Tuckman, "Green Revolution and the Distribution of Agricultural Income in Mexico," 23–24; Sonnenfeld, "Mexico's 'Green Revolution,'" 43.

79. Alcántara, "'Green Revolution' as History," 309.

80. Fitzgerald, "Exporting American Agriculture," 478–79.

81. Anderson, "Green Revolution Lives."

82. Cotter, *Troubled Harvest*, 321–23, 325.

83. Lester R. Brown, *Seeds of Change: The Green Revolution and Development in the 1970's* (New York: Praeger, 1970), vii–ix; Kristen Appendini, "Transforming Food Policy over a Decade: The Balance for Mexican Corn Farmers in 1993," in *Economic Restructuring and Rural Subsistence in Mexico: Corn and Its Crisis of the 1980s*, ed. Cynthia Hewitt de Alcántara, Transformation of Rural Mexico Series, no. 2 (San Diego: Center for US-Mexican Studies, University of California San Diego, 1994), 145, 147–49, 151, 153, 155–57; *Latin America and the Caribbean (LAC) Report* (Washington, DC: Island Press, 2009), 12; John H. Sanders and John K. Lynam, "New Agricultural Technology and Small Farmers in Latin America," *Food Policy* 6 (February 1981): 11, 17–18.

Chapter Two

1. Göran Djurfeldt and Magnus Jirström, "The Puzzle of the Policy Shift—The Early Green Revolution in India, Indonesia and the Philippines," in *The African Food Crisis: Lessons from the Asian Green Revolution*, ed. Göran Djurfeldt, Hans Holmén, Magnus Jirström, and Rolf Larsson (Cambridge, MA: CABI, 2005), 51; Govindan Parayil, "The Green Revolution in India: A Case Study of Technological Change," *Technology and Culture* 33 (October 1992): 737–39.

2. Parayil, "Green Revolution in India," 745, 751; Bandhudas Sen, *The Green Revolution in India: A Perspective* (New York: John Wiley & Sons, 1974), 11; Dana G. Dalrymple, *Imports and Plantings of High-Yielding Varieties of Wheat and Rice in the Less Developed Nations* (Washington, DC: US Department of Agriculture, Foreign Agricultural Service, in cooperation with the Agency of International Development, 1969), 2–4, 6, 13, 15; John H. Perkins, *Geopolitics and the Green Revolution: Wheat, Genes, and the Cold War* (New York: Oxford University Press, 1997), 238.

3. Dalrymple, *Imports and Plantings*, 2–4, 6, 13, 15; Norman E. Borlaug, "Civilization Will Depend More upon Flourishing Crops than on Flowery Rhetoric" (Alfred M. Landon Lecture, March 20, 1979, Kansas State University), 8–9; Homer E. Socolofsky, "The World Food Crisis and Progress in Wheat Breeding," *Agricultural History* 43 (October 1969): 433; Stanley Johnson, *The Green Revolution* (New York: Harper & Row, 1972), 165; Lester R. Brown, *Seeds of Change: The Green Revolution and Development in the 1970's* (New York: Praeger, 1970), 19; Carl E. Pray, "The Green Revolution

as a Case Study in Transfer of Technology," *Annals of the American Academy of Political and Social Science* 458 (November 1981): 71; Parayil, "Green Revolution in India," 752; Perkins, *Geopolitics and the Green Revolution*, 183, 236–37, 240, 244.

4. Parayil, "Green Revolution in India," 746; Monohar Singh Gill, "The Development of Punjab Agriculture, 1977–80," *Asian Survey* 23 (July 1983): 831; Vernon W. Ruttan, "The Green Revolution: Seven Generalizations," *International Development Review* 19, no. 4 (1977): 16–17.

5. Ruttan, "Green Revolution," 16–17; M. S. Randhawa, *Green Revolution* (New York: John Wiley & Sons, 1974), 2; Borlaug, "Civilization Will Depend More upon Flourishing Crops," 8–9.

6. Socolofsky, "World Food Crisis," 433.

7. Sen, *Green Revolution in India*, 2; Brown, *Seeds of Change*, 4–5; Nick Cullather, *The Hungry World: America's Cold War Battle against Poverty in Asia* (Cambridge, MA: Harvard University Press, 2010), 199; Mahmood Hasan Khan, *The Economics of the Green Revolution in Pakistan* (New York: Praeger, 1975), 22, 30–32, 49.

8. M. S. Randhawa, "The Green Revolution in Punjab," *Agricultural History* 51 (October 1977): 659–60; Parayil, "Green Revolution in India," 752–53; Juan de Oniss, "Developers of High-Yielding Grains Report a Victory Over Drought," *New York Times*, September 16, 1969; Socolofsky, "World Food Crisis," 433; Dalrymple, *Imports and Plantings*, 4, 6; Perkins, *Geopolitics and the Green Revolution*, 183–85, 245.

9. "Madras Is Reaping a Bitter Harvest of Rural Terrorism: Rice Growers' Feud with Field Workers Has Fiery Climax Labor Seeks Bigger Share of Gain from Crop Innovations," *New York Times*, January 15, 1969; Joseph Lelyveld, "'Green Revolution' Transforming Indian Farming, but It Has a Long Way to Go," *New York Times*, May 28, 1969; Francine R. Frankel, *India's Green Revolution: Economic Gains and Political Costs* (Princeton, NJ: Princeton University Press, 1971), 7–8.

10. Lelyveld, "'Green Revolution' Transforming Indian Farming."

11. Lelyveld, "'Green Revolution' Transforming Indian Farming"; Joseph Lelyveld, "India's New Hope Fades," *New York Times*, January 1, 1970; "The Green Revolution Turns Red," *New York Times*, January 8, 1970; Sydney H. Schanberg, "Cost of Food Is Becoming a Political Issue in India," *New York Times*, October 23, 1970.

12. Robert R. R. Brooks, "India's Central Problem Is How to Improve Ratio of Food to Population," *New York Times*, January 19, 1970; Israel Shenker, "'Green Revolution' Has Sharply Increased Grain Yields but May Cause Problems," *New York Times*, October 22, 1970; Erich H. Jacoby, "Effects of the 'Green Revolution' in South and South-East Asia," *Modern Asian Studies* 6, no. 1 (1972): 69; Cullather, *Hungry World*, 240.

13. A. K. Chakravarti, "Green Revolution in India," *Annals of the Association of American Geographers* 63 (September 1973): 326–27; Wolf Ladejinsky, "Ironies of India's Green Revolution," *Foreign Affairs* 48, no. 4 (July 1970): 759; Walter P. Falcon, "The Green Revolution: Generations of Problems," *American Journal of Agricultural Economics* 52 (December 1970): 698–700.

14. Schanberg, "Cost of Food"; Donald K. Freebairn, "Did the Green Revolution Concentrate Incomes? A Quantitative Study of Research Reports," *World Development* 23, no. 2 (1995): 267; Harry M. Cleaver Jr., "The Contradictions of the Green Revolution," *American Economic Review* 62 (March 1, 1972): 182; Jacoby, "Effects of the 'Green Revolution,'" 65–66, 68–69.

15. Sydney H. Schanberg, "For Some in India Drought Persists," *New York Times*, February 23, 1971; Kasturi Ragan, "Land Disputes Thwarting Green Revolution in India," *New York Times*, October 12, 1971; Bernard Weinraub, "New Delhi Is Blamed for Worsening Food Crisis," *New York Times*, September 13, 1974.

16. Kasturi Ragan, "The Rains Came and India Eats," *New York Times*, January 30, 1977.

17. Frankel, *India's Green Revolution*, 192–93, 196–97; Leslie Stein, "The Green Revolution and Asian Development Strategy," *Studies in Comparative International Development* 12, no. 12 (1977): 60; Leslie Nulty, *The Green Revolution in West Pakistan: Implications of Technological Change* (New York: Praeger, 1972), 121–22; Socolofsky, "World Food Crisis," 434.

18. Chakravarti, "Green Revolution in India," 319; Stein, "Green Revolution and Asian Development Strategy," 62–63; Falcon, "Green Revolution," 705, 708–9; Frank C. Child and Hiromitsu Kaneda, "Links to the Green Revolution: A Study of Small-Scale, Agriculturally Related Industry in the Pakistan Punjab," *Economic Development and Cultural Change* 23 (January 1975): 262.

19. Magnus Jirström, "The State and Green Revolutions in East Asia," in Djurfeldt et al., *African Food Crisis*, 38–40; Randhawa, "Green Revolution in Punjab," 657–58.

20. Frankel, *India's Green Revolution*, 200–201, 205.

21. Djurfeldt and Jirström, "Puzzle of the Policy Shift," 51–52; Randhawa, "Green Revolution in Punjab," 656; Parayil, "Green Revolution in India," 746; Gill, "Development of Punjab Agriculture," 831; Harry W. Blair, "The Green Revolution and 'Economic Man': Some Lessons for Community Development in South Asia?," *Pacific Affairs* 44 (Autumn 1971): 360; Lester R. Brown, "India's Outlook for Grain Brightens," *New York Times*, January 24, 1972; Kasturi Ragan, "Surplus of Grain Reported in India," April 30, 1972; Partap C. Aggarwal, *The Green Revolution and Rural Labour: A Study of Ludhiana* (New Delhi: Shri Ram Centre for Industrial Relations and Human Resources, 1973), 13–22; Randhawa, *Green Revolution*, 67.

22. Randhawa, "Green Revolution in Punjab," 660–61.

23. Rattan, "Green Revolution," 16–23; Randhawa, "Green Revolution in Punjab," 660–61.

24. Frankel, *India's Green Revolution*, 191; Child and Kaneda, "Links to the Green Revolution," 249, 271; Jeffry M. Pilcher, *Food in World History* (New York: Routledge, 2006), 100; Khan, *Economics of the Green Revolution in Pakistan*, 13, 128–32; Harry M. Cleaver Jr., "The Contradictions of the Green Revolution," *American Economic Review* 62 (March 1, 1972): 181; Sen, *Green Revolution in India*, 103.

25. Sen, *Green Revolution in India*, 102–3.

26. Parayil, "Green Revolution in India," 743, 752–53; Gill, "Development of Punjab Agriculture," 832; Jirström, "The State and Green Revolutions in East Asia," 25–26.

27. Nicholas Wade, "Green Revolution (I): A Just Technology, Often Unjust in Use," *Science* 186 (December 20, 1974): 1093–95.

28. Frankel, *India's Green Revolution*, 196.

29. Wade, "Green Revolution (I)," 1093–96; Nicholas Wade, "Green Revolution (II): Problems of Adopting Western Technology," *Science* 186 (December 27, 1974): 1186–92; James N. Wallace, "Green Revolution Hits Double Trouble," *U.S. News & World Report*, July 28, 1980, https://www.lexisnexis.com.

30. Ruttan, "Green Revolution," 17–18.

31. Frankel, *India's Green Revolution*, 191; Ruttan, "Green Revolution," 19.

32. Ruttan, "Green Revolution," 20.

33. Pray, "Green Revolution as a Case Study," 68–69, 71, 74–75; Rita Sharma and Thomas T. Poleman, *The New Economics of India's Green Revolution: Income and Employment Diffusion in Uttar Pradesh* (Ithaca, NY: Cornell University Press, 1993), 240–55.

34. George Blyn, "The Green Revolution Revisited," *Economic Development and Cultural Change* 31 (July 1983): 717–20.

35. Pray, "Green Revolution as a Case Study," 74–78, 80.

36. Lester R. Brown, "The Browning of the Green Revolution: Today's Droughts Worsen a World Food Shortfall," *Washington Post*, July 3, 1988; William K. Stevens, "Green Revolution Is Not Enough, Study Finds," *New York Times*, September 6, 1994.

37. Freebairn, "Did the Green Revolution Concentrate Agricultural Incomes?," 269.

38. Parayil, "Green Revolution in India," 755–56; Sen, *Green Revolution in India*, 108, 110–12; K. P. Prabhaksaran, "Malnutrition in South Asia: The Future Shock?," *Hindu Business Line* (Chennai, India), January 7, 1998, https://global-factiva.com.

39. Djurfeldt and Jirström, "Puzzle of the Policy Shift," 55; Sydney H. Schanberg, "With Economy in Ruins, Bangladesh Faces Food Crisis," *New York Times*, March 30, 1972; Mahabub Hossain, *Nature and Impact of the Green Revolution in Bangladesh*, Research Report No. 67 (Washington, DC: International Food Policy Research Institute in collaboration with the Bangladesh Institute of Development Studies, July 1988), 11–13; Naila Kabeer and Simeen Mahmud, "Globalization, Gender and Poverty: Bangladeshi Women Workers in Export and Local Markets," *Journal of International Development* 16 (January 2004): 94; Mohammad Alauddin and Clem Tisdell, "Has the Green Revolution Destabilized Food Production? Some Evidence from Bangladesh," *Developing Economies* 26, no. 2 (June 1988): 141.

40. Hossain, *Nature and Impact of the Green Revolution*, 11–12, 15; Alastair Orr, "Why Were So Many Social Scientists Wrong about the Green Revolution? Learning from Bangladesh," *Journal of Development Studies* 48, no. 11 (2012): 1575, 1577–80.

41. Sen, *Green Revolution in India*, 102–3; Mohammad Alauddin and Clem Tisdell, "Welfare Consequences of Green Revolution Technology: Changes in Bangladeshi

Food Production and Diet," *Development and Change* 22 (1991): 503, 505–6, 511–13; Hossain, *Nature and Impact of the Green Revolution*, 24–29, 36.

42. Djurfeldt and Jirström, "Puzzle of the Policy Shift," 56–58, 60; Harry W. Blair, "Rural Development, Class Structure and Bureaucracy in Bangladesh," *World Development* 6, no. 1 (1978): 71–73.

43. Alauddin and Tisdell, "Has the Green Revolution Destabilized Food Production?," 158; Hossain, *Nature and Impact of the Green Revolution*, 23; Djurfeldt and Jirström, "Puzzle of the Policy Shift," 56–58, 60; Blair, "Rural Development, Class Structure and Bureaucracy," 71–73.

44. Orr, "Why Were So Many Social Scientists Wrong," 1565–66.

45. Orr, "Why Were So Many Social Scientists Wrong," 2, 1570–71.

46. Sarwar Md Sarfullah Khaled, "Bangladesh Agriculture—Prevailing Realities," *Financial Express* (Bangladesh), May 25, 2014, https://global-factiva.com.

47. Freebairn, "Did the Green Revolution Concentrate Agricultural Incomes?," 276.

48. Ladejinsky, "Ironies of India's Green Revolution," 758; Sen, *Green Revolution in India*, 3, 104; Parayil, "Green Revolution in India," 738.

49. Freebairn, "Did the Green Revolution Concentrate Incomes?," 268–69, 275–76; Abe Goldman and Joyotee Smith, "Agricultural Transformations in India and Northern Nigeria: Exploring the Nature of Green Revolutions," *World Development* 23, no. 2 (1995): 257.

50. Cleaver, "Contradictions of the Green Revolution," 177–78; Sigrid Schmalzer, *Red Revolution, Green Revolution: Scientific Farming in Socialist China* (Chicago, IL: University of Chicago Press), 5–6.

51. Schmalzer, *Red Revolution, Green Revolution*, 5–6.

52. Peter R. Jennings, "Rice Breeding and World Food Production," *Science* 186 (December 20, 1974): 1085; Ladejinsky, "Ironies of India's Green Revolution," 759.

53. Michael Lipton with Richard Longhurst, *New Seeds and Poor People* (Baltimore, MD: Johns Hopkins University Press, 1989), 3.

54. Amy Waldman, "Poor in India Starve as Surplus Wheat Rots," *New York Times*, December 2, 2002.

55. "India to Import 3mt Wheat, Pay Rs 2k cr," *Economic Times* (New Delhi), April 22, 2006, http://find.galegroup.com/grnr/infomark.do?; Jim Yardley, "As India Grows, Rural Areas Left in the Dust," *New York Times*, September 5, 2009; Celia W. Dugger, "Chidambaram Subramaniam, India's 'Green' Rebel, 90, Dies," *New York Times*, November 10, 2000; "Proper Storage of Grain Needed for Food Security, Says Expert," *Times of India* (Gurugram), September 27, 2010, http://find.galegroup.com/grnr/infomark .do?; Bijay Kumar Singh, "India Needs a Second Green Revolution, Says President Pratibha Patil," *Tehelka* (New Delhi), December 6, 2010, http://search.proquest.comdocview /817223602?accountid=13360.

56. Freebairn, "Did the Green Revolution Concentrate Incomes?," 268, 275–76.

57. Daniel Zwerdling, "India's Farming 'Revolution' Heading for Collapse," Na-

tional Public Radio, April 13, 2009; Daniel Zwerdling, "'Green Revolution' Trapping India's Farmers in Debt," National Public Radio, April 17, 2009.

58. Saurabh Bhatt, "Chinese Agri-Lessons for Indian Policy Makers," *Hindu Business Line* (Chennai, India), December 19, 2011, https://global-factiva.com; "Detailed Land Use System to Raise Grain Yield," *Times of India* (Gurugram), June 28, 2014, http://find.galegroup.com/grnr/infomark.do?; "A Bigger Rice Bowl, The New Green Revolution," *The Economist*, 411 (May 10, 2014): 21–23.

59. P. K. Joshi, Ashok Gulati, Pratap S. Birthal, and Laxmi Tewari, "Agriculture Diversification in South Asia: Patterns, Determinants and Policy Implications," *Economic and Political Weekly* 39 (June 12, 2004): 2466; Pratiksha Ramkumar, "Bring More Women Farmers On Board to Eliminate Hunger, M.S. Swaminathan Says," *Times of India* (Gurugram), November 7, 2014, http://find.galegroup.com/grnr/infomark.do?.

60. Ramkumar, "Bring More Women Farmers On Board."

61. Boro Baski, "Indian Agriculture and Green Revolution: Huge Challenges Ahead," *Kashmir Times* (Srinagar, India), July 3, 2014, https://global-factiva.com.

62. Tarique Niazi, "Rural Poverty and the Green Revolution: The Lessons from Pakistan," *Journal of Peasant Studies* 31 (January 2004): 246–50, 256.

63. Niazi, "Rural Poverty and the Green Revolution," 250–52, 254–56.

64. Sen, *Green Revolution in India*, 108, 111–12; Parayil, "Green Revolution in India," 754; Goldman and Smith, "Agricultural Transformations," 259–60.

65. Chakravarti, "Green Revolution in India," 320; J. S. Kanwar, "Research for Effective Use of Land and Water Resources," in *National Agricultural Research Systems in Asia*, ed. A. H. Moseman (New York: Agricultural Development Council, 1971), 214.

66. Chakravarti, "Green Revolution in India," 320; Kanwar, "Research for Effective Use," 214.

67. Goldman and Smith, "Agricultural Transformations," 259–60; Cullather, *Hungry World*, 230–31.

68. Cullather, *Hungry World*, 230–31.

69. W. Klatt, "Reflections on Agricultural Modernisation in Asia," *Pacific Affairs* 46 (Winter 1973–1974): 534, 536; B. H. Farmer, "The 'Green Revolution' in South Asian Rice Fields: Environment and Production," *Journal of Development Studies* 15, no. 4 (1979): 317.

CHAPTER THREE

1. Yujiro Hayami, "Conditions for the Diffusion of Agricultural Technology: An Asian Perspective," *Journal of Economic History* 34 (March 1974): 135–36, 144, 146, 148; Dana G. Dalrymple, "The Development and Adoption of High-Yielding Varieties of Wheat and Rice in Developing Countries," *American Journal of Agricultural Economics* 67, no. 5 (December 1985): 1067–73.

2. Magnus Jirström, "The State and Green Revolutions in East Asia," in *The Af-*

rican Food Crisis: Lessons from the Asian Green Revolution, ed. Göran Djurfeldt, Hans Holmén, Magnus Jirström, and Rolf Larsson (Cambridge, MA: CABI, 2005), 28–31; Hayami, "Conditions for the Diffusion of Agricultural Technology," 145–48.

3. Hayami, "Conditions for the Diffusion of Agricultural Technology," 145; Jirström, "The State and Green Revolutions in East Asia," 32–34.

4. Hayami, "Conditions for the Diffusion of Agricultural Technology," 145; Jirström, "The State and Green Revolutions in East Asia," 32–34.

5. Jirström, "The State and Green Revolutions in East Asia," 34–35.

6. Jirström, "The State and Green Revolutions in East Asia," 37.

7. Jirström, "The State and Green Revolutions in East Asia," 37.

8. Govindan Parayil, "The Green Revolution in India: A Case Study of Technological Change," *Technology and Culture* 33 (October 1992): 743, 745; Shaobing Peng and Gurdev S. Khush, "Four Decades of Breeding for Varietal Development of Irrigated Lowland Rice in the International Rice Research Institute," *Plant Production Science* 6, no. 3 (2003): 157–60; Julian Borger, "Global Food Crisis: Greener and Leaner," *The Guardian.com* (London), April 18, 2014, https://global-factiva.com; Pamela G. Hollie, "Spread of 'Miracle' Rice Lagging in Asia," *New York Times*, March 12, 1981; K. G. Cassman and P. K. Pingali, "Intensification of Irrigated Rice Systems: Learning from the Past to Meet Future Challenges," *GeoJournal* 25, no. 3 (1995): 299, 305; Kuei-Mei Lo and Hsin-Hsing Chen, "Technological Momentum and the Hegemony of the Green Revolution: A Case Study of an Organic Rice Cooperative in Taiwan," *East Asian Science, Technology and Society* 5, no. 2 (2011): 137–38; "Rice Crop Drops in Ravaged Asia," *New York Times*, January 14, 1973; "Save the Good Revolution," *New York Times*, July 18, 1968; Philip Shabecoff, "Rice Boom in Asia Raises Doubts," *New York Times*, April 6, 1970.

9. B. H. Farmer, "The Green Revolution in South Asian Rice Fields: Environment and Production," *Journal of Development Studies* 15, no. 4 (1979): 306–8, 316–17.

10. Jirström, "The State and Green Revolutions in East Asia," 38–40.

11. Jirström, "The State and Green Revolutions in East Asia," 39.

12. Larry L. Burmeister, "The South Korean Green Revolution: Induced or Directed Innovation?," *Economic Development and Culture Change* 35 (July 1978): 770, 772–79, 783; Shabecoff, "Rice Boom in Asia Raises Doubts"; Lo and Chen, "Technological Momentum," 137–38; Cassman and Pingali, "Intensification of Irrigated Rice Systems," 305; "Rice Crop Drops in Ravaged Asia."

13. Shabecoff, "Rice Boom in Asia Raises Doubts"; Gladwin Hill, "World Parley Warned of Short Food Supplies," *New York Times*, August 11, 1970; Israel Shenker, "'Green Revolution' Has Sharply Increased Grain Yields but May Cause Problems," *New York Times*, October 22, 1970.

14. Joko Mariyono, Tom Kompas, and R. Quentin Grafton, "Shifting from Green Revolution to Environmentally Sound Policies: Technological Change in Indonesian Rice Agriculture," *Journal of the Asia Pacific Economy* 15, no. 2 (2010): 134–40; Marina

Welker, "The Green Revolution's Ghost: Unruly Subjects of Participatory Development in Rural Indonesia," *American Ethnologist* 39 (May 2012): 391–92.

15. Welker, "Green Revolution's Ghost," 391–92; Gary E. Hansen, "Indonesian Green Revolution: The Abandonment of a Non-Market Strategy toward Change," *Asian Survey* 12 (November 1972): 932, 934–36, 940, 943–46.

16. Welker, "Green Revolution's Ghost," 391–92; Hansen, "Indonesian Green Revolution," 932, 934–36, 940, 943–46; "Famine Ravages War-Torn Continent," *New York Times*, January 21, 1973.

17. Joseph Lelyveld, "Resistant Rice Plants Sought for Asia," *New York Times*, October 11, 1973.

18. Erich H. Jacoby, "Effects of the 'Green Revolution' in South and Southeast Asia," *Modern Asian Studies* 6, no. 1 (1972): 66, 68–69.

19. "Filipinos Expect New Rice Scarcity," *New York Times*, February 14, 1972; Lelyveld, "Resistant Rice Plants Sought for Asia"; Bruce Koppel, "Sustaining the Green Revolution," *Asian Survey* 16 (April 1976): 355.

20. Marvine Howe, "Mansholt Calls for Inquiry into Problem of Pesticides," *New York Times*, November 11, 1971.

21. "U.N. Group Calls for Farm Reform," *New York Times*, November 21, 1971.

22. Robert Trumbull, "Experts See a Gloomy Outlook for Asia," *New York Times*, January 13, 1971; Paul Hofmann, "Food Production Gains in Far East," *New York Times*, August 23, 1971.

23. "Vanishing Glut," *New York Times*, January 2, 1973; "Famine Ravages War-Torn Continent."

24. "Rice Crop Drops in Ravaged Asia"; "Famine Ravages War-Torn Continent"; James P. Sterba, "The Green Revolution Hasn't Ended Hunger," *New York Times*, April 15, 1973.

25. William J. C. Logan, "How Deep Is the Green Revolution in South Vietnam? The Story of the Agricultural Turn-Around in South Vietnam," *Asian Survey* 11, no. 4 (April 1971): 321–26, 328.

26. "Rice Crop Drops in Ravaged Asia"; "Famine Ravages War-Torn Continent"; Tran Thi Ut and Kei Kajisa, "The Impact of Green Revolution on Rice Production in Vietnam," *Developing Economies* 44 (June 2006): 168.

27. Ut and Kajisa, "Impact of Green Revolution," 167, 182.

28. Monika Barthwal-Datta, "Low Prices Aren't a Food Security Panacea," *Nikkei Report* (Japan), April 22, 2015, https://global.factiva.com; Ut and Kajisa, "Impact of Green Revolution," 167, 174, 182, 189.

29. Alec Gordon, "The 'Green Revolution' in North Vietnam," *Journal of Contemporary Asia*, 4, no. 1 (1974): 129.

30. Gordon, "'Green Revolution' in North Vietnam," 128–33.

31. Hofmann, "Food Production Gains in Far East"; "Filipinos Expect New Rice Scarcity."

32. Victor K. McElheny, "Green Revolution Passes over Asia without Expected Up-heaval," *New York Times*, September 23, 1974; Walter Sullivan, "Social Ills Tied to Mal-nutrition," *New York Times*, August 26, 1975.

33. Edwin L. Dale Jr., "American Grain Crop: A Life or Death Matter," *New York Times*, May 19, 1974; Seth King, "Governors Told of Food Crisis," *New York Times*, July 31, 1974; McElheny, "Green Revolution Passes over Asia without Expected Upheaval"; Joseph Lelyveld, "Burma and Thailand Seen as Possible Rice Suppliers to Neighbors," *New York Times*, January 6, 1975. Pakistan and India were included in the study.

34. McElheny, "Green Revolution Passes over Asia without Expected Upheaval"; Victor K. McElheny, "New Miracle in Rice Seen by Some in Asia," *New York Times*, November 1, 1974; Lelyveld, "Burma and Thailand Seen as Possible Rice Suppliers to Neighbors."

35. Lelyveld, "Burma and Thailand Seen as Possible Rice Suppliers to Neighbors."

36. "For Asian Agronomists, Hope Lingers," *New York Times*, January 26, 1975; "Huge Rice Crop Leaves Philippines Short of Storage," *New York Times*, September 16, 1975.

37. "An Endless Quest," *New York Times*, May 1, 1973; "For Asian Agronomists, Hope Lingers."

38. Hollie, "Spread of 'Miracle' Rice Lagging in Asia"; Steven Lohr, "New Varieties of Hardy Rice Hold Promise," *New York Times*, August 14, 1984; Tumari Jatileksono and Keijiro Otsuka, "Impact of Modern Rice Technology on Land Prices: The Case of Lampung in Indonesia," *American Journal of Agricultural Economics* 75 (August 1993): 664.

39. Hollie, "Spread of 'Miracle' Rice Lagging in Asia"; Jules Pretty and Rachel Hine, "The Promising Spread of Sustainable Agriculture in Asia," *Natural Resources Forum* 24 (2000): 119.

40. Hollie, "Spread of 'Miracle' Rice Lagging in Asia"; Lohr, "New Varieties of Hardy Rice Hold Promise."

41. Jirström, "The State and Green Revolutions in Southeast Asia," 25–26, 39–40; Paul Lewis, "The Green Revolution Bears Fruit," *New York Times*, June 2, 1985; Cass-man and Pingali, "Intensification of Irrigated Rice Systems," 299–301.

42. Kieran Cooke, "Commodities and Agriculture, Indonesia's Rice 'Miracle'/Boom in Production," *Financial Times* (London), July 5, 1985, https://global.factiva.com.

43. John Stackhouse, "Indonesian Farmers Learn Pest Control Is More Effective without Chemicals," *Globe and Mail* (Toronto), August 12, 1996, https://global.factiva.com; Mariyono, Kompas, and Grafton, "Shifting from Green Revolution," 128–29, 131, 134, 137, 140.

44. Jirström, "The State and Green Revolutions in East Asia," 25–26, 39–40; Welker, "Green Revolution's Ghost," 397; Wilfrido Cruz and Christopher Gibbs, "Resource Policy Reform in the Context of Population Pressure: The Philippines and Nepal," *American Journal of Agricultural Economics Resource Policy Forum* 72 (December 1990):

1265; Cooke, "Commodities and Agriculture"; Marc R. Crowe Bloomberg, "Philippines Scrambling to Solve Its Growing Rice Shortage," *Financial Post* (London), August 19, 1995, https://global.factiva.com; Gemma Cruz Arante, "Green Revolution Revisited," *Manila Bulletin*, April 22, 2008, https://global-factiva.com; "Lack of Philippine Industrial Culture," *Manila Bulletin*, October 18, 2011, https://global-factiva.com.

45. Paul Lewis, "Food Production and the Birth Rate Are in a New Race," *New York Times*, May 10, 1992.

46. Peter Ungphakarn, "Survey of Thailand: Rice Fields Hit by Pests and Climate," *Financial Times* (London), December 5, 1990, https://global.factiva.com.

47. "Future of Agriculture Takes on Even More Importance," *The Nation* (Thailand), February 4, 2000, https://global.factiva.com; Pennapa Hongthong, "Agriculture Ministry Helped Put Farmers into Debt, Official Says," *The Nation* (Thailand), September 9, 2000, https://global.factiva.com; "The Rice That Nearly Wasn't," *Bangkok Post*, October 1, 2000. https://global.factiva.com.

48. Pretty and Hine, "Promising Spread of Sustainable Agriculture," 119; Jessica Hamburger, "Pesticides in China: A Growing Threat to Food Safety, Public Health, and the Environment," *China Environment Series* 5 (2002): 29.

49. Romeo M. Bautista, "Income and Equity Effects of the Green Revolution in the Philippines: A Macroeconomic Perspective," *Journal of International Development* 9, no. 2 (1997): 153, 164; Keijiro Otsuka, Fe Gascon, and Seki Asano, "Green Revolution and Labour Demand in Rice Farming: The Case of Central Luzon, 1966–90," *Journal of Development Studies* 31, no. 1 (1994): 82, 89, 92; Keijiro Otsuka, Fe Gascon, and Deki Asano, "'Second-Generation' MVs and the Evolution of the Green Revolution: The Case of Central Luzon, 1966–90," *Agricultural Economics* 10 (1994): 283–87, 293; Jonna P. Estudillo, Yasuyuki Sawada, and Keijiro Otsuka, "The Green Revolution, Development of Labor Markets, and Poverty Reduction in the Rural Philippines, 1985–2004," *Agricultural Economics* 35, no. s3 (November 2006): 401–2; Jonna P. Estudillo and Keijiro Otsuka, "Green Revolution, Human Capital, and Off-Farm Employment: Changing Sources of Income among Farm Households in Central Luzon, 1966–1994," *Economic Development and Cultural Change* 47, no. 3 (1999): 503–4. The first-generation varieties that proved susceptible to disease included IR-5 to IR-34 and C4 developed at the University of the Philippines.

50. Bautista, "Income and Equity Effects," 153, 164; Otsuka, Gascon and Asano, "Green Revolution and Labour Demand," 82, 89, 92; Otsuka, Gascon, and Asano, "'Second-Generation' MVs," 283–87, 293; Estudillo, Sawada, and Otsuka, "Green Revolution, Development of Labor Markets, and Poverty Reduction," 401–2; Estudillo and Otsuka, "Green Revolution, Human Capital, and Off-Farm Employment," 503–4.

51. Pretty and Hine, "Promising Spread of Sustainable Agriculture," 107, 110–11, 115–17, 119; Hamburger, "Pesticides in China," 30–31; Xiaobai Shen, "Understanding the Evolution of Rice Technology in China—From Traditional Agriculture to GM Rice Today," *Journal of Development Studies* 46 (July 2010): 1027.

52. Keith Bradsher and Andrew Martin, "World's Poor Pay Price as Crop Research Is Cut," *New York Times*, May 18, 2008.

53. W. Klatt, "Reflections on Agricultural Modernisation in Asia," *Pacific Affairs* 46 (Winter 1973–1974): 545; Jikun Huang, Carl Pray, and Scott Rozelle, "Enhancing the Crops to Feed the Poor," *Nature* 418 (August 8, 2002): 678, 680, 683.

54. Cassman and Pingali, "Intensification of Irrigated Rice Systems," 305.

55. "Rice Policies Misguided," *Bangkok Post*, August 6, 2012, https://global.factiva .com; Borger, "Global Food Crisis: Greener and Leaner"; "Forty Years after the 'Green Revolution,'" *Jakarta Post*, June 30, 2009, https://global.factiva.com.

56. Carlos Cortes, "A Rush for Rice: Philippine Scientists Are Developing New Strains to Combat Growing Population and Shrinking Farmland in Asia," *Pittsburgh Post-Gazette*, August 21, 1998, https://global.factiva.com; "New Green Revolution Needed," *New Straits Times* (Berhad, Malaysia), January 7, 2013, https://global.factiva.com; Edward Luce, "Rice Experts to Beat Asia Shortage: Failing Crops and Rising Populations Have Resulted in a Rice Shortfall—And Prices That Have Doubled since January," *National Post* (London), December 8, 1995, https://global.factiva.com.

57. John Vidal, "Philippine Experts Divided over Climate Change Action," *The Guardian.com* (London), April 8, 2014, https://global.factiva.com.

58. "Food Security: A Tough Question for President Jokowi," *Jakarta Post*, November 9, 2014, https://global.factiva.com.

59. Peter B. R. Hazell and C. Ramasamy, *The Green Revolution Reconsidered: The Impact of High-Yielding Rice Varieties in South India* (Baltimore, MD: Johns Hopkins University Press, 1991), xiii.

60. Peng and Khush, "Four Decades of Breeding," 157.

61. "Save the Good Revolution" *New York Times*, July 18, 1968; Göran Djurfeldt and Magnus Jirström, "The Puzzle of the Policy Shift—The Early Green Revolution in India, Indonesia and the Philippines," in Djurfeldt et al., *African Food Crisis*, 43–63.

Chapter Four

1. Sterling Wortman, "Agriculture in China," *Scientific American* 232 (June 1975): 13.

2. Gonçalo Santos, "Rethinking the Green Revolution in South China: Technological Materialities and Human-Environment Relations," *East Asian Science, Technology and Society* 5, no. 4 (2011): 484, 487; Sigrid Schmalzer, *Red Revolution, Green Revolution: Scientific Farming in Socialist China* (Chicago, IL: University of Chicago Press, 2016), 4.

3. Xiaobai Shen, "Understanding the Evolution of Rice Technology in China—From Traditional Agriculture to GM Rice Today," *Journal of Development Studies* 46 (July 2010): 1035.

4. Joshua Eisenman, *Red China's Green Revolution: Technological Innovation, Institutional Change, and Economic Development under the Commune* (New York: Colum-

bia University Press, 2018), 33; Ramon H. Myers, "Agricultural Development," in *The People's Republic of China: A Handbook*, ed. Harold C. Hinton (Boulder, CO: Westview Press, 1979), 176–77, 179–80; Roderick MacFarquhar and John K. Fairbank, eds., *The People's Republic, Part 1: The Emergence of Revolutionary China, 1949–1965*, vol. 14 of *The Cambridge History of China*, ed. Denis Twitchett and John K. Fairbank (New York: Cambridge University Press, 1987), 70–71, 87–88; Nicholas R. Lardy, *Agriculture in China's Modern Economic Development* (New York: Cambridge University Press, 1985), 12; Chao Kuo Chün, ed., *Agrarian Policies of Mainland China: A Documentary Study (1949–1956)* (Cambridge, MA: East Asian Research Center, Harvard University, 1963), 6–7, 38–51; Benedict Stavis, "Rural Institutions in China," in *The Chinese Agricultural Economy*, ed. Randolph Barker and Radha Sina with Beth Rose (Boulder, CO: Westview Press, 1982), 86.

5. MacFarquhar and Fairbank, *The People's Republic, Part 1*, 84; Frederick C. Teiwes, "Establishment and Consolidation of the New Regime," in *The Politics of China: The Eras of Mao and Deng*, ed. by Roderick MacFarquhar, 2nd ed. (New York: Cambridge University Press, 1997), 56–57; Dali L. Yang, *Calamity and Reform in China: State, Rural Society, and Institutional Change since the Great Leap Famine* (Stanford, CA: Stanford University Press, 1996), 22; Myers, "Agricultural Development," 180.

6. Harry Harding, *China's Second Revolution: Reform after Mao* (Washington, DC: Brookings Institution, 1987), 16; MacFarquhar and Fairbank, *The People's Republic, Part 1*, 14, 110–11, 115–19, 157, 160–63, 169–71; Yang, *Calamity and Reform in China*, 24–29, 32, 39, 96; Myers, "Agricultural Development," 182–84; Chün, *Agrarian Policies of Mainland China*, 54–60, 127–33; Lardy, *Agriculture in China's Modern Economic Development*, 16.

7. Eisenman, *Red China's Green Revolution*, 30–32; MacFarquhar, *Politics of China*, 86; Myers, "Agricultural Development," 182–83; MacFarquhar and Fairbank, *The People's Republic, Part 1*, 301–2, 320, 364–65; Stavis, "Rural Institutions in China," 90–91.

8. Shen, "Understanding the Evolution of Rice Technology," 1035.

9. Santos, "Rethinking the Green Revolution," 488–89; Schmalzer, *Red Revolution, Green Revolution*, 73–129.

10. Santos, "Rethinking the Green Revolution," 488, 498, 500; Schmalzer, *Red Revolution, Green Revolution*, 71–72, 219–20.

11. Leslie T. C. Kuo, *The Technical Transformation of Agriculture in Communist China* (New York: Praeger Publishers, 1972), 143–48; Y. Y. Kueh, *Agricultural Instability in China, 1931–1991: Weather, Technology, and Institutions* (Oxford: Clarendon Press, 1995), 204–5; 207; Bruce Stone, "Developments in Agricultural Technology," *China Quarterly* 116 (December 1988): 790–92; Schmalzer, *Red Revolution, Green Revolution*, 8–9, 12; Rakhal Datta, "Technological Choice in Collectivized Agriculture: Farm Mechanization Policy of the People's Republic of China," *China Report* 16 (September 1, 1980): 21–22; Robert C. Hsu, "Agricultural Mechanization in China: Policies, Problems, and Prospects," *Asian Survey* 19 (May 1979): 439.

12. Kueh, *Agricultural Instability in China*, 204–5, 207, 215–16 219–21.

13. Eisenman, *Red China's Green Revolution*, 40–46; MacFarquhar and Fairbank, *The People's Republic, Part 1*, 318–19, 322, 388–90; MacFarquhar, *Politics of China*, 335; Roderick MacFarquhar and John K. Fairbank, eds., *The People's Republic, Part 2: Revolutions within the Chinese Revolution, 1966–1982*, vol. 15 of *The Cambridge History of China*, ed. Denis Twitchett and John K. Fairbank (Cambridge: Cambridge University Press, 1991), 389, 478, 483, 524–25; Yang, *Calamity and Reform in China*, 103, 106–7; Myers, "Agricultural Development," 183–84, 192–93; Feng-hwa Mah, "Agricultural Reform in Mainland China: Problems and Prospects," in *Mainland China: Politics, Economics, and Reform*, ed. Yu-ming Shaw (Boulder, CO: Westview Press, 1986), 448; Benedict Stavis, *Making Green Revolution: The Politics of Agricultural Development in China*, Rural Development Monograph No. 1 (Ithaca, NY: Rural Development Committee, Cornell University, 1974), 110–19; Benedict Stavis, "Turning Point in China's Agricultural Policy" (Working Paper No. 1, Department of Agricultural Economics, Michigan State University, May 1979), 1; Cheng Xu, Han Chunru, and Donald C. Taylor, "Sustainable Agricultural Development in China," *World Development* 20, no. 8 (1992): 1129.

14. MacFarquhar and Fairbank, *The People's Republic, Part 1*, 318–19, 322, 388–90; Yang, *Calamity and Reform in China*, 103, 106–7; Myers, "Agricultural Development," 183–84, 192–93; MacFarquhar and Fairbank, *The People's Republic, Part 2*, 389, 478, 483, 524–25; Mah, "Agricultural Reform in Mainland China," 448; Stavis, *Making Green Revolution*, 110–19; Stavis, "Turning Point in China's Agricultural Policy," 1.

15. Santos, "Rethinking the Green Revolution," 488; Stavis, *Making Green Revolution*, 98–99, 102–4.

16. Eisenman, *Red China's Green Revolution*, 47; Stavis, *Making Green Revolution*, 95–97, 105–8; Shen, "Understanding the Evolution of Rice Technology," 1036–37; Schmalzer, *Red Revolution, Green Revolution*, 27, 29, 39–41.

17. Eisenman, *Red China's Green Revolution*, 55–58; Stavis, *Making Green Revolution*, 95–97, 105–8; Shen, "Understanding the Evolution of Rice Technology," 1036–37.

18. Eisenman, *Red China's Green Revolution*, xvi; Xu, Chunru, and Taylor, "Sustainable Agricultural Development," 1130–31; Jikun Huang and Scott Rozelle, "Technological Change: Rediscovering the Engine of Productivity Growth in China's Rural Economy," *Journal of Development Economics* 49, no. 2 (1996): 339; Stavis, *Making Green Revolution*, 250; Santos, "Rethinking the Green Revolution," 489; Schmalzer, *Red Revolution, Green Revolution*, 53.

19. Eisenman, *China's Green Revolution*, xv, xxi; Santos, "Rethinking the Green Revolution," 489; Tillman Durdin, "New Grains Help Chinese Farmers," *New York Times*, May 16, 1971; Paul Hofmann, "Food Production Gains in Far East," *New York Times*, August 23, 1971; Shen, "Understanding the Evolution of Rice Technology," 1027, 1036–37.

20. Sterling Wortman, "Agriculture in China," *Scientific American* 232 (June 1975): 13, 15.

21. Wortman, "Agriculture in China," 15–17; Stone, "Developments in Agricultural Technology," 795–96.

22. Wortman, "Agriculture in China," 15–17.

23. Wortman, "Agriculture in China," 15, 18–19.

24. Eisenman, *Red China's Green Revolution*, 48; Stavis, *Making Green Revolution*, 252–53, 256–57, 262.

25. Stavis, *Making Green Revolution*, 266–68.

26. Stavis, *Making Green Revolution*, 264, 278–79.

27. Ben Stavis, "A Preliminary Model for Grain Production in China, 1974," *China Quarterly* 65 (March 1976): 82–84, 86; Stavis, *Making Green Revolution*, 279–80.

28. Myers, "Agricultural Development," 184, 187; Harding, *China's Second Revolution*, 18–197.

29. Myers, "Agricultural Development," 185–91.

30. Eisenman, *Red China's Green Revolution*, 66–72; Wortman, "Agriculture in China," 19–21.

31. Eisenman, *Red China's Green Revolution*, 82; Shen, "Understanding the Evolution of Rice Technology," 1037–39.

32. Shen, "Understanding the Evolution of Rice Technology," 1037–39.

33. Eisenman, *Red China's Green Revolution*, 90–91; Shen, "Understanding the Evolution of Rice Technology," 1038–39, 1041; Stone, "Developments in Agricultural Technology," 798; Santos, "Rethinking the Green Revolution," 498; Schmalzer, *Red Revolution, Green Revolution*, 207.

34. Schmalzer, *Red Revolution, Green Revolution*, 80; Santos, "Rethinking the Green Revolution," 500; Weixing Chen, *The Political Economy of Rural Development in China, 1978–1999* (Westport, CT: Praeger, 1999), 37–38; John McMillan, John Whally, and Lijing Shu, "The Impact of China's Economic Reforms on Agricultural Productivity Growth," *Journal of Political Economy* 97 (August 1989): 800; Mah, "Agricultural Reform in Mainland China," 446, 451; Yang, *Calamity and Reform in China*, 451; Thomas P. Bernstein, "Farmer Discontent and Regime Responses," in *The Paradox of China's Post-Mao Reforms*, ed. Merle Goldman and Roderick MacFarquhar (Cambridge, MA: Harvard University Press, 1999), 204, 206; Stavis, "Rural Institutions in China," 94.

35. Eisenman, *Red China's Green Revolution*, 133–38, 210–13, 244; C. T. Wu, "Impacts of Rural Reforms," in *China's Economic Reforms*, Selected Seminar Papers on Contemporary China 7, ed. Joseph C. H. Chai and Chi-Keung Leung (Hong Kong: Centre for Asian Studies, University of Hong Kong, 1987), x, 275; Mah, "Agricultural Reform in Mainland China," 462; Justin Yifu Lin, "Agricultural Development and Reform in China," in *International Agricultural Development*, 3rd ed., ed. Cark K. Eicher and John M. Staatz (Baltimore, MD: Johns Hopkins University Press, 1998), 528–31; Ting-chung Ch'en, "Agriculture in Mainland China: Reform and Problems," in *Mainland China: Politics, Economics, and Reform*, ed. Yu-ming Shaw (Boulder, CO: Westview Press, 1986), 471–96, 473, 479–80; George C. Chow, China's Economic Trans-

formation, 3rd ed. (Malden, MA: Wiley Blackwell, 2015), 45–46, 81, 355–56; Harding, *China's Second Revolution*, 72, 103; Wu, "Impacts of Rural Reforms," 266–67; Lin, "Agricultural Development and Reform in China," 523–38; James K. S. Kung, "Beyond Subsistence: The Role of the Collectives in Rural Economic Development in Post-Mao China—An Exploratory Village Study in South China," in Chai and Leung, *China's Economic Reforms*, 294, 310; MacFarquhar and Fairbank, *The People's Republic, Part 2*, 526–28; Bernstein, "Farmer Discontent and Regime Responses," 206; Mah, "Agricultural Reform in Mainland China," 473–74, 479–80; Schmalzer, *Red Revolution, Green Revolution*, 87, 90.

36. Eisenman, *Red China's Green Revolution*, 193; Santos, "Rethinking the Green Revolution," 489; Mah, "Agricultural Reform in Mainland China," 453–54.

37. Jean C. Oi, *State and Peasant in Contemporary China: The Political Economy of Village Government* (Berkeley: University of California Press, 1989), 162–89, 199–200; Lin, "Agricultural Development and Reform in China," 532; Harding, *China's Second Revolution*, 72, 103–4; Wu, "Impacts of Rural Reforms," 267, 271.

38. Wu, "Impacts of Rural Reforms," 284; Bernstein, "Farmer Discontent and Regime Responses," 213–15; Harding, *China's Second Revolution*, 72, 101–2; Mah, "Agricultural Reform in Mainland China," 454.

39. Lin, "Agricultural Development and Reform in China," 524; Hong Yang, "Growth in China's Grain Production, 1978–1997: A Disaggregation Analysis," *World Development* 27, no. 12 (1999): 2144; Huang and Rozelle, "Technological Change," 339, Xu, *Sustainable Agriculture in China*, 1131; Richard Critchfield, "Asia: China's Agricultural Success Story," *Wall Street Journal*, January 13, 1986; James Kaising Kung, "Food and Agriculture in Post-Reform China: The Market Surplus Problem Revisited," *Modern China* 18 (April 1992): 139.

40. Wu, "Impacts of Rural Reforms," 271; Kung, "Food and Agriculture," 139, 141–42, 144–45.

41. Xu, "Sustainable Agriculture in China," 1133–34.

42. Kung, "Food and Agriculture," 148–49, 151–52.

43. Kung, "Food and Agriculture," 159, 167.

44. Bruce Stone, "Developments in Agricultural Technology," *China Quarterly* 116 (December 1988): 803–4, 807–8; Xu, Chunru, and Taylor, "Sustainable Agricultural Development," 1129.

45. Santos, "Rethinking the Green Revolution," 490.

46. Lester R. Brown, "The Browning of the Green Revolution: Today's Droughts Worsen a World Food Shortfall," *Washington Post*, July 3, 1988; Steve Connor, "Crop Problems May Be Helped by Western Technology," *Independent on Sunday* (London), July 29, 1990, https://global.factiva.com.

47. Ji-Liang Fu, Ernest H. Y. Chu, and Jia-Zhen Tan, "Perspectives on Genetics in China," *Annual Review of Genetics* 29 (1995): 10; Connor, "Crop Problems May Be Helped by Western Technology"; Han Chunru, "Recent Changes in the Rural Envi-

ronment in China," *Journal of Applied Ecology* 26 (December 1989): 804–8; Huang and Rozelle, "Technological Change," 339, 342; Xu, Chunru, and Taylor, "Sustainable Agricultural Development," 1127–28.

48. Critchfield, "Asia: China's Agricultural Success Story."

49. Alejandro Ninn Pitt, Bingxin Yu, and Shenggen Fan, "The Total Factor Productivity in China and India: New Measures and Approaches," *China Agricultural Economic Review* 1, no. 1 (2009): 9–10, 15; Yang, "Growth in China's Grain Production," 2149–50.

50. Devinder Sharma, "Pesticides—Ugly Side of Chinese Reforms," *Hindu Business Line* (Chennai), February 9, 1997, https://global.factiva.com; K. P. Prabhakaran Nair, "Relevance of New Biotechnologies in the Third World," *Hindu Business Line* (Chennai), March 16, 1998, https://global.factiva.com.

51. K. G. Cassman and P. L. Pingali, "Intensification of Irrigated Rice Systems: Learning from the Past to Meet Future Challenges," *GeoJournal* 35, no. 3 (1995): 299–300, 305.

52. Bernstein, "Farmer Discontent and Regime Responses," 215–18; Yang, "Growth in China's Grain Production," 2138–41, 2145, 1251.

53. Bernstein, "Farmer Discontent and Regime Responses," 197–98, 201–3.

54. Colin A. Carter, "The Urban-Rural Income Gap in China: Implications for Global Food Markets," *American Journal of Agricultural Economics* 79, no. 5 (1997): 1410, 1412.

55. Motoki Yasushi, "Transformation of Grain Production and the Rice Frontier in Modernizing China," *Geographical Review of Japan* 77, no. 12 (2004): 839–40, 842.

56. Jikun Huang, Carl Pray, and Scott Rozelle, "Enhancing the Crops to Feed the Poor," *Nature* 148 (August 2002): 678.

57. Bert Hofman, Mik Zhou, and Yoichiro Ishihara, "Asian Development Strategies: China and Indonesia Compared," *Bulletin of Indonesian Economic Studies* 43, no. 2 (2007): 171–72, 181, 183–85, 190.

58. Sukhadeo Thorat and Shenggen Fan, "Public Investment and Poverty Reduction: Lessons from China and India," *Economic and Political Weekly*, February 24, 2007, 704–5; Benjavan Rerkasem, "Transforming Subsistence Cropping in Asia," *Plant Production Science* 8, no. 3 (2005): 275.

59. Jianguo Li and Jared Diamond, "China's Environment in a Global World," *Nature* 435 (June 30, 2005): 181–82; Santos, "Rethinking the Green Revolution," 491–92, 500, 502.

60. Yongqiang Yu, Yao Huang, and Wen Zhang, "Changes in Rice Yields in China since 1980 Associated with Cultivar Improvement, Climate, and Crop Management," *Field Crops Research* 136 (2012): 65–66, 70.

61. Yu, Huang, and Zhang, "Changes in Rice Yields," 71–73.

62. Mingsheng Fan, Rattan Lal, Jian Cao, Lei Qiao, Rongfeng Jiang, and Fusuo Zhang, "Plant-Based Assessment of Inherent Soil Productivity and Contributions to

China's Crop Yield Increase since 1980," *PLOS ONE* 8 (September 2013): 1, 6; Mingsheng Fan, Jianbo Shen, Lixing Yuan, Rongfeng Jiang, Xinping Chen, William J. Davies, and Fusuo Zhang, "Improving Crop Productivity and Resource Use Efficiency to Ensure Food Security and Environmental Quality in China," *Journal of Experimental Botany* 63, no. 1 (2012): 13; Malcolm J. Hawkesford, Jose-Luis Araus, Robert Park, Daniel Calderini, Daniel Miralles, Tianmin Shen, Jianping Zhang, and Martin A. J. Parry, "Prospects of Doubling Global Wheat Yields," *Food and Energy Security* 2 (May 2013): 34; Wang Maohua, "Possible Adoption of Precision Agriculture for Developing Countries at the Threshold of the New Millennium," *Computers and Electronics in Agriculture* 30 (February 2001): 49.

63. Sauraabh Bhatt, "Chinese Agri-Lessons for Indian Policymakers," *Hindu Business Line* (Chennai), December 19, 2011, https://global.factiva.com; Mshahidul Islam, "Silent Tsunami Sends Shock Waves over Asia," *Business Times* (Singapore), May 27, 2008, https://global.factiva.com; Nui Shuping and Mayank Bhardwaj, "China and India Eat More but Consume Less Rice," *International New York Times*, May 20, 2008, https://global.factiva.com.

64. Shuping and Bhardwaj, "China and India Eat More but Consume Less Rice"; Islam, "Silent Tsunami Sends Shock Waves over Asia."

65. Hong Yang and Alexander Zehnder, "China's Regional Water Scarcity and Implications for Grain Supply and Trade," *Environment and Planning*, no. 1 (2001): 84–87; Fan et al., "Improving Crop Productivity and Resource Use Efficiency," 16.

66. Vladimir Novotny, Xiaoyan Wang, Andrew J. Englande Jr., David Bedoya, Luksamee Promakasikorn, and Reyes Tirado, "Comparative Assessment of Pollution by the Use of Industrial Agricultural Fertilizers in Four Rapidly Developing Asian Countries," *Environment, Development, and Sustainability* 12, no. 4 (2010): 496–97, 499; Yu, Huang, Zhang, "Changes in Rice Yields," 71–73.

67. Novotny et al., "Comparative Assessment of Pollution," 496–97, 499; Zhenling Cui, Xinping Chen, and Fusuo Zhang, "Current Nitrogen Management Status and Measures to Improve the Intensive Wheat–Maize System China," *AMBIO* 39 (2010): 378–80.

68. Jessica Hamburger, "Pesticides in China: A Growing Threat to Food Safety, Public Health, and the Environment," *China Environment Series* 5 (2002): 31–34, 36.

69. Amy Zader, "Technologies of Quality: The Role of the Chinese State in Guiding the Market for Rice," *East Asian Science, Technology and Society* 5, no. 4 (2011): 466–67; Shaobing Peng and Gurdev S. Khush, "Four Decades of Breeding for Varietal Improvement of Irrigated Lowland Rice in the International Rice Research Institute," *Plant Production Science* 6, no. 3. (2003): 157, 160.

70. Santos, "Rethinking the Green Revolution," 493, 499.

71. Nair, "Relevance of New Biotechnologies in the Third World"; Colin A. Carter and Scott Rozelle, "Will China Become a Major Force in World Food Markets?," *Re-*

view of Agricultural Economics 23 (Autumn–Winter 2001): 320, 322, 325; Schmalzer, *Red Revolution, Green Revolution*, 208.

72. Law of the People's Republic of China on Land Contract in Rural Areas (Order of the President No. 73), August 29, 2002; Schmalzer, *Red Revolution, Green Revolution*, 210, 224.

73. Peter Rosset, Joseph Collins, and Frances Moore Lappé, "Lessons from the Green Revolution," *Tikkun* 15 (March/April 2000): 53; Fan et al., "Improving Crop Productivity and Resource Use Efficiency," 13–14.

CHAPTER FIVE

1. Paul Lewis, "The Green Revolution Bears Fruit," *New York Times*, June 2, 1985; Philip M. Boffey, "New Crop Varieties Lift Hopes for Africa," *New York Times*, August 20, 1985; Martin Meredith, *The Fate of Africa: A History of the Continent since Independence* (New York: Public Affairs, 2011), 289–90; An Ansoms, "A Green Revolution for Rwanda? The Political Economy of Poverty and Agrarian Change" (Discussion Paper 2008.06, Institute of Development Policy, University of Antwerp, June 2008), 6, 9; Norman E. Borlaug and Christopher R. Dowswell, "The Second Green Revolution," in *Agriculture, Human Security, and Peace: A Crossroad in African Development*, ed. M. Taeb and A. H. Zakri (West Lafayette, IN: Purdue University Press, 2008), 136; Jeffrey M. Pilcher, *Food in World History* (New York: Routledge, 2006), 104; Douglas Brinkley, "Bringing the Green Revolution to Africa: Jimmy Carter, Norman Borlaug, and the Global 2000 Campaign," *World Policy Journal* 13 (Spring 1996): 61–62; Charles Mann, "Reseeding the Green Revolution," *Science* 277 (August 1997): 1040.

2. Beverly D. McIntyre, Hans R. Herren, Judi Wakhungu, and Robert T. Watson, eds., *Sub-Saharan Africa (SSA) Report* (Washington, DC: Island Press, 2009), 3; Borlaug and Dowswell, "Second Green Revolution," 136–37; Meredith, *Fate of Africa*, 289–90.

3. Brendan Jones, "Chinese Teaching Africans Better Farming Methods," *New York Times*, November 9, 1970; Boffey, "New Crop Varieties Lift Hopes for Africa"; McIntyre, Herren, Wakhungu, and Watson, *Sub-Saharan Africa (SSA) Report*, 20.

4. Borlaug and Dowswell, "Second Green Revolution," 137–38; Jones, "Chinese Teaching Africans Better Farming Methods"; Boffey, "New Crop Varieties Lift Hopes for Africa"; Pilcher, *Food in World History*, 104.

5. Hans Holmén, "The State and Agricultural Intensification in Sub-Saharan Africa," in *The African Food Crisis: Lessons from the Asian Green Revolution*, ed. Göran Djurfeldt, Hans Holmén, Magnus Jirström, and Rolf Larsson (Cambridge, MA: CABI, 2005), 94–95, 100–102.

6. Constance Holden, "Ethiopia: Did Aid Speed an Inevitable Upheaval?," *Science* 186 (December 27, 1974): 1192; John M. Cohen, "Effects of Green Revolution Strate-

gies on Tenants and Small-Scale Landowners in the Chilalo Region of Ethiopia," *Journal of Developing Areas* 9 (April 1975): 335, 339–40.

7. Cohen, "Effects of Green Revolution Strategies," 335, 338, 344–48; Mesfin Bezuneh and Carl C. Mabbs-Zeno, "The Contribution of the Green Revolution to Social Change in Ethiopia," *Northeast Africa Studies* 6, no. 3 (1984): 12–13.

8. Cohen, "Effects of Green Revolution Strategies," 349–52; Pilcher, *Food in History*, 104; Bezuneh and Mabbs-Zeno, "Contribution of the Green Revolution to Social Change in Ethiopia," 13, 16; Andrea Useem, "Ethiopia's Green Revolution," *Multinational Monitor* (Washington, DC), November 1997, 8; Mann, "Reseeding the Green Revolution," 1038.

9. Cohen, "Effects of Green Revolution Strategies," 348, 353–54, 357–58; Pilcher, *Food in History*, 104.

10. Kidane Mengisteab, *Ethiopia: Failure of Land Reform and Agricultural Crisis* (New York: Greenwood Press, 1990), 1, 147–49, 154–55, 158–59, 162–63, 169. See also Jason W. Clay and Bonnie K. Holcomb, *Politics and the Ethiopian Famine, 1984–1985* (Cambridge, MA: Cultural Survival, 1986).

11. William I. Jones, "Small Farmers and the Green Revolution in Kenya," *African Economic History*, no. 4 (1977): 182–84.

12. Seth King, "Even Miracles Have Their Price, Green Revolutionaries Discover," *New York Times*, January 11, 1981; Willis Oluoch-Korsura and Joseph T. Karugia, "Why the Early Promise for Rapid Increase in Maize Productivity in Kenya Was Not Sustained: Lessons for Sustainable Investment Agriculture," in Djurfeldt et al., *African Food Crisis*, 183.

13. Aida C. Isinika, Gasper C. Ashimogo, and James E. D. Mlangwa, "From Ujamaa to Structural Adjustment—Agricultural Intensification in Tanzania," in Djurfeldt et al., *African Food Crisis*, 198–99.

14. Carl K. Eicher and Bernard Kupfuma, "Zimbabwe's Maize Revolution: Insights for Closing Africa's Food Gap," in *International Agricultural Development*, 3rd ed., ed. Carl K. Eicher and John M. Staatz (Baltimore, MD: Johns Hopkins University Press, 1998), 550–58; Carl K. Eicher, "Zimbabwe's Maize-Based Green Revolution: Preconditions for Replication," *World Development* 23, no. 5 (1995): 806.

15. Lionel Cliffe, "Zimbabwe's Agricultural 'Success' and Food Security in Southern Africa," *Review of African Political Economy* 15, no. 43 (1988): 5–6, 8, 11.

16. Jack Goody, "Rice Burning and the Green Revolution in Northern Ghana," *Journal of Development Studies* 16, no. 2 (1980): 136, 138–39, 142, 149, 151–53; Alice Wiemers, "A 'Time of Agric': Rethinking the 'Failure' of Agricultural Programs in 1970s Ghana," *World Development* 66 (February 2015): 106.

17. Brinkley, "Bringing the Green Revolution to Africa," 59–60; A. Wayo Seini and V. Kwame Nyanteng, "Smallholders and Structural Adjustment in Ghana," in Djurfeldt et al., *African Food Crisis*, 225–26, 230, 232.

18. Tunji Akande, "The Role of the State in the Nigerian Green Revolution," in Djurfeldt et al., *African Food Crisis*, 161–62, 166; Abe Goldman and Joyotee Smith, "Agricultural Transformations in India and Northern Nigeria: Exploring the Nature of Green Revolutions," *World Development* 23, no. 2 (1995): 251–52.

19. Akande, "Role of the State in the Nigerian Green Revolution," 169–70; Remi Adeyemo, "The Food Marketing System: Implications of the Green Revolution Programme in Nigeria," *Agricultural Systems* 14 (1984): 143–57; Segun Famoriyo and M. Rafique Raza, "The Green Revolution in Nigeria: Prospects for Agricultural Development," *Food Policy* 7 (February 1982): 36–37.

20. Meredith, *Fate of Africa*, 279–82.

21. Meredith, *Fate of Africa*, 290–91; Pilcher, *Food in World History*, 104; *Famine: A Man-Made Disaster? A Report for the Independent Commission on International Humanitarian Issues* (New York: Vintage Books, 1985), 2, 14–15.

22. *Famine*, 25–27; Boffey, "New Crop Varieties Lift Hopes for Africa."

23. *Famine*, 34–36, 51–53; "The Myths Surrounding Global Hunger," *New York Times* September 7, 1981.

24. *Famine*, 62.

25. *Famine*, 64–65, 87, 91–92, 94–95, 104.

26. *Famine*, 120, 129, 132–33, 136–37; Boffey, "New Crop Varieties Lift Hopes for Africa."

27. Boffey, "New Crop Varieties Lift Hopes for Africa"; Pilcher, *Food in World History*, 104.

28. Oluoch-Korsura and Karugia, "Early Promise for Rapid Increase," 200; Isinika, Ashimogo, and Mlangwa, "From Ujamaa to Structural Adjustment," 197, 201.

29. Eicher and Kupfuma, "Zimbabwe's Maize Revolution," 565; Meredith, *Fate of Africa*, 620, 633–47.

30. Eicher "Zimbabwe's Maize-Based Revolution," 808–10; Eicher and Kupfuma, "Zimbabwe's Maize Revolution," 550–61, 808; Meredith, *Fate of Africa*, 620, 633–47.

31. Meredith, *Fate of Africa*, 620, 633–47; Kofi Akwabi-Ameyaw, "Producer Cooperative Resettlement Projects in Zimbabwe: Lessons from a Failed Agricultural Development Strategy," *World Development* 25, no. 3 (1997): 437–38.

32. Melinda Smale, "'Maize Is Life': Malawi's Delayed Green Revolution," *World Development* 23, no. 5 (1995): 823–28.

33. David Hirschmann and Megan Vaughan, *Women Farmers of Malawi: Food Production in the Zomba District*, Research Series No. 58 (Berkeley: Institute of International Studies, University of California, Berkeley), 5–7, 33–34, 40–41, 74, 77–81.

34. Bryson Gwiyani-Nkhoma, "Irrigation Development and Its Socioeconomic Impact on Rural Communities in Malawi," *Development Southern Africa* 28 (June 2011): 210–11, 213–14, 217, 219, 222.

35. William G. Moseley, Judith Carney, and Lawrence Becker, "Neoliberal Policy,

Rural Livelihoods, and Urban Food Security in West Africa: A Comparative Study of The Gambia, Côte d'Ivoire, and Mali," *Proceedings of the National Academy of Science* 107, no. 13 (2010): 5775–79.

36. Pamela G. Hollie, "Spread of 'Miracle' Rice Lagging in Asia," *New York Times*, March 12, 1981; Alan Cowell, "Nigeria, Rich with Oil Is Dependent on U.S. and Other Nations for Food," *New York Times*, August 15, 1981; Flora Lewis, "Back to Food Basics," *New York Times*, March 25, 1982.

37. Akande, "Role of the State in the Nigerian Green Revolution," 168, 176, 181; Goldman and Smith, "Agricultural Transformations," 255–56, 260.

38. Margaret A. Novicki, "Going for a Green Revolution," *Africa Report* 33, no. 5 (September 1, 1988): 19–22.

39. Brinkley, "Bringing the Green Revolution to Africa," 59–61.

40. James S. Butty, "The Liberian Green Revolution Initiative: A Policy Perspective," *Liberia-Forum* 3, no. 4 (1987): 39–44.

41. Butty, "Liberian Green Revolution Initiative," 40, 47–50; Daniel Ogbaharya and Aregia Tede, "Community-Based Natural Resources Management in Eretria and Ethiopia: Toward a Comparative Institutional Analysis," *Journal of East African Studies* 4 (November 2010): 497, 501–2.

42. Oluoch-Korsura and Karugia, "Early Promise for Rapid Increase," 187–88.

43. Oluoch-Korsura and Karugia, "Early Promise for Rapid Increase," 188–89, 191–94.

44. Smale, "'Maize Is Life,'" 819–21.

45. Eicher and Kupfuma, "Zimbabwe's Maize Revolution," 805, 813–14; Anthony Leiman and Alexander Behar, "A Green Revolution Betrayed? Seed Technology and Small-Scale Maize Farmers in Zimbabwe," *Development in Southern Africa* 28 (October 2011): 446, 448; Pilcher, *Food in World History*, 104; Borlaug and Dowswell, "Second Green Revolution," 136–37.

46. Eicher and Kupfuma, "Zimbabwe's Maize Revolution," 550, 805.

47. Steven Wiggins, "Interpreting Changes from the 1970s to the 1990s in African Agriculture through Village Studies," *World Development* 28, no. 4 (2000): 631, 637.

48. Wiggins, "Interpreting Changes," 636, 638; Pilcher, *Food in World History*, 104.

49. Andrew Martin, "So Much Food. So Much Hunger," *New York Times*, September 20, 2009; Borlaug and Dowswell, "Second Green Revolution," 139; Holmén, "The State and Agricultural Intensification," 65.

50. Holmén, "The State and Agricultural Intensification," 65–68.

51. Holmén, "The State and Agricultural Intensification," 100–103.

52. Holmén, "The State and Agricultural Intensification," 104–5.

53. Holmén, "The State and Agricultural Intensification," 105.

54. Holmén, "The State and Agricultural Intensification," 105.

55. Holmén, "The State and Agricultural Intensification," 107–8; Rolf Larsson, "Crisis and Potential in Smallholder Food Production—Evidence from Micro Level," in Djurfeldt et al., *African Food Crisis*, 132; Steven Haggblade, "From Roller Coasters

to Rocketships: The Role of Technology in African Agricultural Success," in Djurfeldt et al., *African Food Crisis*, 156.

56. Isinika, Ashimogo, and Mlangwa, "From Ujamaa to Structural Adjustment," 207–10.

57. Isinika, Ashimogo, and Mlangwa, "From Ujamaa to Structural Adjustment," 211–12, 214; "New Agricultural Plan Ignores Small Farmers," Africa News Service, March 17, 2011, http://find.galegroup.com/grnr/infomark.do?, accessed March 30, 2015.

58. "Shrubby Crops Help Fuel Africa's Green Revolution," *Science Letter*, December 7, 2010, http://find.galegroup.com/grnr/infomark.do?, accessed March 30, 2015; Morton Jerven, "The Political Economy of Agricultural Statistics and Import Subsidies: Evidence from India, Nigeria, and Malawi," *Journal of Agrarian Change* 14 (January 2014): 137; "Public Private Partnership Stressed for Africa's Green Revolution," Africa News Service, September 10, 2013, http://find.galegroup.com/grnr/infomark.do?, accessed March 30, 2015.

59. Marie Javdani, "Malawi's Agricultural Input Subsidy: Study of a Green Revolution-Style Strategy for Food Security," *International Journal of Agricultural Sustainability* 10 (May 2012): 150, 152–54, 57, 61–62.

60. Sally Brooks, "Enabling Adoption? Lessons from the New 'Green Revolution' in Malawi and Kenya," *Climatic Change* 122 (January 2014): 15–16, 18–20, 24.

61. Clemens Breisinger, Xinshen Diao, James Thurlow, and Ramatu M. Al Hassan, "Potential Impacts of a Green Revolution in Africa—The Case of Ghana," *Journal of International Development* 23 (2011): 83–86, 94.

62. Teferi Abate Adem, "The Local Politics of Ethiopia's Green Revolution in South Wollo," *African Studies Review* 55 (December 2012): 82–83, 90–91, 93, 95.

63. Roger Thurow, "The Fertile Continent," *Foreign Affairs* 89 (December 2010): 104–7; Scott Kilmand, "Africa Could Feed Itself but Many Ask: Should It?," *Wall Street Journal*, December 3, 2002, http://www.wsj.com/articles/SB1038868837843204913, accessed March 9, 2015.

64. Celia W. Dugger, "World Bank Report Puts Agriculture at Core of Antipoverty Effort," *New York Times*, October 20, 2007; Elisabeth Rosenthal and Andrew Martin, "Leaders Speak of Their Own Issues at a Conference Addressing Food Shortage," *New York Times*, June 5, 2008; Tina Rosenberg, "A Green Revolution, The Time for Africa," *New York Times*, April 9, 2014; "Scaling Seeds and Technologies Partnership Will Accelerate Progress to Reduce Poverty and Hunger," Africa News Service, July 1, 2003, http://find.galegroup.com/grnr/infomark.do?, accessed March 30, 2015; "USAID, Agra Partner to Reduce Hunger, Poverty in Africa," Africa News Service, July 4, 2013, http://find.galegroup.com/grnr/infomark.do?, accessed March 30, 2015.

65. Yoko Kjima, Keijiro Otsuka, and Dick Sserunkuuma, "An Inquiry into Constraints on the Green Revolution in Sub-Saharan Africa: The Case of NERICA Rice in Uganda," *World Development* 39, no. 1 (2011): 84–85; Tunji Akande, Göran Djurfeldt, Hans Holmén, and Aida C. Isinika, "Conclusions and a Look Ahead," in Djurfeldt et al.,

African Food Crisis, 255–56; Robert Paarlberg, "Attention Whole Food Shoppers," *Foreign Policy* 179 (May/June 2010): 82.

66. Eicher, "Zimbabwe's Maize-Based Green Revolution," 806.

67. Eicher, "Zimbabwe's Maize-Based Green Revolution," 807.

68. Kei Kajisa and Ellen Payongayong, "Potential of Aid Contributions to the Rice Green Revolution in Mozambique: A Case Study of the Chokwe Irrigation Scheme," *Food Policy* 36 (2011): 615–16, 623; Benedito Cunguara, "An Exposition of Development Failures in Mozambique," *Review of African Political Economy* 39 (March 2012): 161–67.

69. Jikun Huang, Carl Pray, and Scott Rozelle, "Enhancing the Crops to Feed the Poor," *Nature* 418 (August 8, 2002): 678; Kjima, Otsuka, and Sserunkuuma, "Constraints on the Green Revolution," 77–79, 84.

70. John H. Sanders, "Agricultural Research and Cereal Technology Introduction in Burkina Faso and Niger," *Agricultural Systems* 30, no. 2 (1989): 140–43, 151–52. See also H. van Keulen and H. Breman. "Agricultural Development in the West African Sahelian Region: A Cure against Land Hunger?" *Agriculture, Ecosystems and Environment* 32 (1990): 177–97. For a study of grazing problems, see Matthew Turner, "Overstocking the Range: A Critical Analysis of the Environmental Science of Sahelian Pastoralism," *Economic Geography* 69 (October 1993): 402–21.

71. Ruth Oneang'o, "What Opportunities Do We Have Not to End Hunger in the World?," *African Journal of Food, Agriculture, Nutrition and Development*, September 1, 2013, http://find.galegroup.com/grnr/infomark.do?, accessed June 2, 2014.

72. Behrooz Morvaridei, "Capitalist Philanthropy and Hegemonic Partnerships," *Third World Quarterly* 33, no. 7 (2012): 1191, 1196–98, 1210; John Getter, "For Good, Measure," *New York Times*, March 9, 2008; Carol B. Thompson, "Africa: Green Revolution or Rainbow Evolution?," *Review of African Political Economy* 34, no. 113 (September 2007): 562–65; Gary Toenniessen, Akinwumi Adesina, and Joseph DeVries, "Building an Alliance for a Green Revolution in Africa," *Annals of the New York Academy of Sciences*, no. 1136 (2008): 234–35, 239–42; Jean-Jacques Dethier and Alexander Effenberger, "Agriculture and Development: A Brief Review of the Literature," *Economic Systems* 36 (2012): 200.

73. Javier Blas, "Africa: In Search of a Green Revolution," *Financial Times.com* (United Kingdom), January 21, 2014, https://global-factiva-com, accessed July 7, 2015; Richard J. Blaustein, "The Green Revolution Arrives in Africa," *BioScience* 58 (January 2008): 8–14; Thurow, "Fertile Continent," 107, 110.

74. Paul Mosley, "The African Green Revolution as a Pro-Poor Policy Instrument," *Journal of International Development* 14 (August 2002): 696; McIntyre, Herren, Wakhungu, and Thompson, *Sub-Saharan Africa (SSA) Report*, 50, 55; Borlaug and Dowswell, "Second Green Revolution," 137; Michael Johnson, Peter Hazell, and Ashok Gulati, "The Role of Intermediate Factor Markets in Asia's Green Revolution: Lessons from Africa?," *American Journal of Agricultural Economics* 85 (December 2003): 1211, 1214–15.

75. Thurow, "Fertile Continent," 109–10; Keynote opening address delivered by Dr. Akinwumi Adesina, Honourable Minister of Agriculture of Nigeria at the Africa Green Revolution Forum, September 2, 2014, Africa Union, Addis Ababa, Ethiopia, http://find.galegroup.com, accessed March 13, 2015; Ewout Frankema, "Africa and the Green Revolution: A Global Historical Perspective," *NJAS - Wageningen Journal of Life Sciences* 70–71 (2014): 22–23; McIntyre, Herren, Wakhungu, and Thompson, *Sub-Saharan Africa (SSA) Report*, 50.

76. Keneng Hilton Ndukong, "The Tall Order of Self-Sufficiency," *Financial Times*, June 23, 2014, https://global-factiva-com; Borlaug and Dowswell, "Second Green Revolution," 137; Blas, "Africa: In Search of a Green Revolution."

Chapter Six

1. David Sprinkle, "The Non-GMO Market: Waiting for the Dust to Settle," *Nutraceuticals World*, April 2014, 31; Carl E. Pray and Anwar Naseem, "Supplying Crop Biotechnology to the Poor: Opportunities and Constraints," *Journal of Development Studies* 43, no. 1 (2007): 192; "Food Fight: A Fierce Public Debate over GM Food Exposes Concerns about America," *The Economist* (United Kingdom), December 14, 2013, http://www.economist.com/news/china/21591577-fierce-public-debate-over-gm-food -exposes-concerns-about-america-food-fight, accessed July 7, 2014.

2. Zhonghu He, Xiachun Xia, Shaobing Peng, and Thomas Adam Lumpkin, "Meeting Demands for Increased Cereal Production in China," *Journal of Cereal Science* 59, no. 3 (2014): 235–36; Xiaobai Shen, "Understanding the Evolution of Rice Technology in China—From Traditional Agriculture to GM Rice Today," *Journal of Development Studies* 46 (July 2010): 1026–27.

3. He et al., "Meeting Demands," 236–37.

4. Cong Cao, *GMO China: How Global Debates Transformed China's Agricultural Biotechnology Policies* (New York: Columbia University Press, 2018), xviii, 92, 109, 159; Zhang Tao and Zhou Shudong, "The Economic and Social Impact of GMOs in China," *China Perspectives* 47 (May–June 2003): 50–57; He et al., "Meeting Demands," 241–42.

5. He et al., "Meeting Demands," 241–42.

6. Tiziano Gomiero, David Pimentel, and Maurizio G. Paoletti, "Is There a Need for a More Sustainable Agriculture?," *Critical Reviews in Plant Sciences* 30 (2011): 17–18; Pray and Naseem, "Supplying Crop Biotechnology," 193–96.

7. Gomiero, Pimentel, and Paoletti, "Is There a Need for a More Sustainable Agriculture?," 17–18; Pray and Naseem, "Supplying Crop Biotechnology," 193–96.

8. Cao, *GMO China*, xvii, 77–79; Gomiero, Pimentel, and Paoletti, "Is There a Need for a More Sustainable Agriculture?," 17–18; Pray and Naseem, "Supplying Crop Biotechnology," 193–96; Aarti Gupta and Robert Falkner, "The Influence of the Cartagena Protocol on Biosafety: Comparing Mexico, China and South Africa," *Global Environmental Politics* 6 (November 2006): 38–39. As of 2015, India did not permit GM crop production. In India, GM cotton constituted almost all of the nation's 11.6 million hectares

planted with biotech seeds, which Monsanto supplied. See Op Rana, "GM Is a Question of Public or Private Good," *China Daily* (Beijing), February 9, 2015, https://global-factiva-com. In India, critics charged that the intellectual property rights (that is, patents) of GM seeds gave corporations a monopoly over scientific agricultural knowledge. See Sambit Mallick, Haribabu Ejnavarzala, Reedy B. Bhoopathi, "Industrialization of Seed Production: Implications for Agriculture in India," *Perspectives on Global Development and Technology* 10 (201): 455. Thailand, the world's largest exporter of rice, also did not permit cultivation of this GM crop. Nanchanok Wongsamuth, "Food for Thought," *Bangkok Post*, August 24, 2013, https://global-factiva-com.

9. Gomiero, Pimentel, and Paoletti, "Is There a Need for a More Sustainable Agriculture?," 18; Jikun Huang, Ruifa Hu, Scott Rozelle, and Carl Pray, "Genetically Modified Rice, Yields, and Pesticides: Assessing Farm-Level Productivity Effects in China," *Economic Development and Culture Change* 56 (January 2008): 242; Cao, *GMO China*, 76.

10. Huang et al., "Genetically Modified Rice, Yields, and Pesticides," 242–44, 251; Cao, *GMO China*, 27, 56, 100.

11. Cheng Xu, Han Chunru, and Donald C. Taylor, "Sustainable Agricultural Development in China," *World Development* 20, no. 8 (1992): 1130; Shen, "Understanding the Evolution of Rice Technology," 1027, 1040; Jikun Huang, Ruifa Hu, Scott Rozelle, and Carl Pray, "Insect-Resistant GM Rice in Farmers' Fields: Assessing Productivity and Health Effects in China," *Science* 308 (April 29, 2005): 688–90.

12. Shen, "Understanding the Evolution of Rice Technology," 1027.

13. Tao and Shudong, "Economic and Social Impact of GMOs," 47; Huang et al., "Insect-Resistant GM Rice in Farmers' Fields," 688, 690; Cao, *GMO China*, 69.

14. Jim Harkness, "The Politics of GMO in China," Institute for Agriculture and Trade Policy, October 21, 2011, http://www.iatp.org/blog/2011, accessed August 18, 2014.

15. Niu Shuping and Ken Wells, "Origin Expects to Grow China's First GMO Corn in 2013," Reuters News Release, February 10, 2012, http://.reuters.com/article, accessed August 19, 2014.

16. Chuin-Wei Yap, "It's China vs. China in Genetically Modified Food Fight," *Wall Street Journal*, September 3, 2013, http://blogs.wsj.com/chinarealtime/2013/09/03/its-china-vs-china-in-gmo-food-fight, accessed August 18, 2014; "Fierce Public Debate over GM Food Exposes Concerns about America"; Cao, *GMO China*, xvi, 185.

17. Yap, "China vs. China in Genetically Modified Food Fight"; "Fierce Public Debate over GM Food Exposes Concerns about America"; Cao, *GMO China*, xvi, 185.

18. Yap, "China vs. China in Genetically Modified Food Fight"; "Fierce Public Debate over GM Food Exposes Concerns about America"; Cao, *GMO China*, xvi–xvii.

19. Adam Miner, "Why Are the Chinese Scared of American Corn?," *Bloomberg View*, December 18, 2013; "US Corn Exports to China Drop 85% after Ban on GMO Strain," April 12, 2014, http://www.RT.com, accessed August 18, 2014; Liyan Qi and Chuin-Wei Yap, "China Seeks Its Own GMO-Food Path," *Wall Street Journal*, March 7,

2014, http://blogs.wsj.com/chinarealtime/2014/03/07/china-seeks-its-own-gmo-food
-path, accessed August 18, 2014; Chuin-Wei Yap, "Claims That U.S. Soybeans Cause
Infertility Stoke China's GMO Battle," *Wall Street Journal*, May 14, 2014, http://blogs
.wsj.com/chinarealtime/2014/05/14/claims-that-u-s-soybeans-cause-infertility-stoke
-chinas-gmo-battle, accessed August 8, 2014; Cao, *GMO China*, 185.

20. Tao and Shudong, "Economic and Social Impact of GMOs," 55–56; Niu Shuping and David Stanway, "Food for Thought," *Huffington Post*, December 4, 2013, http://
www.huffingtonpost.com, accessed August 18, 2014; Lawrence Woodward, "China
Bans More US Imports to Stop GMO Contamination," http://www.gmeducation.org,
accessed August 18, 2014; Cao, *GMO China*, 99, 183.

21. Shuping and Stanway, "Food for Thought"; Tom Polansek, "China's Rejection
of GMO Corn Has Cost U.S. up to $2.9 Billion," *Huffington Post*, April 16, 2014, http://
huffingtonpost.com, accessed August 18, 2014; "Fierce Public Debate over GM Food
Exposes Concerns about America."

22. Niu Shuping and David Stanway, "China Delays GMO Corn, Rice to Woo the
Public," Reuters News Release, March 7, 2013, http://www.reuters.com, accessed August 18, 2014; Qi and Yap, "China Seeks Its Own GMO-Food Path"; "Chinese Army
Bans All GMO Grains," *Eco Watch*, May 5, 2014, http://ecowatch.com, accessed August 18, 2014; Cao, *GMO China*, 49.

23. Robert Falkner, "International Sources of Environmental Policy Change in
China: The Case of Genetically Modified Food," *Pacific Review* 19 (December 2006):
473–74, 477; Cao, *GMO China*, 182.

24. Falkner, "Environmental Policy Change in China," 474–76; Pray and Naseem,
"Supplying Crop Biotechnology," 193.

25. Tao and Shudong, "Economic and Social Impact of GMOs," 54; Cao, *GMO
China*, 15, 37.

26. Falkner, "Environmental Policy Change in China," 477–78; Gupta and Falkner,
"Influence of the Cartagena Protocol on Biosafety," 40; Robert Falkner and Aarti Gupta,
"The Limits of Regulatory Convergence: Globalization and GMO Politics in the South,"
International Environmental Agreements 9 (2016): 118–19; Cao, *GMO China*, 40–43. In
2002, China signed the Cartagena Protocol and ratified it in 2005.

27. Falkner, "Environmental Policy Change in China," 482, 484.

28. Falkner, "Environmental Policy Change in China," 485–87; Tao and Shudong,
"Economic and Social Impact of GMOs," 54–55; Gupta and Falkner, "Influence of the
Cartagena Protocol on Biosafety," 41; Cao, *GMO China*, 101.

29. Falkner, "Environmental Policy Change in China," 488–89; Gupta and Falkner,
"Influence of the Cartagena Protocol on Biosafety," 39–40; Tao and Shudong, "Economic and Social Impact of GMOs," 57.

30. Falkner and Gupta, "Limits of Regulatory Convergence," 118; Dayuan Xue and
Clem Tisdell, "Global Trade in GM Food and the Cartagena Protocol on Biosafety:
Consequences for China," *Journal of Agricultural and Environmental Ethics* 15, no. 4

(2002): 338; Gupta and Falkner, "Influence of the Cartagena Protocol on Biosafety," 39; Falkner, "Environmental Policy Change in China," 490.

31. Gupta and Falkner, "Influence of the Cartagena Protocol on Biosafety," 42; Falkner and Gupta, "Limits of Regulatory Convergence," 128–29; Huang et al., "Insect-Resistant GM Rice in Farmers' Fields," 690.

32. Rana, "GM Is a Question of Public or Private Good"; D. Gale Johnson, "Biotechnology Issues for Developing Economies," *Economic Development and Cultural Change* 51 (October 2002): 2–3.

33. Johnson, "Biotechnology Issues," 2–3.

34. Jikun Huang, Deliang Zhang, Jun Yang, Scott Rozelle, and Nicholas Kalaitzandonakes, "Will the Biosafety Protocol Hinder or Protect the Developing World: Learning from China's Experience," *Food Policy* 33 (2008): 5–6, 9; Xue and Tisdell, "Global Trade in GM Food," 352, 354.

35. Jennifer Clapp, "The Political Economy of Food Aid in an Era of Agricultural Biotechnology," *Global Governance* 11 (October–December 2005): 467, 470–73, 475, 477–79.

36. Robert L. Paarlberg, "Reinvigorating Genetically Modified Crops: Poor Farmers in Developing Nations Will Benefit If the United States Asserts Itself in the International Area to Develop and Promote Biotechnology," *Issues in Science and Technology* 19 (Spring 2003): 86–92.

37. "Gates Foundation–Led Green Revolution Promotes False Solutions to Hunger in Africa," Africa News Service, September 26, 2012, http://find.galegroup.com/grnr/infomark.do?, accessed March 30, 2015; Carol B. Thompson, "Alliance for a Green Revolution in Africa (AGRA): Advancing the Theft of African Genetic Wealth," *Review of African Political Economy* 39 (June 2012): 345–46, 348–49; Sjoerd Bazuin, Hossein Azadi, and Frank Witlox, "Application of GM Crops in Sub-Saharan Africa: Lessons Learned from the Green Revolution," *Biotechnology Advances* 29 (2011): 909–11.

38. Scott Zhuge, "Durban Dilemma: A Second Green Revolution?," *Harvard International Review* 33 (Spring 2012): 6–7; James A. Okeno, Jeffery D. Wolt, Manjit K. Misra, and Lulu Rodriquez, "Africa's Inevitable Walk to Genetically Modified (GM) Crops: Opportunities and Challenges for Commercialization," *New Biotechnology* 30 (January 2013): 124–25, 128; Areola A. Adele, E. Jane Morris, and Govindan Parayil, "Status of Development, Regulation and Adoption of GM Agriculture in Africa: Views and Positions of Stakeholder Groups," *Food Policy* 43 (2013): 159, 165.

39. Okeno et al., "Africa's Inevitable Walk," 125; Jane Karuku, "Africa Should Not Ignore the Potential of GM Crops," Africa News Service, October 4, 2013, http://find.galegroup.com/grnr/infomark.do?, accessed March 30, 2015; Stan Okenwa, "NGOs Review Gates's Initiative for Africa," Africa News Service, November 5, 2009, http://find.galegroup.com/grnr/infomark.do?, accessed March 30, 2015; "Gates Foundation–Led Green Revolution Promotes False Solutions to Hunger in Africa."

40. "Countering Africa's Green Revolution," *Africa News Service*, July 8, 2013, http://find.galegroup.com/grnr/infomark.do?, accessed March 30, 2015; H. I. Miller, Ariane Koenig, Philip Aerni, M. Ann Tutwiler, and Peter Hazell, "GM Crop Controversies," *Issues in Science and Technology* 20 (Fall 2003): 14–19.

41. James Klepek, "Selling Guatemala's Next Green Revolution: Agricultural Modernization and the Politics of GM Maize Regulation," *International Journal of Agricultural Sustainability* 10 (May 2012): 117, 120–21.

42. Liza Grandia, "Modified Landscapes: Vulnerabilities to Genetically Modified Corn in Northern Guatemala," *Journal of Peasant Studies* 41, no. 1 (2014): 82, 94–95; Klepek, "Selling Guatemala's Next Green Revolution," 125.

43. Klepek, "Selling Guatemala's Next Green Revolution," 126–30; Grandia, "Modified Landscapes," 81, 83, 90, 92; James Klepek, "Against the Grain: Knowledge Alliances and Resistance to Agricultural Biotechnology in Guatemala," *Canadian Journal of Development Studies* 33 (September 2012): 310–11, 314, 316, 320–21.

44. Norman Borlaug, "Ending World Hunger: The Promise of Biotechnology and the Threat of Antiscience Zealotry," *Plant Physiology* 124 (October 2000): 487–90; Ingo Potrykus, "Golden Rice and Beyond," *Plant Physiology* 125 (March 2001): 1157–61; Michael Lipton, "Plant Breeding and Poverty: Can Transgenic Seeds Replicate the 'Green Revolution' as a Source of Gains for the Poor?," *Journal of Development Studies* 43 (January 2007): 50–54; Yap, "Claims That U.S. Soybeans Cause Infertility Stoke China's GMO Battle"; Tao and Shudong, "Economic and Social Impact of GMOs," 53; Xue and Tisdell, "Global Trade in GM Food," 350–51; Cao, *GMO China*, xvii, 5–6, 27, 115–18, 123. China's concerns about the political and economic ramifications of the release of GM crops into the global marketplace proved well founded. In 1988, China became the first nation to produce a commercially ready GM crop with the production of a virus-resistant tobacco. Several years later, it removed this tobacco from production due to resistance from importers, particularly the United States and European nations. In 1997, China introduced an insect-resistant GM cotton that included a gene that killed bollworms. This GM cotton permitted a 60–80 percent decrease in pesticide use, thereby reducing the environmental and human health risks. This GM cotton variety also decreased expenditures for labor and insecticides. Cotton, however, is not a food crop and transgenetic research to develop disease- and insect-resistant as well as herbicide-tolerant rice, maize, and soybean varieties had not met many international certification standards for commercial production by the early twenty-first century. Moreover, GM cotton destroyed the natural enemies of the cotton bollworm, but it did not prevent the increase of nontarget insects. In time, the bollworm developed a resistance to GM cotton, which then required the application of pesticides for control.

45. "A Call for a Green Revolution," *New York Times*, May 24, 2004.

46. Tao and Shudong, "Economic and Social Impact of GMOs," 53–56; Cao, *GMO China*, 8, 12–13.

CHAPTER SEVEN

1. Carl E. Pray, "The Green Revolution as a Case Study in Transfer of Technology," *Annals of the American Academy of Political and Social Science* 458 (November 1981): 68–70, 76–77; R. E. Evenson and D. Gollin, "Assessing the Impact of the Green Revolution, 1977 to 2000," *Science* 300 (May 2, 2003): 761.

2. Jeffrey M. Pilcher, *Food in World History* (New York: Routledge, 2006), 100.

3. Abe Goldman and Joyotee Smith, "Agricultural Transformations in India and Northern Nigeria: Exploring the Nature of Green Revolutions," *World Development* 23, no. 2 (1995): 260.

4. Goldman and Smith, "Agricultural Transformations," 257; Donald K. Freebairn, "Did the Green Revolution Concentrate Incomes? A Quantitative Study of Research Reports," *World Development* 23, no. 2 (1995): 267–69, 275–76.

5. Pilcher, *Food in World History*, 104.

6. Bandhudas Sen, *The Green Revolution in India: A Perspective* (New York: John Wiley & Sons, 1974), 102.

7. Bekele Shiferaw, Melinda Smale, Hans-Joachim Braun, Etienne Duveiller, Mathew Reynolds, and Geoffrey Muricho, "Crops That Feed the World 10: Past Success and Future Challenges to the Role Played by Wheat in Global Food Security," *Food Security* 5 (June 2013): 291; Sumithra Muthayya, Jonathan D. Sugimoto, Scott Montgomery, and Alan F. Maberly, "An Overview of Global Rice Production, Supply, Trade, and Consumption," *Annals of the New York Academy of Sciences* 1324 (September 2014): 7.

8. Shiferaw et al., "Crops That Feed the World," 292–93, 296.

9. Shiferaw et al., "Crops That Feed the World," 292; Pilcher, *Food in World History*, 103.

10. Pray, "Green Revolution as a Case Study," 72–74.

11. Clifton R. Wharton Jr., "The Green Revolution: Cornucopia or Pandora's Box?," *Foreign Affairs* 47 (April 1969): 465–66, 475.

12. Wharton, "Green Revolution," 465–66.

13. Wharton, "Green Revolution," 467.

14. Wharton, "Green Revolution," 467–75.

15. Kenneth W. Thompson, "The Green Revolution: Leadership and Partnership in Agriculture," *Review of Politics* 34 (April 1972): 185, 187–89; Sen, *Green Revolution in India*, 102–3.

16. Pray, "Green Revolution as a Case Study," 68–80.

17. Pray, "Green Revolution as a Case Study," 75–77. By 2014, Malawi, Cameroon, Ghana, Kenya, Nigeria, and Uganda had begun field tests of GM crops.

18. Magnus Jirström, "The State of the Green Revolution in East Asia," in *The African Food Crisis: Lessons from the Asian Green Revolution*, ed. Göran Djurfeldt, Hans Holmén, Magnus Jirström, and Rolf Larsson (Cambridge, MA: CABI, 2005), 25–26.

19. Goldman and Smith, "Agricultural Transformations," 243, 257.

20. Goldman and Smith, "Agricultural Transformations," 243, 259–60.

21. Freebairn, "Did the Green Revolution Concentrate Incomes?," 268, 275–76.

22. John H. Perkins, *Geopolitics and the Green Revolution: Wheat, Genes and the Cold War* (New York: Oxford University Press, 1997), 256–58.

23. Perkins, *Geopolitics and the Green Revolution*, 259–61.

24. Michael Lipton with Richard Longhurst, *New Seeds and Poor People* (Baltimore, MD: Johns Hopkins University Press, 1989), 7–9; Evenson and Gollin, "Impact of the Green Revolution," 762; Daniel Zwerdling, "India's Farming Revolution Heading for Collapse," National Public Radio, April 13, 2009, http://www.npr.org/templates/story /story.php?storyId=102893816; Daniel Zwerdling, "'Green Revolution': Trapping India's Farmers in Debt," National Public Radio, April 17, 2009, http://www.npr.org/templates /story/story.php?storyId=102944731.

25. Göran Djurfeldt and Magnus Jirström, "The Puzzle of the Policy Shift—The Early Green Revolution in India, Indonesia and the Philippines," in Djurfeldt et al., *African Food Crisis*, 58, 60; Keijiro Otsuka and Takashi Yamano, "Green Revolution and Regional Inequality: Implications of Asian Experience for Africa," in Djurfeldt et al., *African Food Crisis*, 239–41; Pratyusha Basu and Bruce A. Scholten, "Technological and Social Dimensions of the Green Revolution: Connecting Pasts and Futures," *International Journal of Agricultural Sustainability* 10 (May 2012): 110.

26. Frederick Kaufman, "The Second Green Revolution," *Popular Science* (February 2011): 64, 67.

27. Shiferaw et al., "Crops That Feed the World," 311–12.

28. Wharton, "Green Revolution," 476; William I. Jones, "Small Farmers and the Green Revolution in Kenya," *African Economic History* 77, no. 4 (1977): 182.

29. Goldman and Smith, "Agricultural Transformations," 244; Raj Patel, Eric Holt-Gimenez, and Annie Shattuck, "Ending Africa's Hunger: Bill Gates's Fortune Is Funding a New Green Revolution. But Is That What Africans Need?," *The Nation* 289, no. 8 (September 21, 2009): 17; Catherine Higgs, "Land Reform, Betterment Schemes, and the Green Revolution in South Africa, 1913–2013" (paper presented at the 130th Annual Meeting of the American Historical Association, Atlanta, Georgia, January 10, 2015). By 2013, 80 percent of the white maize, 55 percent of the yellow maize, and 85 percent of the soybeans raised in South Africa came from GM seed varieties. South Africa "equated national food security with large-scale farming" and the use of GM crops.

30. Norman E. Borlaug, "The Green Revolution Revisited and the Road Ahead" (Special 30th Anniversary Lecture, the Norwegian Nobel Institute, Oslo, September 8, 2000), 11; Patel, Holt-Gimenez, and Shattuck, "Ending Africa's Hunger," 17.

31. B. H. Farmer, "The 'Green Revolution' in South Asian Rice Fields: Environment and Production," *Journal of Development Studies* 15, no. 4 (1979): 307–9, 315–17.

32. Farmer, "'Green Revolution,'" 307, 316–17.

33. "The Myths Surrounding Global Hunger," *New York Times*, September 7, 1981.

34. Peter B. R. Hazell, "The Asian Green Revolution," in *Proven Successes in Agricultural Development: A Technical Compendium to Millions Fed*, edited by David J. Spielman and Rajul Pandya-Lorch (Washington, DC: International Food Policy Research Institute, 2010), 68, 80; Cao, *GMO China*, xvii, 184.

Selected Bibliography

Adem, Teferi Abate. "The Local Politics of Ethiopia's Green Revolution in South Wollo." *African Studies Review* 55 (December 2012): 81–102.

Adenle, Ademola. "Response to Issues of GM Agriculture in Africa: Are Transgenetic Crops Safe?" *BMC Research Notes*, no. 4 (2011): 2–6.

Adenle, Ademola A., E. Jane Morris, and Govindan Parayil. "Status of Development, Regulation and Adoption of GM Agriculture in Africa: Views and Positions of Stakeholder Groups." *Food Policy* 43 (December 2013): 159–66.

Adeyemo, Remi. "The Food Marketing System: Implications of the Green Revolution Programme in Nigeria." *Agricultural Systems* 14 (1984): 143–57.

Aggarwal, Partap C. *The Green Revolution and Rural Labour: A Study in Ludhiana*. New Delhi: Shri Ram Centre for Industrial Relations and Human Resources, 1973.

Ahlberg, Kristin L. *Transplanting the Great Society: Lyndon Johnson and Food for Peace*. Columbia: University of Missouri Press, 2008.

Akande, Tunji. "The Role of the State in the Nigerian Green Revolution." In Djurfeldt et al., *African Food Crisis*, 161–79.

Akwabi-Ameyaw, Kofi. "Producer Cooperative Resettlement Projects in Zimbabwe: Lessons from a Failed Agricultural Development Strategy." *World Development* 25, no. 3 (1997): 437–56.

Alauddin, Mohammad, and Clem Tisdell. "Has the Green Revolution Destabilized Food Production? Some Evidence from Bangladesh." *Developing Economies* 26, no. 2 (June 1988): 141–60.

———. "Welfare Consequences of Green Revolution Technology: Changes in Bangladeshi Food Production and Diet." *Development and Change* 22, no. 3 (1991): 497–517.

Anderson, Kym, and Shunli Yao. "China, GMOs and World Trade in Agricultural and Textile Products." *Pacific Economic Review* 8, no. 2 (2003): 157–69.

Ansoms, An. "A Green Revolution for Rwanda? The Political Economy of Poverty and Agrarian Change." Discussion Paper 2008.06, Institute of Development Policy, University of Antwerp, June 2008.

Basu, Pratyusha, and Bruce A. Scholten. "Technological and Social Dimensions of the

Green Revolution: Connecting Pasts and Futures." *International Journal of Agricultural Sustainability* 10 (May 2012): 109–16.

Bautista, Romeo M. "Income and Equity Effects of the Green Revolution in the Philippines: A Macroeconomic Perspective." *Journal of International Development* 9, no. 2 (1997): 151–68.

Bazuin, Sjoerd, Hossein Azadi, and Frank Witlox. "Application of GM Crops in Sub-Saharan Africa: Lessons Learned from Green Revolution." *Biotechnology Advances* 29 (2011): 908–12.

Bernstein, Thomas P. "Farmer Discontent and Regime Responses." In *The Paradox of China's Post-Mao Reforms*, edited by Merle Goldman and Roderick MacFarquhar, 197–219. Cambridge, MA: Harvard University Press, 1999.

Bezuneh, Mesfin, and Carl C. Mabbs-Zeno. "The Contribution of the Green Revolution to Social Change in Ethiopia." *Northeast African Studies* 6, no. 3 (1984): 9–17.

Blair, Harry W. "The Green Revolution and 'Economic Man': Some Lessons for Community Development in South Asia?" *Pacific Affairs* 44 (Autumn 1971): 353–67.

———. "Rural Development, Class Structure and Bureaucracy in Bangladesh." *World Development* 6, no. 1 (1978): 65–82.

Blaustein, Richard J. "The Green Revolution Arrives in Africa." *BioScience* 58 (January 2008): 8–14.

Blyn, George. "The Green Revolution Revisited." *Economic Development and Cultural Change* 31 (July 1983): 705–25.

Borlaug, Norman E. "A Choice for Mankind: Adequate Food Production with Equitable Distribution or Hunger and Poverty for Millions." Sterling B. Hendricks Memorial Lectureship Award, sponsored by the Agricultural Research Service, US Department of Agriculture, presented August 24, 1981, at the American Chemical Society Meeting in New York.

———. "Civilization Will Depend More upon Flourishing Crops than on Flowery Rhetoric." Alfred M. Landon Lectures on Public Issues, Kansas State University, March 20, 1979.

———. "The Current Crisis in Global Perspective." In *Agricultural Distress in the Midwest Past & Present*, edited by Lawrence E. Gelfand and Robert J. Neymeyer, 93–111. Iowa City: Center for the Study of the Recent History of the United States, University of Iowa, 1986.

———. "Ending World Hunger: The Promise of Biotechnology and the Threat of Antiscience Zealotry." *Plant Physiology* 124 (October 2000): 487–90.

———. "Feeding a World of 10 Billion People: The Miracle Ahead." Lecture presented at De Montfort University, Leicester, United Kingdom, May 6, 1997.

———. "Genetic Improvement of Crop Foods." *Nutrition Today* 7 (January/February 1972): 20–25.

———. "The Green Revolution: For Peace and Bread." *Bulletin of the Atomic Scientists* 27 (June 1971): 6–9, 42–48.

———. "The Green Revolution, Peace and Humanity." Speech delivered upon receipt of the 1970 Nobel Peace Prize. Oslo, Norway, December 11, 1970. *CIMMYT Reprint and Translation Series*, no. 3 (January 1972).

———. "The Green Revolution Revisited and the Road Ahead." Special 30th Anniversary Lecture, The Norwegian Nobel Institute, Oslo, Norway, September 2000.

———. "The Impact of Agricultural Research on Mexican Wheat Production." *Transactions of the New York Academy of Sciences*, ser. 2, 20, no. 3 (January 1958): 278–95.

———. "Living History Interview with Dr. Norman E. Borlaug." *Transnational Law & Contemporary Problems* 1 (Fall 1991): 539–54.

———. "Mexican Wheat Production and Its Role in the Epidemiology of Stem Rust in North America." *Phytopathology* 44 (1954): 398–404.

———. "Reaching Sub-Saharan Africa's Small-Scale Farmers with Improved Technology: The Sasakawa-Global 2000 Experience." Presented at the World Bank Agricultural Symposium, January 9, 1991.

———. "World Hunger: What to Do." Inaugural York Distinguished Lecture Series, University of Florida, September 11, 1985.

Borlaug, Norman E., and Oddvar H. Aresvik. "The Green Revolution—An Approach to Agricultural Development and Some of Its Economic Implications." *International Journal of Agrarian Affairs* 5 (March 1973): 385–403.

Borlaug, Norman E., and Christopher R. Dowswell. "The Importance of Agriculture and a Stable Adequate Food Supply to the Well-Being of Humankind." *Research in Domestic and International Agribusiness Management* 11 (1995): 1–32.

———. "The Second Green Revolution." In *Agriculture, Human Security, and Peace: A Crossroad in African Development*, edited by M. Taeb and A. H. Zakri, 131–55. West Lafayette, IN: Purdue University Press, 2008.

Breisinger, Clemens, Xinshen Diao, James Thurlow, and Ramatu M. Al Hassan. "Potential Impacts of a Green Revolution in Africa—The Case of Ghana." *Journal of International Development* 23 (2011): 82–102.

Brooks, Sally. "Enabling Adaptation? Lessons from the New 'Green Revolution' in Malawi and Kenya." *Climatic Change* 122 (January 2014): 15–26.

Brown, Lester R. *Seeds of Change: The Green Revolution and Development in the 1970's*. New York: Praeger, 1970.

———. *Who Will Feed China? Wake-Up Call for a Small Planet*. New York: W. W. Norton, 1995.

Burmeister, Larry L. "The South Korean Green Revolution: Induced or Directed Innovation?" *Economic Development and Culture Change* 35 (July 1978): 769–90.

Butty, James S. "The Liberian Green Revolution Initiative: A Policy Analysis Perspective." *Liberia-Forum* 3, no. 4 (1987): 38–52.

Cao, Cong. *GMO China: How Global Debates Transformed China's Agricultural Biotechnology Policies*. New York: Columbia University Press, 2018.

Carey, David, Jr. "Guatemala's Green Revolution: Synthetic Fertilizer, Public Health, and Economic Autonomy in the Mayan Highland." *Agricultural History* 83, no. 3 (2009): 283–322.

Carter, Colin A. "The Urban-Rural Income Gap in China: Implications for Global Food Markets." *American Journal of Agricultural Economics* 79, no. 5 (1997): 1410–18.

Chakravarti, A. K. "Green Revolution in India." *Annals of the Association of American Geographers* 63 (September 1973): 319–30.

Ch'en, Ting-chung. "Agriculture in Mainland China: Reform and Problems." In *Mainland China: Politics, Economics, and Reform*, edited by Yu-ming Shaw, 471–96. Boulder, CO: Westview Press, 1986.

Chen, Weixing. *The Political Economy of Rural Development in China, 1978–1999*. Westport, CN: Praeger, 1999.

Child, Frank C., and Hiromitsu Kaneda. "Links to the Green Revolution: A Study of Small-Scale, Agriculturally Related Industry in the Pakistan Punjab." *Economic Development and Cultural Change* 23 (January 1975): 249–75.

Chow, George C. *China's Economic Transformation*. 3rd ed. Malden, MA: Wiley Blackwell, 2015.

Chunru, Han. "Recent Changes in the Rural Environment in China." *Journal of Applied Ecology* 26 (December 1989): 803–12.

Clawson, David L., and Don R. Hoy. "Nealtican, Mexico: A Peasant Community That Rejected the 'Green Revolution.'" *American Journal of Economics and Sociology* 38 (October 1979): 371–87.

Clay, Jason W., and Bonnie K. Holcomb. *Politics and the Ethiopian Famine, 1984–1995*. Cambridge, MA: Cultural Survival, 1986.

Cliffe, Lionel. "Zimbabwe's Agricultural 'Success' and Food Security in Southern Africa." *Review of African Political Economy* 15, no. 43 (1988): 4–25.

Cohen, John M. "Effects of Green Revolution Strategies on Tenants and Small-Scale Landowners in the Chilalo Region of Ethiopia." *Journal of Developing Areas* 9 (April 1975): 355–58.

Conway, Gordon. *The Doubly Green Revolution: Food for All in the 21st Century*. Ithaca, NY: Cornell University Press, 1998.

Cotter, Joseph. *Troubled Harvest: Agronomy and Revolution in Mexico, 1880–2002*. Westport, CT: Praeger, 2003.

Cui, Zhenling, Xinping Chen, and Fusuo Zhang. "Current Nitrogen Management Status and Measures to Improve the Intensive Wheat–Maize System in China." *AMBIO* 39 (2010): 376–84.

Cullather, Nick. *The Hungry World: America's Cold War Battle against Poverty in Asia*. Cambridge, MA: Harvard University Press, 2010.

———. "Miracles of Modernization: The Green Revolution and the Apotheosis of Technology." *Diplomatic History* 28 (April 2004): 227–54.

Cunguara, Benedito. "An Exposition of Development Failures in Mozambique." *Review of African Political Economy* 39 (March 2012): 161–70.

Dalrymple, Dana G. "Changes in Wheat Varieties and Yields in the United States, 1919–1984." *Agricultural History* 62 (Autumn 1988): 20–36.

———. "The Development and Adoption of High-Yielding Varieties of Wheat and Rice in Developing Countries." *American Journal of Agricultural Economics* 67, no. 5 (December 1985): 1067–73.

Day, Richard H., and Inderjit Singh. *Economic Development as an Adaptive Process: The Green Revolution in the Indian Punjab.* Cambridge: Cambridge University Press, 1977.

De Alcántara, Cynthia Hewitt. "The 'Green Revolution' as History: The Mexican Experience." *Development and Change* 5 (May 1974): 25–44.

———. *Modernizing Mexican Agriculture: Socioeconomic Implications of Technological Change, 1940–1970.* Geneva, Switzerland: United Nations Research Institute for Social Development, 1976.

DeGregori, Thomas R. "Green Revolution Myth and Agricultural Reality?" *Journal of Economic Issues* 38 (June 2004): 503–8.

DeWalt, Billie R. "Mexico's Green Revolution: Food for Feed." *Mexican Studies / Estudios Mexicanos* 1 (Winter 1985): 29–60.

Djurfeldt, Göran, Hans Holmén, Magnus Jirström, and Rolf Larsson, eds. *The African Food Crisis: Lessons from the Asian Green Revolution.* Cambridge, MA: CABI, 2005.

Djurfeldt, Göran, and Magnus Jirström. "The Puzzle of the Policy Shift—The Early Green Revolution in India, Indonesia and the Philippines." In Djurfeldt et al., *African Food Crisis*, 43–63.

Eicher, Carl K. "Zimbabwe's Maize-Based Green Revolution: Preconditions for Replication." *World Development* 23, no. 5 (1995): 805–18.

Eicher, Carl K., and Bernard Kupfuma. "Zimbabwe's Maize Revolution: Insights for Closing Africa's Food Gap." In *International Agricultural Development*, 3rd ed., edited by Carl K. Eicher and John M. Staatz, 550–70. Baltimore, MD: Johns Hopkins University Press, 1998.

Eisenman, Joshua. *Red China's Green Revolution: Technological Innovation, Institutional Change, and Economic Development under the Commune.* New York: Columbia University Press, 2018.

Ellahi, Mahbob, Euan Fleming, and Renato Villano. "Explaining Inter-Provincial Inequality in Productivity Growth in Crop Production in Pakistan." *Spatial Economic Analysis* 4 (December 2010): 441–61.

Estudillo, Jonna P., and Keijiro Otsuka. "Green Revolution, Human Capital, and Off-Farm Employment: Changing Sources of Income among Farm Households in Central Luzon, 1966–1994." *Economic Development and Cultural Change* 47, no. 3 (1999): 497–523.

Estudillo, Jonna P., Yasuyuki Sawada, and Keijiro Otsuka. "The Green Revolution, Development of Labor Markets, and Poverty Reduction in the Rural Philippines, 1985–2004." *Agricultural Economics* 35, no. s3 (November 2006): 399–407.

Evenson, R. E. "Besting Malthus: The Green Revolution." *Proceedings of the American Philosophical Society* 149 (December 2005): 469–86.

Evenson, R. E., and D. Gollin. "Assessing the Impact of the Green Revolution, 1960 to 2000." *Science* 300 (May 2, 2003): 758–62.

Falcon, Walter P. "The Green Revolution: Generations of Problems." *American Journal of Agricultural Economics* 52 (December 1970): 698–710.

Falkner, Robert. "International Sources of Environmental Policy Change in China: The Case of Genetically Modified Food." *Pacific Review* 19 (December 2006): 473–94.

Falkner, Robert, and Aarti Gupta. "The Limits of Regulatory Convergence: Globalization and GMO Politics in the South." *International Environmental Agreements* 9 (2009): 113–33.

Famine: A Man-Made Disaster? A Report for the Independent Commission on International Humanitarian Issues. New York: Vintage Books, 1985.

Famoriyo, Segun, and M. Rafique Raza. "The Green Revolution in Nigeria: Prospects for Agricultural Development." *Food Policy* 7 (February 1982): 27–38.

Fan, Mingsheng, Jianbo Shen, Lixing Yuan, Rongfeng Jiang, Xinping Chen, William J. Davies, and Fusuo Zhang. "Improving Crop Productivity and Resource Use Efficiency to Ensure Food Security and Environmental Quality in China." *Journal of Experimental Botany* 63, no. 1 (2012): 13–24.

Farmer, B. H. *Green Revolution? Technology and Change in Rice-Growing Areas of Tamil Nadu and Sri Lanka.* Boulder, CO: Westview Press, 1977.

———. "The 'Green Revolution' in South Asian Rice Fields: Environment and Production." *Journal of Development Studies* 15, no. 4 (1979): 304–19.

———. "Perspectives on the 'Green Revolution' in South Asia." *Modern Asian Studies* 20, no. 1 (1986): 175–99.

Fitzgerald, Deborah. "Exporting American Agriculture: The Rockefeller Foundation in Mexico, 1943–53." *Social Studies Science* 16 (August 1986): 457–83.

Frankel, Francine R. *India's Green Revolution: Economic Gains and Political Costs.* Princeton, NJ: Princeton University Press, 1971.

Frankema, Ewout. "Africa and the Green Revolution: A Global Historical Perspective." *NJAS - Wageningen Journal of Life Sciences* 70–71 (2014): 17–24.

Freebairn, Donald K. "Did the Green Revolution Concentrate Incomes? A Quantitative Study of Research Reports." *World Development* 23, no. 2 (1995): 265–79.

Gana, Alia, Thora Martina Herrmann, and Sophia Huyer. "Women in Agriculture." In *Agriculture at a Crossroads: Synthesis Report International Assessment of Agricultural Knowledge, Science and Technology Development*, edited by Beverly D. McIntyre, Hans R. Herren, Judi Wakhungu, and Robert T. Watson, 75–80. Washington, DC: Island Press, 2009.

Gill, Monohar Singh. "The Development of Punjab Agriculture, 1977–80." *Asian Survey* 23 (July 1983): 830–44.

Goldman, Abe, and Joyotee Smith. "Agricultural Transformations in India and Northern Nigeria: Exploring the Nature of Green Revolutions." *World Development* 23, no. 2 (1995): 243–63.

Goody, Jack. "Rice-Burning and the Green Revolution in Northern Ghana." *Journal of Development Studies* 16, no. 2 (1980): 136–55.

Gordon, Alec. "The 'Green Revolution' in North Vietnam." *Journal of Contemporary Asia* 4, no. 1 (1974): 128–33.

Grandia, Liza. "Modified Landscapes: Vulnerabilities to Genetically Modified Corn in Northern Guatemala." *Journal of Peasant Studies* 41, no. 1 (2014): 79–105.

Griffin, E. B. *Political Economy of Agrarian Change: An Essay on the Green Revolution.* Cambridge, MA: Harvard University Press, 1974.

Gudmundson, Lowell. "On Green Revolutions and Golden Beans: Memories and Metaphors of Costa Rican Coffee Co-op Founders." *Agricultural History* 88 (Fall 2014): 538–65.

Gupta, Aarti, and Robert Falkner. "The Influence of the Cartagena Protocol on Biosafety: Comparing Mexico, China and South Africa." *Global Environmental Politics* 6 (November 2006): 23–55.

Gwiyani-Nkhoma, Bryson. "Irrigation Development and Its Socioeconomic Impact on Rural Communities in Malawi." *Development Southern Africa* 28 (June 2011): 209–13.

Hamburger, Jessica. "Pesticides in China: A Growing Threat to Food Safety, Public Health, and the Environment." *China Environment Series* 5 (2002): 29–44.

Hansen, Gary E. "Indonesia's Green Revolution: The Abandonment of a Non-Market Strategy toward Change." *Asian Survey* 12 (November 1972): 932–46.

Harding, Harry. *China's Second Revolution: Reform after Mao.* Washington, DC: Brookings Institution, 1987.

Hart, Keith. *The Political Economy of West African Agriculture.* Cambridge: Cambridge University Press, 1982.

Harwood, Jonathan. "Peasant Friendly Plant Breeding and the Early Years of the Green Revolution in Mexico." *Agricultural History* 83 (Summer 2009): 384–410.

Hayami, Yujiro. "Conditions for the Diffusion of Agricultural Technology: An Asian Perspective." *Journal of Economic History* 34 (March 1974): 131–48.

Hayami, Yujiro, and Masao Kikuchi. *A Rice Village Saga: Three Decades of Green Revolution in the Philippines.* Lanham, MD: Barnes & Noble, 2000.

Hazell, Peter B. R. "The Asian Green Revolution." In *Proven Successes in Agricultural Development: A Technical Compendium to Millions Fed*, edited by David J. Spielman and Rajul Pandya-Lorch, 67–98. Washington, DC: International Food Policy Research Institute, 2010.

Hazell, Peter B. R., and C. Ramasamy. *The Green Revolution Reconsidered: The Impact of High Yielding Rice Varieties in South India.* Baltimore, MD: Johns Hopkins University Press, 1991.

Hirschmann, David, and Megan Vaughan. *Women Farmers of Malawi: Food Production in the Zomba District.* Research Series No. 58. Berkeley: Institute of International Studies, University of California, Berkeley, 1984.

Hofman, Bert, Min Shao, and Yoichiro Ishihara. "Asian Development Strategies: China and Indonesia Compared." *Bulletin of Indonesian Economic Studies* 43, no. 2 (2007): 171–99.

Holden, Constance. "Ethiopia: Did Aid Speed an Inevitable Upheaval?" *Science* 186 (December 27, 1974): 1192, 1225–26.

Holmén, Hans. "Spurts in Production—Africa's Limping Green Revolution." In Djurfeldt et al., *African Food Crisis*, 65–85.

———. "The State and Agricultural Intensification in Sub-Saharan Africa." Djurfeldt et al., *African Food Crisis*, 87–112.

Hossain, Mahabub. *Nature and Impact of the Green Revolution in Bangladesh.* Research Report 67. Washington, DC: International Food Policy Research Institute in collaboration with the Bangladesh Institute of Development Studies, July 1988.

Hossain, Mahabub, Manik L. Bose, and Bazlul A. A. Mustafi. "Adoption and Productivity Impact of Modern Rice Varieties in Bangladesh." *Developing Economies* 44 (June 2006): 149–66.

Huang, Jikun, Ruifa Hu, Scott Rozelle, and Carl Pray. "Genetically Modified Rice, Yields, and Pesticides: Assessing Farm-Level Productivity Effects in China." *Economic Development and Cultural Change* 56 (January 2008): 241–63.

———. "Insect-Resistant GM Rice in Farmers' Fields: Assessing Productivity and Health Effects in China." *Science* 308 (April 29, 2005): 688–90.

Huang, Jikun, Carl Pray, and Scott Rozelle. "Enhancing Crops to Feed the Poor." *Nature* 418 (August 2002): 678–84.

Huang, Jikun, and Scott Rozelle. "Technological Change: Rediscovering the Engine of Productivity Growth in China's Rural Economy." *Journal of Development Economics* 49, no. 2 (1996): 337–69.

Hurt, R. Douglas, and Mary Ellen Hurt. *The History of Agricultural Science and Technology: An International Annotated Bibliography.* New York: Garland, 1994.

Isinika, Aida C., Gasper C. Ashimogo, and James E. D. Mlangwa. "From Ujamaa to Structural Adjustment—Agricultural Intensification in Tanzania." In Djurfeldt et al., *African Food Crisis*, 197–218.

Jacoby, Erich H. "Effects of the 'Green Revolution' in South and South-East Asia." *Modern Asian Studies* 6, no. 1 (1972): 63–69.

Jai, Shirong, and Yufa Peng. "GMO Biosafety Research in China." *Environmental Biosafety Research* 1 (2002): 5–8.

Jain, H. K. *The Green Revolution: History, Impact and Future.* Houston, TX: Studium Press, 2010.

Javdani, Marie. "Malawi's Agricultural Input Subsidy: Study of a Green Revolution-Style Strategy for Food Security." *International Journal of Agricultural Sustainability* 10 (May 2012): 150–63.

Jennings, Bruce H. *Foundations of International Agricultural Research: Science and Politics in Mexican Agriculture.* Boulder, CO: Westview Press, 1988.

Jennings, Peter R. "Rice Breeding and World Food Production." *Science* 186 (December 20, 1974): 1085–88.

Jerven, Morten. "The Political Economy of Agricultural Statistics and Input Subsidies: Evidence from India, Nigeria and Malawi." *Journal of Agrarian Change* 14 (January 2014): 129–45.

Jirström, Magnus. "The State and Green Revolutions in East Asia." In Djurfeldt et al., *African Food Crisis,* 25–42.

Johnson, D. Gale. "Biotechnology Issues for Developing Economies." *Economic Development and Cultural Change* 51 (October 2002): 1–4.

Johnson, Michael, Peter Hazell, and Ashok Gulati. "The Role of Intermediate Factor Markets in Asia's Green Revolution: Lessons for Africa?" *American Journal of Agricultural Economics* 85 (December 2003): 1211–16.

Johnson, Stanley. *The Green Revolution.* New York: Harper & Row, 1972.

Jones, David M. "The Green Revolution in Latin America: Success or Failure." *International Aspects of Development in Latin America: Geographic Aspects* 6 (1977): 53–63.

Jones, William I. "Small Farmers and the Green Revolution in Kenya." *African Economic History,* no. 4 (1977): 182–85.

Kabeer, Naila, and Simeen Mahmud. "Globalization, Gender and Poverty: Bangladeshi Women Workers in Export and Local Markets." *Journal of International Development* 16 (January 2004): 93–109.

Kajisa, Kei, and Ellen Payongayong. "Potential of and Constraints to the Rice Green Revolution in Mozambique: A Case Study of the Chokwe Irrigation Scheme." *Food Policy* 36 (October 2011): 615–26.

Karim, M. Bazlul. *The Green Revolution: An International Bibliography.* New York: Greenwood Press, 1986.

Kerr, Rachel Bezner. "Lessons from the Old Green Revolution for the New: Social, Environmental and Nutritional Issues for Agricultural Change in Africa." *Progress in Development Studies* 12, nos. 2–3 (October 2012): 213–29.

Keulen, H. van, and H. Breman. "Agricultural Development in the West African Sahelian Region: A Cure against Land Hunger?" *Agriculture, Ecosystems and Environment* 32 (1990): 177–97.

Khan, Mahmood Hasan. *The Economics of the Green Revolution in Pakistan.* New York: Praeger, 1975.

Kijima, Yoko, Keijiro Otsuka, and Dick Sserunkuuma. "An Inquiry into Constraints on a Green Revolution in Sub-Saharan Africa: The Case of NERICA Rice in Uganda." *World Development* 39, no. 1 (2011): 77–86.

Klatt, W. "How Green a Revolution?" *Pacific Affairs* 49 (Autumn 1976): 516–22.

Klepek, James. "Against the Grain: Knowledge Alliances and Resistance to Agricultural Biotechnology in Guatemala." *Canadian Journal of Development Studies* 33 (September 2012): 310–25.

———. "Selling Guatemala's Next Green Revolution: Agricultural Modernization and the Politics of GM Maize Regulation." *International Journal of Agricultural Sustainability* 10 (May 2012): 117–34.

Kloppenburg, Jack Randolph. *First Seed: The Political Economy of Plant Biotechnology.* 2nd ed. Madison: University of Wisconsin Press, 2004.

Koopman, Jeanne. "Will Africa's Green Revolution Squeeze African Family Farmers to Death? Lessons from Small-Scale High-Cost Production in the Senegal River Valley." *Review of African Political Economy* 39 (September 2012): 500–511.

Kung, James Kaising. "Food and Agriculture in Post-Reform China: The Market Surplus Problem Revisited." *Modern China* 18 (April 1992): 138–70.

Kung, James K. S. "Beyond Subsistence: The Role of the Collectives in Rural Economic Development in Post-Mao China—An Exploratory Village Study in South China." In *China's Economic Reforms*, Selected Seminar Papers on Contemporary China 7, edited by Joseph C. H. Chai and Chi-Keung Leung, 293–328. Hong Kong: Centre for Asian Studies, University of Hong Kong, 1987.

Kuo, Leslie T. C. *The Technical Transformation of Agriculture in Communist China.* New York: Praeger, 1972.

Ladejinsky, Wolf. "Ironies of India's Green Revolution." *Foreign Affairs* 48, no. 4 (July 1970): 758–68.

Lawrence, Peter. "The Political Economy of the 'Green Revolution' in Africa." *Review of African Political Economy* 15 (February 2007): 59–75.

Leaf, Murray J. "The Green Revolution in a Punjab Village, 1965–1978." *Pacific Affairs* 53 (Winter 1980–1981): 617–25.

Leiman, Anthony, and Alexander Behar. "A Green Revolution Betrayed? Seed Technology and Small-Scale Maize Farmers in Zimbabwe." *Development Southern Africa* 28 (October 2011): 445–60.

Lin, Justin Yifu. "Agricultural Development and Reform in China." In *International Agricultural Development*, 3rd ed., edited by Carl K. Eicher and John M. Staatz, 523–38. Baltimore, MD: Johns Hopkins University Press, 1998.

Lipton, Michael. "Plant Breeding and Poverty: Can Transgenic Seeds Replicate the 'Green Revolution' as a Source of Gains for the Poor?" *Journal of Development Studies* 43 (January 2007): 31–62.

Lipton, Michael, with Richard Longhurst. *New Seeds and Poor People.* Baltimore, MD: Johns Hopkins University Press, 1989.

Liu, Jianguo, and Jared Diamond. "China's Environment in a Globalizing World." *Nature* 435 (June 2005): 1179–86.

Lo, Kuei-Mei, and Hsin-Hsing Chen. "Technological Momentum and the Hegemony of the Green Revolution: A Case Study of an Organic Rice Cooperative in Taiwan." *East Asian Science, Technology and Society* 5, no. 2 (2011): 135–72.

Logan, William J. C. "How Deep Is the Green Revolution in South Vietnam? The Story of the Agricultural Turn-Around in South Vietnam." *Asian Survey* 11, no. 4 (April 1971): 321–30.

Mah, Feng-hwa. "Agricultural Reform in Mainland China: Problems and Prospects." In *Mainland China: Politics, Economics, and Reform*, edited by Yu-ming Shaw, 443–69. Boulder, CO: Westview Press, 1986.

Mann, Charles. "Reseeding the Green Revolution." *Science* 277 (August 1997): 1038–43.

Mariyono, Joko, Tom Kompas, and R. Quentin Grafton. "Shifting from Green Revolution to Environmentally Sound Policies: Technological Change in Indonesian Rice Agriculture." *Journal of the Asia Pacific Economy* 15, no. 2 (2010): 128–47.

Matchett, Karin. "At Odds over Inbreeding: An Abandoned Attempt at Mexico / United States Collaboration to 'Improve' Mexican Corn, 1940–1950." *Journal of the History of Biology* 39, no. 2 (2006): 345–72.

Mengisteab, Kidane. *Ethiopia: Failure of Land Reform and Agricultural Crisis.* New York: Greenwood Press, 1990.

Meredith, Martin. *The Fate of Africa: A History of the Continent since Independence.* Rev. ed. New York: Public Affairs, 2011.

Mosley, Paul. "The African Green Revolution as a Pro-Poor Policy Instrument." *Journal of International Development* 14 (August 2002): 695–724.

Myers, Ramon H. "Agricultural Development." In *The People's Republic of China: A Handbook*, edited by Harold C. Hinton, 175–99. Boulder, CO: Westview Press, 1979.

Niazi, Tarique. "Rural Poverty and the Green Revolution: The Lessons from Pakistan." *Journal of Peasant Studies* 31 (January 2004): 242–60.

Nicholls, Clara Ines, and Miguel A. Altieri. "Conventional Agricultural Development Models and the Persistence of the Pesticide Treadmill in Latin America." *International Journal of Sustainable Development and World Ecology* 4, no. 2 (1997): 93–11.

Novotny, Vladimir, Xiaoyan Wang, Andrew J. Englande Jr., David Bedoya, Luksamee Promakasikorn, and Reyes Tirado. "Comparative Assessment of Pollution by the Use of Industrial Agricultural Fertilizers in Four Rapidly Developing Asian Countries." *Environment, Development, and Sustainability* 12, no. 4 (2010): 491–509.

Nulty, Leslie. *The Green Revolution in West Pakistan: Implications of Technological Change.* New York: Praeger, 1972.

Oi, Jean C. *State and Peasant in Contemporary China: The Political Economy of Village Government.* Berkeley: University of California Press, 1989.

Okeno, James A., Jeffrey D. Wolt, Manjit K. Misra, and Lulu Rodriquez. "Africa's Inevitable Walk to Genetically Modified (GM) Crops: Opportunities and Challenges for Commercialization." *New Biotechnology* 30 (January 2013): 124–30.

Olsson, Tore C. *Agrarian Crossings: Reformers and the Remaking of the US and Mexican Countryside.* Princeton, NJ: Princeton University Press, 2017.

Orr, Alastair. "Why Were So Many Social Scientists Wrong about the Green Revolution? Learning from Bangladesh." *Journal of Development Studies* 48, no. 11 (2012): 1565–86.

Otsuka, Keijiro, Fe Gascon, and Seki Asano. "Green Revolution and Labour Demand in Rice Farming: The Case of Central Luzon, 1966–90." *Journal of Development Studies* 31, no. 1 (1994): 82–109.

———. "'Second-Generation' MVs and the Evolution of the Green Revolution: The Case of Central Luzon, 1966–90." *Agricultural Economics* 10 (1994): 283–95.

Otsuka, Keijiro, and Takashi Yamano. "Green Revolution and Regional Inequality: Implications of Asian Experience for Africa." In Djurfeldt et al., *African Food Crisis*, 239–52.

Paarlberg, Don. *Norman Borlaug—Hunger Fighter*. PA 969. Washington, DC: Foreign Economic Development Service, US Department of Agriculture, cooperating with the US Agency for International Development, 1970.

Parayil, Govindan. "The Green Revolution in India: A Case Study of Technological Change." *Technology and Culture* 33 (October 1992): 737–56.

Paul, Satya. "Green Revolution and Income Distribution among Farm Families in Haryana, 1969–70 to 1982–83." *Economic and Political Weekly* (December 23–30): 1989.

Perkins, John H. *Geopolitics and the Green Revolution: Wheat, Genes, and the Cold War*. New York: Oxford University Press, 1997.

———. "The Rockefeller Foundation and the Green Revolution, 1941–1956." *Agriculture and Human Values* 7, no. 3–4 (1990): 6–18.

Pilcher, Jeffrey M. *Food in World History*. New York: Routledge, 2006.

Pingali, Prabhu. "From the Green to the Gene Revolution: How Will the Poor Fare?" *Indian Journal of Agricultural Marketing* 19, no. 1 (1998): 1–4.

Postgate, W. D. "Fertilizers for India's Green Revolution: The Shaping of Government Policy." *Asian Survey* 14 (August 1974): 733–50.

Potrykus, Ingo. "Golden Rice and Beyond." *Plant Physiology* 125 (March 2001): 1157–61.

Prändl-Zika, Veronika. "From Subsistence Farming towards a Multifunctional Agriculture: Sustainability in the Chinese Rural Reality." *Journal of Environmental Management* 87 (2008): 236–48.

Pray, Carl E. "The Green Revolution as a Case Study in Transfer of Technology." *Annals of the American Academy of Political and Social Science* 458 (November 1981): 68–80.

Pray, Carl E., and Anwar Naseem. "Supplying Crop Biotechnology to the Poor: Opportunities and Constraints." *Journal of Development Studies* 43, no. 1 (2007): 192–217.

Pretty, Jules, and Rachel Hine. "The Promising Spread of Sustainable Agriculture in Asia." *Natural Resources Forum* 24 (2000): 107–21.

Randhawa, M. S. *Green Revolution*. New York: John Wiley & Sons, 1974.

———. "Green Revolution in Punjab." *Agricultural History* 51 (October 1977): 656–61.

Renkow, Mitch. "Differential Technology Adoption and Income Distribution in Pakistan: Implications for Research Resource Allocation." *American Journal of Agricultural Economics* 75 (February 1993): 33–43.

Reveles, Irma Lorena Acosta. "The Limits and Contradictions of Agricultural Technology in Latin America: Lessons from Mexico and Argentina." *Perspectives on Global Development Technology* 11, no. 3 (2012): 386–400.

Robertson, Claire C. "Black, White, and Red All Over: Beans, Women, and Agricultural Imperialism in Twentieth-Century Kenya." *Agricultural History* 71 (Summer 1997): 259–99.

Ruttan, Vernon W. "Controversy about Agricultural Technology Lessons from the Green Revolution." *International Journal of Biotechnology* 6, no. 1 (2004): 43–54.

———. "The Green Revolution: Seven Generalizations." *International Development Review* 19 (1977): 16–23.

Saha, Madhumita. "The State, Scientists, and Staple Crops: Agricultural 'Modernization' in Pre-Green Revolution India." *Agricultural History* 87 (Spring 2003): 201–23.

Sanders, John H. "Agricultural Research and Cereal Technology Introduction in Burkina Faso and Niger." *Agricultural Systems* 30, no. 2 (1989): 139–54.

Sanders, John H., and John K. Lynam. "New Agricultural Technology and Small Farmers in Latin America." *Food Policy* 6 (February 1981): 11–18.

Sanders, Richard. "Organic Agriculture in China: Do Property Rights Matter?" *Journal of Contemporary China* 15 (February 2006): 113–32.

Sanderson, Steven E. *The Transformation of Mexican Agriculture: International Structure and the Politics of Rural Change.* Princeton, NJ: Princeton University Press, 1986.

Santos, Gonçalo. "Rethinking the Green Revolution in South China: Technological Materialities and Human-Environment Relations." *East Asian Science, Technology and Society* 5, no. 4 (2011): 479–504.

Schmalzer, Sigrid. *Red Revolution, Green Revolution: Scientific Farming in Socialist China.* Chicago, IL: University of Chicago Press, 2016.

———. "Towards a Transnational, Trans-1978 History of Food Politics in China: An Exploratory Paper." *PRC History Review* 3 (January 2018): 1–14.

Seini, A. Wayo, and V. Kwame Nyanteng. "Smallholders and Structural Adjustment in Ghana." In Djurfeldt et al., *African Food Crisis*, 219–37.

Sen, Bandhudas. *The Green Revolution in India: A Perspective.* New York: John Wiley & Sons, 1974.

Sharma, Rita, and Thomas T. Poleman. *The New Economics of India's Green Revolution: Income and Employment Diffusion in Uttar Pradesh.* Ithaca, NY: Cornell University Press, 1993.

Shen, Xiaobai. "Understanding the Evolution of Rice Technology in China—From Traditional Agriculture to GM Rice Today." *Journal of Development Studies* 46 (July 2010): 1026–46.

Shiferaw, Bekele, Melinda Smale, Hans-Joachim Braun, Etienne Duveiller, Mathew Reynolds, and Geoffrey Muricho. "Crops That Feed the World 10: Past Successes and Future Challenges to the Role Played by Wheat in Global Food Security." *Food Security* 5 (June 2013): 291–317.

Smale, Melinda. "'Maize Is Life': Malawi's Delayed Green Revolution." *World Development* 23, no. 5 (1995): 819–31.

Socolofsky, Homer E. "The World Food Crisis and Progress in Wheat Breeding." *Agricultural History* 43 (October 1969): 423–38.

Sonnenfeld, David A. "Mexico's 'Green Revolution,' 1940–1980: Towards an Environmental History." *Environmental History Review* 16 (Winter 1992): 28–52.

Stakman, E. C., Richard Bradfield, and Paul C. Mangelsdorf. *Campaigns against Hunger.* Cambridge, MA: The Belknap Press of Harvard University Press, 1967.

Stavis, Ben. "A Preliminary Model for Grain Production in China, 1974." *China Quarterly* 65 (March 1976): 82–96.

Stavis, Benedict. *Making Green Revolution: The Politics of Agricultural Development in China.* Rural Development Monograph No. 1. Ithaca, NY: Rural Development Committee, Cornell University, 1974.

Stein, Leslie. "The Green Revolution and Asian Development Strategy." *Studies in Comparative International Development* 12, no. 2 (1977): 58–69.

Stone, Bruce. "Developments in Agricultural Technology." *China Quarterly* 116 (December 1988): 767–822.

Tao, Zhang, and Zhou Shudong. "The Economic and Social Impact of GMOs in China." *China Perspectives* 47 (May–June 2003): 2–10.

Thiesenhusen, William C. "Green Revolution in Latin America: Income Effects, Policy Decisions." *Monthly Labor Review* 95 (March 1972): 20–27.

Thompson, Carol B. "Alliance for a Green Revolution in Africa (AGRA): Advancing the Theft of African Genetic Wealth." *Review of African Political Economy* 39 (June 2012): 345–50.

Thompson, Kenneth W. "The Green Revolution: Leadership and Partnership in Agriculture." *Review of Politics* 34 (April 1972): 174–89.

Thurow, Roger. "The Fertile Continent." *Foreign Affairs* 89 (December 2010): 102–10.

Toenniessen, Gary, Akinwumi Adesina, and Joseph DeVries. "Building an Alliance for a Green Revolution in Africa." *Annals of the New York Academy of Sciences* 1136 (2008): 233–42.

Tuckman, Barbara H. "The Green Revolution and the Distribution of Agricultural Income in Mexico." *World Development* 4, no. 1 (1976): 17–24.

Turner, Matthew. "Overstocking the Range: A Critical Analysis of the Environmental Science of Sahelian Pastoralism." *Economic Geography* 69 (October 1993): 402–21.

Ut, Tran Thi, and Kei Kajisa. "The Impact of Green Revolution on Rice Production in Vietnam." *Developing Economies* 44 (June 2006): 167–89.

Wade, Nicholas. "Green Revolution (I): A Just Technology, Often Unjust in Use." *Science* 186 (December 20, 1974): 1093–96.

———. "Green Revolution (II): Problems of Adapting a Western Technology." *Science* 186 (December 27, 1974): 1186–89, 1191–92.

Walsh, John. "Mexican Agriculture: Crisis within Crisis." *Science* 219 (February 18, 1983): 825–26.

Welker, Marina. "The Green Revolution's Ghost: Unruly Subjects of Participatory Development in Rural Indonesia." *American Ethnologist* 39 (May 2012): 389–406.

Wellhausen, Edwin J. "The Agriculture of Mexico." *Scientific American* 235 (September 1976): 128–53.

Wharton, Clifton R., Jr. "The Green Revolution: Cornucopia or Pandora's Box?" *Foreign Affairs* 47 (April 1969): 464–76.

Wiggins, Steve. "Interpreting Changes from the 1970s to the 1990s in African Agriculture through Village Studies." *World Development* 28, no. 4 (2000): 631–62.

Wolfe, Michael D. *Watering the Revolution: An Environmental and Technological History of Agrarian Reform in Mexico.* Durham, NC: Duke University Press, 2017.

Wortman, Sterling. "Agriculture in China." *Scientific American* 232 (June 1975): 13–21.

Wu, C. T. "Impacts of Rural Reforms." In *China's Economic Reforms*, Selected Seminar Papers on Contemporary China 7, edited by Joseph C. H. Chai and Chi-Keung Leung, 265–92. Hong Kong: Centre for Asian Studies, University of Hong Kong, 1987.

Xu, Cheng, Han Chunru, and Donald C. Taylor. "Sustainable Agricultural Development in China." *World Development* 20, no. 8 (1992): 1127–44.

Xue, Dayuan, and Clem Tisdell. "Global Trade in GM Food and the Cartagena Protocol on Biosafety: Consequences for China." *Journal of Agricultural and Environmental Ethics* 15, no. 4 (2002): 337–56.

Yang, Dali L. *Calamity and Reform in China: State, Rural Society, and Institutional Change since the Great Leap Famine.* Stanford, CA: Stanford University Press, 1996.

Yang, Hong, and Alexander Zehnder. "China's Regional Water Scarcity and Implications for Grain Supply and Trade." *Environment and Planning* 33, no. 1 (2001): 79–95.

Yapa, Lakshman. "What Are Improved Seeds? An Epistemology of the Green Revolution." *Economic Geography* 69 (July 1993): 254–73.

Yasushi, Motoki. "Transformation of Grain Production and the Rice Frontier in Modernizing China." *Geographical Review of Japan* 77, no. 12 (2004): 838–57.

Yu, Yongqiang, Yao Huang, and Wen Zhang. "Changes in Rice Yields in China since 1980 Associated with Cultivar Improvement, Climate and Crop Management." *Field Crops Research* 136 (2012): 65–75.

Zader, Amy. "Technologies of Quality: The Role of the Chinese State in Guiding the Market for Rice." *East Asian Science, Technology and Society* 5, no. 4 (2011): 461–77.

Zhu, Z. L., and D. L. Chen. "Nitrogen Fertilizer Use in China—Contributions to Food Production, Impacts on the Environment and Best Management Practices." *Nutrient Cycling in Agroecosystems* 63 (July 2002): 117–27.

Index

Page numbers in italics refer to illustrations.

mental degradation from fertilizers, pesticides, and herbicides, 40; lack of extension services to educate farmers, 40; little benefits of technologies for small-scale farmers, 175; suffering of 75% of children from inadequate food and malnutrition, 40; undermining of farmers with US surplus maize, 40

high-yielding crop varieties (HYVs): consumer rejection of, 185; development of, in India, 22, 56–57; development of, in Mexico, 16–17; expectations for, 1; high-yield and synthetic maize varieties, 12–13; Lerma Rojo 64 high-yielding wheat variety, 22; NERICA, 157; and rust disease, 36; second-generation varieties in East and Southeast Asia, 86, 97; Sonora 63 and 64, semidwarf, high-yielding, disease-resistant spring wheat varieties, 16–17, 17; unsuitability of for environments in East and Southeast Asia, 90–91, 97. See also International Rice Research Institute; IR-8 hybrid rice variety
Honduras, and GM maize, 176

India, pre–Green Revolution issues: Bengal Famine, 45; focus on food production rather than land distribution, 55; food crisis of 1974, 52, 69; hunger as matter of poverty rather than food shortages, 55; lack of incentive for farmers to increase grain production, 45; mismanagement of agriculture and food distribution by Great Britain, 68; social and economic problems caused by class and gender, 52; threat of famine by

1960s, 45, 46; US termination of food aid in 1965, 183; war with Pakistan over Kashmir, 45, 51
India, Green Revolution: approximate scale neutrality of technology in the Punjab, 58; development of high-yielding rice varieties, 22, 56–57; dissemination of HYV wheat by agricultural universities, 184; farmers' use of tube wells for irrigation, 48; field trials of GM crops, 164; government desire to maintain sovereignty and ensure food security, 68; government desire to transform small-scale farmers into profit makers, 68; government price supports, 46, 48; government provision of research and extension programs, 67; increased profits for large-scale landowners, 50, 185, 192; increased worker wages, 46; India Fertilizer Association, 184; invitation to Norman Borlaug to evaluate wheat-breeding program, 46; Lerma Rojo 64 high-yielding wheat variety, 22; multiplier effect in northern region, 55; planting of HYVs and increased wheat production, 46–48, 61, 183, 188; and self-sufficiency in food grains, 67, 188; success of program in northern wheat belt, 50, 54–55, 67, 74; success of rice HYVs in Punjab, 57
India, Green Revolution, negative and unintended consequences: consumer preference for traditional rice varieties and failure of new varieties to adapt to environmental conditions, 49, 51–52; continued problem of hunger and malnutrition, 49, 55; demand for greater share of profits by landless workers, 49; higher rents